BIBLICAL RECEPTION, 5

Biblical Women and the Arts

**Edited by**
**J. Cheryl Exum and David J. A. Clines**

# BIBLICAL WOMEN AND THE ARTS

Guest edited by
Diane Apostolos-Cappadona

LONDON • NEW YORK • OXFORD • NEW DELHI • SYDNEY

T&T CLARK
Bloomsbury Publishing Plc
50 Bedford Square, London, WC1B 3DP, UK

BLOOMSBURY, T&T CLARK and the T&T Clark logo are trademarks of
Bloomsbury Publishing Plc

First published in Great Britain 2018
This paperback edition published 2020



A catalogue record for this book is available from the British Library.

A catalog record for this book is available from the Library of Congress.

ISBN: HB: 978-0-5676-7460-9
PB: 978-0-5676-9291-7
ePDF: 978-0-5676-7461-6
eBook: 978-0-5676-8516-2

Series: Biblical Reception, volume 5

Typeset by Newgen KnowledgeWorks Pvt. Ltd., Chennai, India

To find out more about our authors and books visit www.bloomsbury.com
and sign up for our newsletters.

# CONTENTS

# ABSTRACTS

**Diane Apostolos-Cappadona**, 'Naked or Nurtured: The Breast of Eve, the Breast of Mary'

Available in assorted sizes and ages, female breasts have had a long history of exposure and concealment, appearing not only as symbols of sensual delight and sustenance but also as symbols of shame and perversity. The lore of the breast flourished throughout the visual record of Western cultural history from the Amazons of classical Greek myth who sacrificed their left breasts for protection in battle to St. Agatha who lost her breasts to martyrdom to the modern heroines who survived breast cancer. Perhaps the most famous naked breasts in Christian art are those of Eve and of Mary as the former's desirable 'apple-round' breasts contrast to the latter's bizarrely shaped nursing breast. Mary's exposed breast is seen in only two motifs in Christian art as *Maria lactans* or as the petitioner who bared her breasts in ultimate appeal on behalf of a sinner before her son in his role as judge. As the nursing mother, Mary's breast, when exposed, is not of normal size, shape or position to the rest of her body sometimes jutting forth from her collarbone or placed in the centre of her sternum. This engorged milky mammary is out of proportion to the rest of Mary's body, so the artist draws our eye immediately to it. Her milk not only provided sustenance to her son but offered spiritual sustenance to singular individuals, such as St. Bernard. While it is perfectly natural for Mary as a mother to nurse her son, there is no biblical narrative that affirms this motif. Thereby this present interdisciplinary study begs the question of how an iconographic motif develops in Christian art.

**Zohar Hadromi-Allouche**, 'Images of the First Woman: Eve in Islamic *Fāl-nāma* Paintings'

This chapter discusses the portrayal of Eve in Islamic paintings in relation to her image in textual Islamic sources. The paintings under discussion are taken from the highly influential Iranian and Turkish *Fāl-nāma* volumes (books from which images and text were used for divination) from the sixteenth and early seventeenth centuries. They present Eve in three significant moments of her and Adam's story: being adored by the angels in the garden; the expulsion from paradise; and the moment after the expulsion. Their analysis demonstrates, on the one hand, that the portrayal of Eve in these paintings reflects the textual Islamic traditions of the Qur'an and later sources; while on the other it shows how the images break with these traditions, reinterpret them and introduce new details into the scene. The first part of this chapter surveys the narratives of the transgression in the garden in the Qur'an and Islamic traditions. The second part begins with a short introduction of the *Fāl-Nāma* codices. It then moves on to examine the portrayal of Eve in three *Fāl-Nāma* paintings, discussing them also in the broader context of other contemporaneous works. Applying a combined approach of iconography and close reading, the analysis reveals a complex, ambivalent character of Eve, who is concurrently venerated and sinful, prophetic and demonic, the source of human death and life. While such traits and contradictions also emerge from some of the textual depictions of Eve, the visual images introduce further details, which are not in line with the textual sources. The paintings thus portray Eve in a manner that goes beyond the mainstream textual narratives, and imply towards alternative narratives of Eve, which the textual tradition could not, or would not, explicitly relate.

**Ori Z. Soltes**, 'Beauty and Its Beholders: Envisioning Sarah and Esther'

Sarah and Esther stand at the beginning and end of the Hebrew-Israelite-Judaean narrative within the Hebrew Bible. They play obliquely parallel and very important kinds of roles in the stories of which they are part, from the matter of their physical beauty and assertiveness to the manner in which their actions lead to a salvational outcome – the first on behalf of a son, the second on behalf of the people that constitute his spiritual descendants. Both heroines are shared by the Jewish and Christian traditions. In the latter they are understood as characters whose Hebrew biblical contexts offer significant anticipatory places in the New Testament and Christian world. Esther in particular is understood with Marian prefigurative connotations, but by paradox, this anticipation is more visible in the symbolic details of scenes involving Sarah than those involving Esther. The visual response to both characters has evolved diversely. Sarah emerges as a central figure only in modern and contemporary art – particularly in the hands of Jewish artists who have also emerged to prominence in the past two centuries – after a long history of assuming a secondary place in the imagery centred on others. Esther has been more consistently offered as the centrepiece of her own story. Sarah is depicted more often at moments that underscore her old age, less often when her youthful beauty is a focus; Esther is invariably depicted as young and physically attractive – until some recent works inspired by certain rabbinic discussions. Artists have added visual layers to the history of biblical interpretation.

**Christine E. Joynes**, 'Re-visioning Women in Mark's Gospel through Art'

Art can offer fresh insights for our understanding of New Testament texts, particularly when it comes to assessing the complex roles played by women in the biblical narratives. This chapter argues that engaging with the reception in art of some female characters in Mark's Gospel leads the viewer to recognize the significant diversity of extant interpretations. Such visual interpretations of women in Mark's Gospel suggest that 'women' should not be amassed as a single group, whose experiences of patriarchy are comparable in different historical periods and geographical regions. In some instances encountering biblical women in art conforms to the familiar method of 'redeeming' women from the biblical text, as practised by various notable feminist scholars; but in other examples, these encounters re-inscribe problematic gendered categories. Thus, re-visioning Mark's Gospel women through art provides an important corrective to the universalizing and essentializing tendencies of Western biblical interpreters and points to the need for a much more nuanced approach.

**Ela Nutu**, 'How Salomé Fell for the Baptist, or John the Baptist as *l'homme fatal*: Artistic Interpretations of a Biblical Narrative'

According to the Bible, John the Baptist is executed by decapitation at the request of a little girl. Matthew (14:1–12) and Mark ( 6:14–29) recount that, during one of King Herod's birthday banquets, Salomé dances so pleasingly in front of her step-father and his guests, that Herod promises to give his wife's daughter anything she may desire, 'even half of his kingdom' (Mark 6:23). Salomé asks her mother for advice and at her suggestion declares her wish to be the head of John the Baptist on a charger. Though seemingly disconcerted by the request, Herod follows through on his promise and orders John's execution. When she is presented with John's head, Salomé offers it to her mother. The biblical account is very brief, yet Salomé has become for many the quintessential *femme fatale,* 'the symbolic incarnation of undying Lust, the Goddess of immortal Hysteria, the accursed Beauty exalted above all other beauties' (J.-K. Huysmans, *Against Nature* [trans. Robert Baldick; Harmondsworth: Penguin, 1959], pp. 65–66.). Her metamorphosis is largely due to Salomé's power to inspire artists, whose sensory interpretations of the biblical narrative have in turn left an indelible mark on the readers' imagination. One of the criticisms that Oscar Wilde received for his play *Salomé* (1891) is that it had a 'nauseating' effect on the audience, most strikingly due to Salomé's sexual interest in the Baptist, which culminates in her kissing the decapitated head of the prophet on the mouth. This element is completely absent from the biblical text, so how did it emerge? Is Oscar Wilde responsible for it? Is it typical of his time? And how did John the Baptist become the poster boy for biblical masculinity? Certainly the figure of the Baptist emerging from Auguste Rodin's bronze statue 'Saint John the Baptist' (1880) exudes virility: naked, tall, purposeful, with clearly defined muscles, proud genitalia and legs apart. Pablo Picasso also chose to portray Salomé naked and, intriguingly, placed in the midst of itinerant acrobats, musicians and clowns. Picasso's *Salomé* etching (1905) depicts her dancing in front of Herod; her complete nakedness exposed to him, her left leg kicking the air. This chapter investigates the complex relationships between the biblical text and some of its literary and artistic metamorphoses, with a particular focus on the emergence of Salomé as *femme fatale* and the Baptist's as the archetype of virile masculinity in *fin-de-siècle* Europe.

**Andrea M. Sheaffer**, 'Framing a Heroine: Judith's Counterparts in Biblical Villains'

The Apocrypha's Judith has been celebrated for millennia as the widow who valiantly saves Israel from the Assyrian army. The biblical text leaves no doubt of Judith's status as a heroine and countless works of art have depicted her as such. But what happens when artists conflate Judith with other infamous biblical women, painting Judith in exact likeness to figures whose names have become synonymous with deceit, trickery and traitorous action? This chapter identifies works by several artists, including Lucas Cranach the Elder and Peter Paul Rubens, who depict Judith as a visual counterpart to their renderings of Salome and Delilah. The chapter suggests that these depictions were heavily influenced by a social and cultural mistrust of women who exert power over men. In turn, images of Judith diverge from interpretation of the heroine as saintly and chaste and place emphasis on her use of deceit and seduction to accomplish her mission. By comparing canvas and text, the chapter concludes with reflections on the impact of reading Judith alongside such unlikely visual counterparts, illuminating her role in the text.

**John Nassichuk**, 'Biblical Elegy and *Quattrocento* Marian Encomium: Marcantonio Sabellico's *Carmina de Beata Virgine Mariae*'

This contribution examines a little known collection of Marian elegies written during the second half of the Quattrocento by a major Venetian Latin humanist, Marcantonio Sabellico, professor in the *Scuola di San Marco* and head librarian at the *Biblioteca Marciana*. After a general overview of the collection's contents, comprising thirteen encomiastic poems composed in elegiac distiches, our study shall describe in particular details of the contents of the first two pieces. In the opening elegy, Sabellico sings the praise of Mary's day of birth, describing it, in strains reminiscent of Virgil's fourth and eighth eclogues as a glorious cosmic event worthy of continuous praise. This use of pagan mythological imagery, heavily indebted to Virgil, places the description of Mary's familial origins in a mythical, 'Golden-Age' context and, as such, prepares the way for the following elegy, in which Sabellico tackles the same topic from a different angle, trying his hand at precise biblical paraphrase. This second elegy takes its cue from the first chapter of Matthew which evokes Jesus' patrilineal genealogy. Sabellico inserts more precise detail culled from the Books of Kings and Chronicles, thus creating a greatly amplified 'genealogy' of Mary. In fact, his use of this material pictures the Old Testament succession of kings, leading up to the destruction of the Temple of Jerusalem, as a veritable foil against which the unsurpassed splendour of Mary is to be measured.

**Kelley Harness**, 'Theatrical Reliquaries: Afterlives of St. Mary Magdalene in Early Seventeenth-century Florence'

Beginning in 1619 and continuing through the 1620s, Florentine grand duchess Maria Magdalena commemorated her name saint's feast day (22 July) by sponsoring performances of music and short theatrical works on the subject of St. Mary Magdalene in the small octagonal chapel adjacent to her apartment in the Palazzo Pitti. In the years immediately preceding the performances, the grand duchess had ordered a complete renovation of the space, resulting in a chapel in which visual images of St. Mary Magdalene figured prominently, as did the grand duchess's ever-expanding collection of relics, housed in wall niches covered by paintings on religious subjects, including Mary Magdalene. The surviving musical and theatrical works from this era reveal that audience members heard a speaking and singing Mary Magdalene, giving voice to the saint in a manner unavailable to visual representations. The chapel's frescoes encouraged the contextualization of that voice through visual reminders of Mary Magdalene's preaching, and her words, now directed towards a seventeenth-century audience, carried that tradition forward to the present. Although hidden from public view, intended only for the grand duchess and a small circle of her intimates, the Magdalene plays and music – like the relics that surrounded their performance – held the potential for spiritual and political power, activated by whoever possessed them. The saint's voice thus served as the ventriloquizing medium by which the grand duchess reminded courtiers and family members alike of her name saint's efficacy as both devotional object and preaching subject.

**Heidi J. Hornik**, 'Guercino's *Christ and the Woman of Samaria* in the Kimbell Art Museum: The Evolution of Biblical Narrative and Visual Meaning'

The Italian seventeenth-century artist known as Guercino painted the *Christ and the Woman of Samaria at the Well* (Figure 9.1), now in the collection of the Kimbell Art Museum, Fort Worth, Texas. The under-researched painting, dated 1619–20, marks the culmination of Guercino's early (pre-Roman) artistic style. Through a comparative study of the Kimbell version of the painting with four other paintings of the same subject painted either by Guercino or a close follower in his studio, the stylistic differences in the artist's *oeuvre* can be detected. Guercino also selected different moments in the visual narrative to illustrate. Guercino's use of composition and gesture create a rich visual depiction of John 4:1–26 that is critical to our understanding of the theme during the Baroque period of art history. The meaning of the Gospel story to the artist and to his contemporaries is further revealed in the context of biblical interpretation. The declarations regarding works of art made in the twenty-fifth and final session of the Council of Trent and the writings of the theologian Cornelius à Lapide offer a deeper level of meaning by illustrating a theme of conversion in the Kimbell *Christ and the Woman of Samaria* by Guercino.

**Natasha O'Hear**, 'Picturing the Woman Clothed with the Sun (Rev 12): Images of Apocalyptic Conflict, Piety and Strength'

In Revelation 12 we witness a cosmic struggle in which an innocent woman with a new-born baby is attacked by a diabolical Dragon. While in one sense an isolated incident (the woman does not appear again in the text), in her person and in her predicament the Woman Clothed with the Sun encapsulates much of the cyclical drama of Revelation and can be seen as both a structural and thematic hinge. Her centrality to the narrative is reflected in privileged artistic attention that the figure has received through the ages. Her visual history is explored in this chapter via fourteen carefully chosen images, each representing an interpretative trend and ranging from the eleventh to the twenty-first centuries. The early medieval illuminated Apocalypse manuscripts tend to emphasize the cosmic aspects of the woman's struggle, with Marian references coming gradually to the fore. By contrast, Albrecht Dürer and Diego Velázquez emphasize her humanity as well as her centrality to John's vision. William Blake suggests an ambiguity to the vision, intimating that the Dragon figure may not be wholly evil while Odilon Redon, in nineteenth-century fin-de-siècle style, renders his Woman Clothed with the Sun as a seductive dancer. We close our survey with the work of two contemporary Chicana artists for whom the Woman Clothed with the Sun embodies the struggle for social and political liberation and recognition. In these differing visual handlings of Revelation 12 we are thus able to see the power of visual exegesis in developing, emphasizing and even extending the meaning of the biblical source-text, and in doing so offering a more rounded picture of this important biblical woman.

# ILLUSTRATIONS

# CONTRIBUTORS

**Diane Apostolos-Cappadona** is Haub Director of the Catholic Studies Program and Professor of Religious Art and Cultural History at Georgetown University. The author and editor of many books, reference works, scholarly articles, and exhibition catalogues, she served as Consulting Editor for the Arts, Dance, Film and New Media for the *New Catholic Encyclopedia* (2011) and most recently edited *Material Religion* (2016) for the series *Macmillan Interdisciplinary Handbooks: Religion*. She is currently Editor-in-Chief of the new series *Brill Research Perspectives in Religion and the Arts* (first issues forthcoming 2017) and the *Oxford Encyclopedia of Religion and the Arts*, 3 volumes (forthcoming 2020).

**Zohar Hadromi-Allouche** is a lecturer in Religious Studies and Islam at the University of Aberdeen. Her research applies a literary approach to medieval religious Islamic sources; and examines these sources from a comparative perspective. Her recent publications focus on the construction of Eve in Islamic sources. Dr. Hadromi-Allouche is also co-editor of *Fall Narratives: An Interdisciplinary Approach* (Ashgate, 2017) and editor of *Fallen Animals: Art, Literature, Religion* (Lexington Books, 2017).

**Kelley Harness** is associate professor of music (musicology) at the University of Minnesota and past editor-in-chief of the *Journal of Seventeenth-Century Music*. She is the author of *Echoes of Women's Voices: Music, Art, and Female Patronage in Early Modern Florence* (2006) and of articles in numerous scholarly journals and collections of essays, including the *Journal of the American Musicological Society* and *The Routledge Companion to Music and Visual Culture* (2014). She is currently writing a book on the Florentine horse ballets.

**Heidi J. Hornik** is professor of Italian Renaissance and Baroque Art History at Baylor University. She received her BA degree from Cornell University and her MA and doctor of philosophy degrees from the Pennsylvania State University. Hornik's work, *Michele Tosini and the Ghirlandaio Workshop in Cinquecento Florence*, was the first biography on the late Renaissance painter incorporating her primary research from the state archives in Florence and in church archives throughout Italy. She has co-authored four books on art and theology (*Illuminating Luke* trilogy and *The Acts of the Apostles through the Centuries*) with Mikeal C. Parsons, professor of religion at Baylor. Hornik was awarded a visiting scholar fellowship at Harvard University for the spring 2017 semester to complete *The Art of Christian Reflection* (Baylor University Press).

**Christine E. Joynes** is director of the Centre for Reception History of the Bible at the University of Oxford. She also co-chairs 'The Bible and Visual Art' section at the Society of Biblical Literature Annual Meeting. Her research focusses on the reception history of the New Testament and she is currently writing the Wiley-Blackwell Bible Commentary, *Mark's Gospel through the Centuries*. Her edited volumes include *Perspectives on the Passion: Encountering the Bible through the Arts* (2007) and *From the Margins 2: Women of the New Testament and their Afterlives* (2009). In addition, she has written many articles exploring the interpretation of the New Testament in art, music and literature.

**John Nassichuk** is professor of French and Neo-Latin literature at the University of Western Ontario, Canada. His research is in the area of French and Neo-Latin literature of the Renaissance period, with particular attention to the multiple relationships between Italian *Quattrocento* humanism – especially that of Naples – and northern Renaissance culture. He also maintains an interest in biblical paraphrases and adaptations, both in Latin and in the vernacular languages. In 2012 he edited, with Perrine Galand, the Droz volume entitled *Aspects du lyrisme conjugal*. A recent article on devotional Neo-Latin drama in the Parisian colleges has appeared in *Renaissance Studies* (2016).

**Ela Nutu** is the author of *Incarnate Word, Inscribed Flesh: John's Prologue and the Postmodern* and co-editor, with J. Cheryl Exum, of *Between the Text and the Canvas: The Bible and Art in Dialogue*. She has contributed to a number of edited volumes including *Recycled Bible*, edited by Fiona Black and *From the Margins 2: Women of the New Testament and their Afterlives*, co-edited by Christopher Rowland and Christine E. Joynes; and most recently an entry 'Blessing and Benediction in Contemporary Literature' in *Encyclopaedia of the Bible and its Reception*. She collaborated with the British Library and the Lokahi Foundation Sacred Exhibition 'Ways of Reading' project and contributed a chapter titled 'Illuminating Texts, the Bible and Artistic Traditions'. Publications also include a number of articles in *Biblical Reception*, *Biblical Interpretation* and *Semeia*. Nutu is interested in exploring different means of reading biblical texts, particularly the ways in which cultural trends (and specifically the visual arts) affect a recycling of the Bible in terms of the creation of gender identity and ideology. She has given a number of lectures and conference papers in this area, and her current research project focusses on the journeys of Judith and Salome from text into art and culture and investigates the parameters of the *femme forte* and the *femme fatale* in relation to these female characters.

**Natasha O'Hear** is a lecturer in theology and visual art at the Institute for Theology, Imagination and the Arts (ITIA) at the University of St Andrews. Her research interests centre on visualizations of biblical texts, and of Revelation in particular. She completed a DPhil in this field at Oxford University in 2008 and went on to publish it as a monographin 2011 (*Contrasting Images of the Book of Revelation in Late Medieval and Early Modern Art: A Case Study in Visual Exegesis* [Oxford Theological Monographs]). Since then she has published, with Anthony O'Hear, *Picturing the Apocalypse: The Book of Revelation in the Arts over Two Millennia* (2015), as well as several articles on the visual history of Revelation ranging from the middle ages to the twenty-first century. Natasha also teaches at an Academy School in West London.

**Andrea M. Sheaffer** holds a PhD in Hebrew Bible and is the director of Admissions at the Graduate Theological Union in Berkeley, California. Her current research interests focus on women and power in the Bible and visual arts. She is the author of *Envisioning the Book of Judith: How Art Illuminates Minor Characters* (2014) and currently serves as a member of the Bible and Visual Arts steering committee of the Society of Biblical Literature.

**Ori Z. Soltes** teaches at Georgetown University across a range of disciplines, from art history and theology to philosophy and political history. He is the former director of the B'nai B'rith Klutznick National Jewish Museum, and has curated more than eighty-five exhibitions there and in other venues across the country and overseas. Some of his recent books include *Fixing the World: Jewish American Painters in the Twentieth Century; The Ashen Rainbow: The Holocaust and the Arts; Our Sacred Signs: How Jewish, Christian and Muslim Art Draw from the Same Source;* and *Tradition and Transformation: Three Millennia of Jewish Art and Architecture.*

# INTRODUCTION

Diane Apostolos-Cappadona

This current volume of *Biblical Reception* is dedicated to the theme of how biblical women have been interpreted, envisioned and/or re-visioned through the arts in the widest possible considerations from drawings, paintings, prints and sculptures to performance, poetry, literature and music. What began as a conversation among colleagues attending the special session co-sponsored by the AAR Arts, Literature, and Religion Section with the SBL Bible and the Visual Arts Section at the 2014 Annual Meeting in San Diego blossomed into a larger exchange that resulted in the decision to organize this present volume.

Clearly the wealth of creative materials generated by the afterlives of biblical women demands more and more attention from biblical scholars, art historians and those interested in religion and the arts within and beyond the lens of feminism. The larger spectrum of interdisciplinary approaches to this subject facilitates our understanding not simply of the process of the afterlife of a biblical figure or narrative but also the cultural position of women within the societal contexts of the artist or patron's milieu.

Throughout this present collection, then, readers will find a diversity of methodological approaches to the modes and motifs of biblical women throughout the centuries of Western cultural history. From the multiple perspectives provided by this ensemble of contributing scholars, woman – biblical woman in particular – is approached as subject, object, symbol, emblem, sign and illustration from the perspectives of art history, biblical studies, Christian theology, cultural history, feminist studies, comparative literature and music history. This breadth of scholarship and female motifs affirm the human proclivity for making history 'our own', particularly our recognition of the Bible as a living text and the arts as accessible modes of religious and societal reception in daily life.

As guest editor for Volume 5 of *Biblical Reception*, I want to acknowledge the collegial cooperation of all the contributors throughout the process from submission to acceptance to copy-editing and proofreading. Dominic Mattos, editorial director, and Sarah Blake, editorial assistant, both at Bloomsbury, worked closely with me throughout the editorial stages that brought this coalition of diverse manuscripts together into a coherent volume. On behalf of all the contributors, I am grateful to all those archives, galleries, libraries and museums that made so many of the illustrations available through international scholarly access programs. Such a well-illustrated and brilliantly imagined volume as this one has become would have not been possible without their support. To paraphrase Alice, how could a book such as this one be possible without pictures?

*Diane Apostolos-Cappadona*
Georgetown University
Washington, DC

1

# Naked or Nurtured: The Breast of Eve, the Breast of Mary

Diane Apostolos-Cappadona

Female breasts have had a long history of exposure and concealment, appearing not only as symbols of sensual delight and sustenance but also of shame and perversity. Visual and historical records of Western culture abound with the lore of the breast that through vastly contrasting examples announce the symbolic power and significance of the feminine and the female. In terms of biblical women, however, no female breasts are more famous or regularly depicted in Western Christian art than those of Eve and Mary. Oftentimes as a contrast, as in the First Eve/Second Eve discussions, Eve's breast is depicted as an object of desire, like a tempting piece of fruit, while Mary's milk-filled breast was offered as a symbol of maternal love and salvific grace.

Since the publication of cultural historian Margaret Yalom's now classic study *A History of the Breast*, many feminist historians, art historians and theologians have given keen attention to the religious symbolism of the breast, especially of Mary's breast.[1] In several of those texts, the authors have discussed the same images presented here, with, however, divergent interpretations and distinct conclusions that emphasized the reality of the multidimensional and interdisciplinary nature of both this form of study and of these specific images. While there may be minimal or no biblical or patristic basis for this motif, there are clearly social, cultural, liturgical, medical and political dimensions to what might be characterized as the evolution of an idea fundamental to the formation of Marian devotion.

This present investigation then traverses interdisciplinary studies in order to understand the origin and translation of how a human necessity (the nursing breast) is adapted within the 'space between'[2] the lines in biblical and apocryphal texts[3] to become accepted by believers as an 'authentic' biblical motif. While depictions of Mary nursing her Child can be found in Late Antique/Early Christian art and standardized in Byzantine art, this motif was rarely presented in medieval art until the twelfth and thirteenth centuries when it was popularized through the devotional attention to the humanity of Christ and to Marian miracles.

## *Depicting the Exposed Breast*

It is both a natural and universal phenomenon that women – whether divine or human – expose their breasts in order to nurse their children. The Egyptian Isis and the Christian Virgin Mary have been depicted with at least one breast exposed as they suckled their sons. Nonetheless, in the twentieth and twenty-first centuries, the exposed breast is more often than not interpreted as a clear object of shame.

There are visual connectors that identify a cultural and theological milieu that evolved from a classical Mediterranean goddess's celestial milk to become assimilated into early Christian Eucharistic rites and Marian devotion. These visual connectors were then incorporated into the liturgical and pious devotions of the coordinated tradition of the Byzantine liturgy and the icon, and later enmeshed with medieval spiritual and devotional movements such as the *Devotio Moderna*, the Brotherhood of the Common Life and medieval female mystics to become elevated to an art motif in the early Renaissance.

Although it may be impossible to establish empirical evidence for the exact sources for the evolution or transformation of this motif of the 'spirituality of the Virgin's milk'[4] from classical culture, there is a common devotional *Zeitgeist* that coalesced medieval Marian devotionalism with Byzantine piety towards the *Theotokos*.[5] One of the popular influences of this 'conflated' Marian devotionalism was the writings of the medieval mystics, predominately women such as Hildegaard of Bingen (1098–1179) and Mechtild of Magdeburg (c. 1207–1294). Nonetheless, it was the male author of *The Meditations of Bonaventura* who wrote that

> Then the Son of the eternal God came out of the womb of the mother without a murmur or lesion, in a moment; as He had been in the womb so He was now outside, on the hay at His mother's feet. Unable to contain herself, the mother stooped to pick Him up, embraced Him tenderly and, guided by the Holy Spirit, placed Him in her lap and began to wash Him with her milk, her breasts filled up by heaven.[6]

Passages like these from medieval devotional texts were either inspired or accompanied by depictions of the motif of the *Maria lactans* as in the illumination identified as *The Virgin Suckling the Child, with a Kneeling Nun* in the Amesbury Psalter (Figure 1.1). Recent historical scholarship has affirmed that the majority of the audience for these texts and images were women, oftentimes nuns but also laywomen, predominantly from the aristocracy but also of varied classes, who owned, commissioned and used books of hours and psalters.[7] The 'power of images'[8] to coalesce with and strengthen devotional empathy and affective piety was operative in the development of the motifs related to Mary's breasts and their significance in Christian spirituality and liturgy both as fundamental to the humanity of Jesus and to Mary's eventual position, a principal intercessory figure for the Christian collective.

**Figure 1.1** Amesbury Psalter, *The Virgin Suckling the Child; with a Kneeling Nun*, c. 1250–55. MS 6 f.4. Illumination on parchment, 236 x 162 mm. Salisbury, Oxford, All Souls College, © The British Library.

## *Eve and the Virgin*

The depictions of women in Christian art played significant roles in the socialization of women, especially for their roles in both ecclesiastical and everyday life. Typically, these presentations were divided into the motifs of the ideal and the imperfect. The Pauline teachings of the Christ as the 'New Adam' (1 Cor 15:21–22, 45–49 DR[9]) led to the association of a 'first Eve' and Mary as the 'New Eve' by several church fathers.[10] They contrasted the active disobedience of the 'first Eve' with the passive obedience of the 'second Eve'.

Acceptable modes of appearance, attitude and behaviour were prescribed just as unacceptable modes were proscribed for young Christian women through visual images such as the contrast between Eve and the Virgin. The juxtaposition of these two female figures within the same frame such as in the medieval Italian painter Carlo da Camerino's (d. 1439)[11] *The Madonna of Humility with the Temptation of Eve* (Figure 1.2) provided a vehicle through which to consider the duality of the female breast, as Mary's was discreetly uncovered while Eve's was noticeably exposed.

In the centre of his vertical panel, Carlo da Camerino depicted a significant Madonna of Humility with Mary seated humbly on the ground nursing her young Son. They were surrounded, if not protected, by the Christian warrior St. George and the archangels Gabriel and Michael. By contrast, the lower and smaller segment of the panel presented an almost supine figure of a naked Eve who, urged on

**Figure 1.2** Carlo da Camerino, *The Madonna of Humility with the Temptation of Eve*, c. 1400. Tempera and gold on wood panel; framed: 191.50 x 99.00 x 11.00 cm ($75\frac{3}{8}$ x $38\frac{15}{16}$ x $4\frac{5}{16}$ inches); unframed: 181.50 x 88.60 cm ($71\frac{7}{16}$ x $34\frac{7}{8}$ inches). The Cleveland Museum of Art, Holden Collection 1916.795.

by the serpent entwined around her lower extremities, raised the 'forbidden fruit' to her mouth. Thereby, she would damn humanity with her disobedience even as she looked up at the model of female obedience.

Mary was positioned so that she could nurse her young Son comfortably and modestly. Her hands supported and shielded him from the viewers' eyes as the tilt of her head enhanced the aura of maternal protection. Her copious blue mantle encased her body and was available to him for warmth and modesty. He was balanced between her thighs and her lap to signify the natural connection between mother and child – both through gestation and birthing. Their bodily postures and facial expressions connoted a *sacra conversazione*[12] that believers were privileged to witness.

Although his back was turned towards the viewer, the Christ Child's haloed head and right hand were positioned, like those of the interlocutor figure of classical painting, to bring the viewer's eye to his mother's deftly exposed right breast. From a twenty-first-century perspective, with its awareness of modern medical and anatomical knowledge, Mary's displayed breast was misplaced and misshapen in this depiction of her body while her other breast appears to be non-existent.[13] Late medieval artists such as Carlo da Camerino were schooled in and employed the visual vocabulary of signs and symbols. Clearly, the placement and size of the Madonna's breast was more symbolic than naturalistic as in the work of the Sienese painter Paolo di Giovanni Fei (c. 1345–1411), *Madonna and Child* (Figure 1.3).

Among its multiple meanings, the motif of the *Maria lactans* was a devotional image that offered solace to those mothers who lost children to starvation or illness during periods of famine, plague and war.[14] Resting in the arms of *Mater Ecclesia*, those 'lost children' would not thirst, starve or suffer as Mary's enlarged breast provided milk for all. However, obedience to the socio-spiritual convention of Marian modesty encouraged artists such as Carlo da Camerino to situate this nursing breast in an irregular place such as her collarbone or shoulder.

Eve's bodily posture was awkward as she balanced on her elbows and lower torso. Her legs, bent at the knee, were raised as her heels touched the ground in a reverse pattern of *The Temptation of Eve*[15] (c. 1120–35: San Lazare en Autun) by the French Romanesque sculptor Giselbertus of Autun (fl. twelfth century). However, Carlo da Camerino's Eve has uncovered hair that cascaded down her back as one lengthy tendril dripped down between her right arm and breast. The serpent wrapped itself around Eve's legs as far as her loins and with a swirling motion raised its reptilian head directly below those of the Madonna and Child. The serpent's female head had uncovered hair as an allusion to Lilith, the legendary Hebrew female revived in medieval and Renaissance Christian art as a central character in both the Temptation and the Fall narratives.

The Madonna and Child, and their saintly companions, were positioned carefully above the double golden border incised with botanical and geometric patterns. However, Eve and the serpent extended into the foliated separation as if to extend outward and upward in order to better see Mary and her Child. They were positioned in the Garden of Eden restored by Mary's acts of humility and

**Figure 1.3** Paolo di Giovanni Fei, *Madonna and Child*, 1370s. Tempera on wood, gold ground. Overall, with engaged frame, 34¼ x 23¼ in. (87 x 59.1 cm); painted surface 27 x 16⅞ in. (68.6 x 42.9 cm). Bequest of George Blumenthal, 1941. The Metropolitan Museum of Art, New York, 41.190.13.

obedience while Eve (like the serpent) was restricted to the earth having lost her, and our, garden home.

As she had not yet eaten of the forbidden fruit, Carlo da Camerino placed Eve within a partial garden setting, given the pattern of foliated forms on the golden border. Her sightline ran upwards on an angle just past the Madonna and Child to the figures of St. George, the Christian warrior who defended a princess from a monster, and the archangel Michael who guarded the gates of Eden and carried souls for judgment. This path of vision was affirmed by Carlo da Camerino's creation of an upward triangle formed from Eve's right hand in which she held the tantalizing apple and the Madonna's two hands that cradled the fruit of her womb, Jesus.

The classic contrast such as Eve's naked body and Mary's voluminously clothed form would be found in many works of Christian art both before and after Carlo da Camerino, as evidenced most regularly in the sculptural images of the Virgin and Child on the facades of medieval cathedrals and ecclesiastical interiors. Below Mary's feet, there is a carved base with images of Eve, the forbidden fruit and the serpent (or Lilith) like those found on the now unoccupied boxwood base from the Netherlands (Figure 1.4). On this particular base is the typical presentation of the Tree of Knowledge filled with the forbidden fruit in the centre separating the figure of the by then recognizable female-headed serpent (Lilith) slithering on the ground to the viewer's right and the naked body of Eve in a similar posture on the viewer's left. While both female figures have long hair and mirror image faces, this Eve chewed greedily on the apple in her right hand. In her left hand, she cuddled two additional apples carefully positioned as if they were her breasts. The visual analogy between Eve's breasts and the round apples was common in depictions of the Temptation episode.[16] The medieval mind operated typologically on multiple levels to interpret visually, spiritually and culturally the adage, 'Eve authoress of sin, Mary authoress of merit'.

**Figure 1.4** *Base for a Statuette: Eve and Lilith*, 1470–80. Boxwood base, overall: 3½ x 4⅞ x 3⅜ in. (8.9 x 12.4 x 8.6 cm). The Cloisters Collection, 1955. The Metropolitan Museum of Art, New York, 55.116.2.

## *The Nursing Breast: Classical Mediterranean Tradition*

The cosmic and human implications of the goddess as a nursing mother and the visual theology of mother's milk inform the evolution of the Christian iconography of both the First Eve/Second Eve theme and the *Maria lactans* motif from its classical Mediterranean sources. A female symbol for immortality, wisdom, fertility and nourishment, milk is central to the myths and symbols of birth, nurture and renewal. Through association with the cycle of female energies, milk was recognized for its symbolic and natural values. The elemental yet powerful role of milk in human experience can be signified as an ancient and complex symbol for the gift of life and by the Hebraic references to the 'land of milk and honey'. The initial appearance of a mother's milk is as miraculous as the moments of conception and birth. Like honey, milk is a 'perfect food' requiring no preparation and providing nourishment. The transfer of milk from mother to infant is a natural exchange of bodily fluid signifying simultaneously a shared identity as well as shared thoughts.

This topos has religious and ritual connotations in pre-modern cultures. In ancient Egypt, milk from the goddess's breast contained protective and reviving powers, and symbolized life, longevity, salvation and divine adoption. In the period of the Middle Kingdom, each pharaoh partook of the goddess's breast three times: at birth, enthronement and death/rebirth as Horus. The classical Greek images of the *kourotrophoi*[17] emphasized divine adoption, protection and transfer of wisdom. The Greco-Roman cultural practice of a 'wet nurse' signified a separation between mother and nurse. As milk was the source of wisdom, a wet nurse must be selected carefully as her milk was the beginning of the infant's education.[18] The initiation rites of many Greco-Roman mystery religions, which sought sacred knowledge, often included both a baptism in milk and a representation of the initiate as a small adult being suckled at a goddess's breast.[19]

The motif of the nursing mother is perhaps the most obvious and complex of the symbolisms of milk. Following the Egyptian custom, milk was identified simultaneously as a divine and a secular food. The suckling of a mortal infant by a divine mother signified the principles of sacred nurture and divine adoption. The image of the infant pharaoh suckling at the breast of a goddess signified his entry into the divine realm, thereby aligning him with the god Horus.[20]

A second motif is that of nurture, which extends the meaning of milk beyond human and divine existence into the realm of nature. The visual and sensory analogies between milk and semen fused with the primeval recognition of these bodily fluids as central to the mystery of life. Nurture, thereby, indicated not simply the sustenance of life but its procreation, whether human, nature or divine.

A third motif is that of wisdom and thereby spiritual renewal. Just as the drinking of the goddess's milk imbued the suckling infant with immortality and divine energy, so the suckling adult imbibed wisdom and spiritual energy from *mater sapientia*. The Christian mystic identified as Pseudo-Dionysius affirmed milk as a metaphor for God's teachings while a Muslim hadith proclaimed that milk signified an initiation towards knowledge.

In *A History of the Breast*, the cultural historian Margaret Yalom advised that 'In the beginning was the breast'.[21] For all but a small fraction of human history, there was no substitute for a mother's milk. Indeed, until the end of the nineteenth century, when pasteurization made animal milk safe, a maternal breast meant life or death for every new-born babe. Small wonder that our prehistoric ancestors endowed their female idols with awesome bosoms in places as far apart as Spain and the Steppes of Russia long before the creation of agriculture. It takes no great stretch of the imagination to picture a distraught Stone Age mother begging one of those buxom idols for an ample supply of milk.[22]

Offering the breast was, among other things, a sign of the capacity to grant favours. Milk was seen as both a material and a spiritual form of nourishment. To give the breast to one's baby was decidedly more than a simple matter of alimentation: the mother transmitted with her milk a whole religio-ethical belief system.

Sacred representations of mothers with babies at the breast began to appear in archaic Greek society and were probably related to *kourotrophoi* cults.[23] For the most part, the rites practised by these cultic devotees took place in simple shrines or in the open air, and were lacking in the grandeur reserved for the Olympian gods. Nonetheless, these popular cults continued to thrive until the dawn of Christianity.

In neighbouring Egypt, the mother goddess took the form of the awesome Isis, associated with the milk-giving cow, the Tree of Life, and the throne of the pharaohs. In the last capacity, she was equated with the royal throne itself, 'so that ascending the throne was to sit upon her lap, and to suckle from her breast was to receive the divine nourishment that would give the king the qualities of kingship'.[24] Whenever Isis was shown nursing a pharaoh, it was a means of confirming him as her son and attesting to his divinity. Pharaohs were portrayed as nursed by Isis either at their birth, their coronation or their death as these were moments requiring divine intervention for a smooth passage from one form of life to another. No one doubted that milk drunk from Isis's breast would confer immortality.

When Isis offers her breast to her own son Horus, the great goddess was brought closer to the concerns of real people (Figure 1.5). Depictions of a divine mother nursing her child provide a visual metaphor of motherhood as both a continuous with lived reality and a validation of the experience of maternity. This visual image promotes the concept of divine lactation as a metaphor for divine–human communication and the initiation of a male saviour in formative Christianity.

## *Nursing Breast in the Jewish and Early Christian Traditions*

In the world of the Hebrew Bible, women were valued primarily as mothers, and in the Late Antique/Early Christian world, the Virgin Mary was celebrated as the miraculous mother of Jesus of Nazareth. In both the Jewish and Christian traditions, breasts were honoured as milk-producing vessels necessary for the survival of the Hebrew people and, later, the followers of Jesus. The example of the baby

**Figure 1.5** *Statuette of Isis and Horus*, 332–30 BCE. Egyptian faience, H. 17 cm (6 11/16 in.); W. 5.1 cm (2 in.), D. 7.7 cm (3 1/16 in.). Purchase, Joseph Pulitzer Bequest Fund, 1955. The Metropolitan Museum of Art, New York, 55.121.5.

Jesus suckling at his mother's breast became a metaphor for the spiritual nurturance of all Christian souls.

With the advent of Christianity, the special nature of milk and the idea of the Virgin as a sign of purity and sexual innocence were transferred to Mary as that most special of mothers and signified a connection with the reality of women's daily experience and a divine metaphor for Jesus' humanity. The topos of Mary's milk had extraordinary shifts in meaning that parallel a microcosmic history of Christian attitudes towards female physicality. Initially, her milk symbolized knowledge, new life and paradise; and later it was celebrated as a sign of Mary's grace. A symbol of erudition, intercession, salvation, sustenance and paradise, her milk signalled the transfer of wisdom, for Mary was Sophia and her Son the Logos.[25] The medieval accounts of the miraculous bestowal of Mary's milk into the mouths of believers affirmed their devotion.[26]

In the early church, the newly baptized were given a cup of milk and honey to taste as symbolizing their regeneration through baptism (cf. 1 Cor 3:2; Heb 5:12; 1 Peter 2:2).[27] This rite had Hebrew scriptural foretypes and devotional references to all those who were 'children in Christ'. The inclusion of a cup of milk and honey in the ritual of baptism was a recognized practice that could be interpreted devotionally. According to the twenty-third canon of the Third Council of Carthage (397), this milk and honey was to be consecrated at the altar on Easter Eve, the most solemn day for baptism.[28] However, Canon 57 from the Quinisext Synod in Trullo (692) decreed this practice was forbidden.[29]

According to Byzantine tradition, the evangelist Luke wrote the first icons of the *Theotokos* after the Pentecost. He initiated three 'prototypes', the first being the *Theotokos hodigetria*, 'she who leads the way', which visually emphasized the divinity of the Christ Child. Second was the *Theotokos eleousa*, 'Our Mother of Tenderness', which illustrated the humanity of Jesus as well as Mary's foreknowledge of her child's future and the depth of her daily suffering on account of that future. The third was that of the 'Mourning Mother' depicted alone at the foot of the cross, an image later connected with the iconic motif identified as the *Deesis*, or entreaty, preceding the Last Judgment.

These depictions of the *Theotokos* with her infant son by St. Luke were clearly connected to the liturgical tradition of the Fourth Tone, First Hymn of the Virgin, from the Matins sung on the feasts of Mary such as the Annunciation and the *Koimesis*[30]: 'Painting your all-honourable image, the divine Luke, author of the Gospel of Christ, inspired by the divine voice, represented the Creator of all things in your arms.'[31]

The first icons written by St. Luke were prototypes for future icons such as the variant identified as the *Theotokos galaktotrophousa*, that is, 'the giver of milk'. It was also believed that the *Theotokos* approved and conferred her grace and power only to *these* prototypes. Thereby only those images (or icons) that reproduced the authentic traits of the Virgin as represented by St. Luke transmitted her power and grace.

There was both a written tradition to affirm this 'pious practice' in both the Eastern and Western churches into the ninth century, and a liturgical tradition that identified particular icons of the *Theotokos* as those made by St. Luke that were venerated in Constantinople and in Rome.[32] The Western Christian *Maria lactans* (Mary as the Nursing Mother) derived from the Byzantine *Theotokos galaktotrophousa* (Mother of God as the Milk Giver) identified Mary simultaneously as 'mother church' and as the good mother who nursed her child.[33]

## *Medieval Spirituality of the Virgin's Milk*

Medieval relics and pilgrimage traditions coalesced in the formulation of the spirituality of Mary's milk. Popular devotional practices, legends, conciliar documents and liturgical practices were affirmed by the visual presence of the Marian milk relics transferred from the Holy Land to various European churches. Medieval pilgrims travelled throughout the Christian world from Bethlehem to Chartres, Paris, Avignon, Toulon, Rome, Padova, Oviedo, Venice, Naples, Walsingham and the Royal Chapel at Windsor to revere phials of Mary's milk that were reputed to liquefy miraculously on specific Marian feasts.

Her nurturing breast and her milk were promoted in the Marian devotions of medieval women mystics such as the German medieval poet known as Inclusa Ava (d. 1127) and Gertrude the Great (1256–1302). By the twelfth century, this form of effluvial sanctity interconnected with devotional relics and sacramental practice. Venerating a relic was not simply an act of prayer or devotion but one predicated on the ***seeing*** of the spiritual through the physical. While relics such as the drops of Mary's milk existed, this spiritual seeing could also be initiated by images such as the motif of the *Maria lactans*. This understanding of the meaning of Mary's milk highlights effluvial sanctity in medieval Christian practice and shows how iconography endorses such sacrality in the hearts of the Christian collective.

Medieval female mystics were renowned for their keening spirituality and intimate knowledge of God that was most often described in a language filled with bodily metaphor and a sense of sexual intimacy. As with the mystics of all world religious traditions, the medieval female mystics spoke (and wrote) in a language that was simultaneously paradoxical and clear. They placed great emphasis on the eye, on the act of ***seeing*** the invisible and thereby acquiring an intimate and immediate knowledge of the non-empirical reality identified as God or the sacred.

Although revered within the institutional church, Christian mystics have traditionally been categorized as anti-theological, anti-institutional, intuitive and sentimental. For the medieval female mystics, especially those from the northern European regions, their spiritual and devotional centre was a reunion with God premised on the mystery of the Incarnation and the Redemption; thereby they perceived the humanity of Jesus as the essential mediation between God and humanity. As the Romanian philosopher Émile Cioran (1911–1995) noted, 'European mysticism is a religious movement with political overtones…[having a] strong spirit of reform…[and a] fight for the restoration of true faith'.[34] This 'true faith' was tempered by the spiritualties of the mendicant orders, lay devotions and the varied forms of lay spirituality of the Brotherhood of the Common Life and of the *Devotio moderna* whose emphasis on devout meditation fostered an intimacy with the images of sacred subjects.

These varied 'traditions' incorporated elements of folk traditions, pious legends, popular devotions and a mystical spirituality that had begun with the Cistercian shift to the subjective experience of faith and that descended through the mendicant emphasis on the humanity of Jesus. This transfer of the 'power of prayer' from the clergy to the illiterate laity was the basis for the development of the lay breviary and the Book of Hours, as well as such communal/individual prayer forms as the Our Father and the Hail Mary. Such a lay movement emphasized the centrality of the 'act of beholding' as an appropriate mode of devotion, contemplation and meditation, especially for women.

The German Beguine Mechthild of Magdeburg was a mystical writer associated with the monastery of Helfta. Such medieval women mystics functioned as translators to the laity of a theology transformed by a devotional and spiritual emphasis on the humanity of Jesus, not the divinity of Christ. Accordingly, the boundaries of this transformed Christian spirituality expanded beyond the geographical borders of monasteries and convents to the laity. Working in coordination with theologians, monks and clerics, these religious women taught the laity how to pray and how to venerate the saints and the Holy Sacraments outside the physical confines of the ecclesial structures, thereby strengthening the faith and daily devotions of the laity, ergo, the members of 'Mother Church'.

Throughout her popular devotional text, *The Flowing Light of the Godhead*, Mechthild of Magdeburg made regular reference to what might be termed a 'spirituality of the Virgin's Milk'. Consider, for example, the following passage from her text:

> Ah! Lady! thou must still nurture us…till the Last Day. Then shalt thou see how God's children and thy children are weaned and grown up into everlasting life. Then shall we see and know in unspeakable joy, the milk and e'en the self-same breast, which Jesus oft as infant kissed.[35]

In her use of this motif, Mechthild was not alone; in fact, a survey of the writings of thirteenth-century mystics, especially women mystics, reveals a Mariological emphasis in terms of the devotions of Marian spirituality from the attentions to the Virgin's inner feelings during significant scriptural events such as the Annunciation, Nativity and Crucifixion to her role in non-scriptural events, which became central to pious legends and sacred traditions such as the *Pietà* and her *Koimesis*. The sacramental and spiritual focus of these events and feelings became Mary's extraordinary empathy or perhaps, better said, her '*com-passio*'.[36]

As a crucial theological and artistic symbol for 'Mother Church', Mary as the Virgin Mother garnered an increasing position in the spiritual, devotional and liturgical life of the medieval laity. One of the central visual images for this new Mariology was a retrieval and a re-visioning of the Byzantine *Theotokos galaktotrophusa*. Similarly, the writings of the medieval women mystics were a popular vehicle for the teaching on the 'act of beholding' as appropriate to daily devotional practice. Thereby, the icon was both to be beheld, and to be a visual defence, if not explanation, for this connection between salvific word and image.

The motif of the *Maria lactans* was a major intercessory image for medieval Christianity. Mary's pleas for the salvation of a penitent were granted by virtue of the breasts with which she had nursed the Christ Child. This iconographic motif, which effectively illustrated the Saturday Mass for the Virgin as well, was the liturgical counterpart of this same concern and attitude in the writings and devotional practices of the medieval women mystics like Mechthild, who wrote

And the sweet milk flowed from her pure being;
The Child sucked in human fashion;
His mother rejoiced in holiness;
The angels praised God;
And the shepherds came and sought and found
Our true Redeemer.[37]

Mechthild of Magdeburg underscored the labyrinth of theological meaning, spiritual implications and devotion to the spirituality of the Virgin's Milk: 'how her [Mary's] comely breasts were so full of sweet milk that drops of it flowed down to the glory of the Father, for the love of man, that man might be welcomed above all creatures'.[38]

*Effluvial Sanctity: Mary's Milk in Image and Sacrament*

As European interest in Mary's motherliness and compassion increased, so did both the miraculous stories and the iconography of the *Maria lactans*. One of the more popular variations on the theme of Mary nursing her Child was that of her offering her breast milk as a sign of special favour to holy individuals. One such variant is known as the 'Lactation Miracle of St. Bernard'. The son of Burgundian nobles, St. Bernard of Clairvaux (1090/1092–1153) was an austere cleric and author who forswore wealth *and* images. However he had a deep-seated devotion to the Virgin Mary and in a series of significant theological and devotional treatises he supported the Marian cult of the Virgin Birth, the efficacy of Mary's intercession, and proposed that she be identified as the mediatrix of Grace.

According to pious tradition, the Virgin Mary expressed three drops of her milk directly into the saint's mouth as both a sign of her special favour and as a bestowal of grace. There are actually two versions of this legend; in the first Mary appeared to St. Bernard who knelt before a statue of the Madonna and Child as depicted in the illumination of *Saint Bernard's Vision of the Virgin and Child* (Figure 1.6) by the Netherlandish painter Simon Marmion (1425–1489).

As part of his prayer, St. Bernard is reputed to have said *Monstra te esse Matrem*[39]as inscribed in gold letters over the Virgin's golden halo in the manuscript illumination. Marmion positioned St. Bernard's sightline towards the Virgin's nipple as she carefully expressed the first of three drops of her milk, signifying through this gesture that she was his mother and was prepared to mediate for him with her natural son. The bare-headed and kneeling St. Bernard was dressed in an elegant cope that included a hood embroidered with an image of the Annunciation while the Christ Child held the bishop's elegantly decorated golden staff. The saint's bare hands were folded in the Germanic gesture of prayer revealing his episcopal ring on the middle finger of his right hand.

**Figure 1.6** Simon Marmion, *Saint Bernard's Vision of the Virgin and Child*, from a Prayer Book or a Book of Hours, c. 1475–80. Tempera colours and gold on parchment, Leaf: 11.6 x 6.3 cm (4 9/16 x 2½ in.). Detached lead, MS. 32, recto (Alternate number: 88. MS.14.recto [object number]). The Getty Museum, Los Angeles.

The second version of this miraculous lactation to St. Bernard strengthens Mary's medieval reputation as a miracle worker. Suffering from an eye infection, St. Bernard prays to have his health restored. Mary expresses three drops of her milk not into his mouth but rather directly onto the infected eye, and St. Bernard's eye is immediately healed. Miraculous healings involving Mary's milk were reported throughout the era of High Mariology.

The long-standing tradition of Mary's Milk Grotto in Bethlehem was predicated upon two biblical passages: the Flight into Egypt (Matt 2:13–15 DR) and the Massacre of the Innocents (Matt 2:16–18 DR). Following the tradition, the Holy Family took refuge in this cave during the Massacre of the Innocents and just before the Flight into Egypt. While Mary was nursing the infant Jesus there, a drop of her milk fell to the ground, turning it white.[40]

A small oratory for devotion to the Virgin Mary was built by Paula around 404 and later expanded into the Byzantine-style church of St. Paula.[41] From the seventh century forward, as the legend further identifying this site as the burial place of the massacred innocents enhanced its reputation, fragments of the limestone ceiling and walls or rocks from this grotto were sent to churches throughout Europe as holy relics. In 1375, Pope Gregory XI (1331–1378) named the Milk Grotto as a Marian shrine. Like the Sanctuary of the Nativity, Mary's Milk Grotto has been the privilege of the Franciscans since the late thirteenth/early fourteenth century. The present church was erected in 1872 with a new chapel dedicated to the Mother of God built in 2007 that connects to the Milk Grotto via an underground tunnel.

Even in the twenty-first century, this site continues to be visited by Jewish, Christian and Muslim women who believe that by ingesting the scrapings from the white stones in the grotto they can boost the quantity and quality of their milk or enhance their fertility.[42] Mothers usually mix these powdered scrapings in their drinking water, and would-be mothers place the 'rock' under their mattresses before sexual intercourse.

## *The Motif of Mary's Breast in the Double Intercession*

Throughout the Middle Ages as Mariology reached its apogee among theologians, artists and the laity, there was the daily mindfulness of the spiritual path to salvation through pilgrimages to holy sites in Europe – from Compostela to Rome – and ultimately to the Holy Land as well as through the veneration and collecting of relics. While pilgrims could visit Marian shrines, attend prayer services said in her honour, and commission works of art dedicated to her, the lacuna of Mary's corporeal remains presented a challenging vacuum for the medieval believer. Without any bodily vestiges, the most significant Marian relics were quite simply material entities that had been in contact with her physical body either as a form of garment or an object she had touched. The most significant among these were her belt or girdle, and her tunic or veil.[43]

Hence as Marian devotions increased and interest in her earthly existence intensified among the faithful the widely dispersed vials of her milk became even more precious and prized relics. Salvation was not only the promise of Christianity but also an aspiration of those pilgrims who venerated relics, and particular to the reverence of Marian relics was the perception of Mary as *mediatrix*. The motif of the *Maria lactans* became a major intercessory image for medieval Christianity. Mary's plea for the salvation of a penitent was granted by virtue of the breasts that had nursed the Christ Child.

Perhaps as a natural extension, in terms of medieval thinking and theology, the depiction of the *Maria lactans* morphed into the depiction of the Virgin as intercessor at the Last Judgment. As this idea was transformed into image, Mary was represented kneeling before her enthroned Son who was clearly identified as the Resurrected Christ as he displayed both his wounds from the nails and lance, and his cruciform nimbus[44] as seen in the innovative illumination of the single

**Figure 1.7** Huth Psalter, *Detail of Virgin Baring her Breast to Intercede for Humanity*, from *The Last Judgment*, c. 1280. Illumination on parchment, BL Add 38116, f.13v.

intercession from the *Huth Psalter* (Figure 1.7).[45] While her left hand is raised in a gesture of exclamation, Mary's right hand displayed her naked right breast as a reminder of her role in his humanity as echoed in Luke 11:27: 'And it came to pass, as he spoke these things, a certain woman from the crowd, lifting up her voice, said to him: Blessed is the womb that bore thee, and the paps that gave thee suck.' Such a visual and textual interpretation of Mary had classical precedents that reinforced the idea of her displaying her breasts in total appeal as Classical prototypes like Phryne, and perhaps unwillingly but most famously like Hecuba in a desperate attempt to save her son Hektor.[46]

The popular devotion to the Virgin Mother as principal intercessor increased in the thirteenth and fourteenth centuries and transformed into the motif identified as the 'Double Intercession' given the growing influence of the texts attributed to several theologians, most especially St. Bernard of Clairvaux and Bonaventure. While originally found in the writings of the biographer of St. Bernard known as Arnold of Chartres,[47] the Double Intercession most probably garnered the attention of the laity through narrative episodes like the following passage from *The Golden Legend*:

> About the security Bernard says: 'O man, you have sure access to God, when the mother stands before the Son. The Son stands before the Father, the mother shows her Son her bosom her breasts, the Son shows his Father his

side and wounds. Surely then where there are so many marks of love, there can be no refusal.'[48]

Perhaps the most famous depiction of what has become identified as the 'Double Intercession' was initially located in the Santa Maria della Fiore, the Cathedral of Florence, on the fifteenth-century painting *The Intercession of Christ and the Virgin* (Figure 1.8).[49] This slightly larger than life-size work is one of the earliest visualizations of this iconography that can also be identified as a multiple exemplification incorporating Christ as the Man of Sorrows and a depiction of the Trinity.[50]

**Figure 1.8** Attributed to Lorenzo Monaco (Piero di Giovanni), *The Intercession of Christ and the Virgin*, before 1402, c. 1370–1425. Tempera on canvas. Overall: 94¼ x 60¼ x 1 in. (239.4 x 153 x 2.5 cm). The Cloisters Collection, 1953. The Metropolitan Museum of Art, New York, 53.37.

The sumptuous blue background of this painting accentuates the brilliant golden haloes and the white garments worn by Mary and God the Father. Cognizant that the human eye moves first to the light, hence to the colour white in a painting, artists such as Monaco employed it instead of the more traditional blue garment on Mary to emphasis her significance in both this painting and in her role as intercessor. The symphonic interplay of harmonious gestures between God the Father, God the Son and Mary leads the viewers' sightlines across the lower horizon of the painting then upwards to Mary's white robe. Her outstretched right hand gestured to the presence of the individuals who have garnered her grace and for whose sins she now intercedes (Figure 1.9). Following her right hand upwards towards the display of her naked right breast in her left hand (Figure 1.10), the viewer then sees both the golden script that comes from her mouth towards her Son and his extended left hand.

As she asked him, 'Most sweet Son, for the milk I gave you, have mercy on these people', he responded in both a dual upward sweep of his words, 'My Father, let those be saved for whom you wished that I suffer the Passion' and of the display of his side wound to God the Father.[51] As the viewer looked upwards from the wounds and words of Christ towards the white dove, representing the Holy Spirit,

**Figure 1.9** Detail of the penitents between Christ and the Virgin from *The Intercession of Christ and the Virgin*, see Figure 1.8.

**Figure 1.10** Detail of the Virgin holding forth her naked breast from *The Intercession of Christ and the Virgin*, see Figure 1.8.

that hovered between himself and God the Father, she saw the white-clad figure of God the Father who simultaneously gestured welcome and granted mercy.

The continual intersections not simply of the hand gestures and words of the three individual figures but of the multiple series of intersecting triangles formed throughout the painting drew the viewer's attention to the significance of Mary's position as she was included in the major triangles formed at least twice between herself, her son and God the Father, as well as the ones that ran across her displayed breast, his revealed wounds and the Holy Spirit or God the Father.[52] The further, and perhaps penultimate, internal triangle was formed from the diagonal lines as her words reached Christ and his words reached, and hovered over, her extended breast.

In terms of medieval Christian iconography, it would be significant to note that both the kneeling figures of Mary and her Son were represented as if they were equals: they knelt on the same level ground and were of approximately equal stature. As the art historian and theologian Timothy Verdon noted, '...in the most common prayer honouring her, believers ask Mary to "pray for us sinner, now and in the hour of our death".'[53]

*Conclusion: Why Mary's Breast Was Covered Again*

The reality of changing cultural and devotional attitudes that corresponded with the rise of Renaissance Humanism in theology, philosophy and the arts resulted in the road to the Reformation and transformations in the role of Mary. The evolution of the Renaissance artistic emphasis on naturalism in presentations of the human figure initiated a transformation in the depiction of the body from a fundamentally symbolic referent to the one predicated on the then modern perceptions of the human anatomy and medicine. The reintroduction of the classical nude into Renaissance painting and sculpture furthered the public reception of the sexuality and sensuality of the human body.

So Mary's naked breast, for example, was now depicted in a more natural shape and position, and had the possibility of arousing erotic sensibilities among believers. Additionally, the social and cultural attitudes towards modifications in women's costumes, and class attitudes to both breastfeeding and the employment of wet nurses were contributing factors in the 'covering up' of Mary's lactating breast. Instead, however, of a complete abandonment of the motif of the *Maria lactans*, artists initiated or revived earlier gestural symbolism through which the Christ Child indicated his need for his mother's milk, for example either by the insertion into or the tugging by his little hand on the neckline of her garment.

As Reformation thinking began to influence both the political and social consciousness of Europe, the Reformers' concerns over Marian devotions found new venues in the Roman Catholic Church as artists followed the lead of the new spirituality that moved from the imagery of the Madonna and Child to the motifs of the suffering and bereaved mother that further emphasized Mary's subservience to her Son. Catholic iconography found inspiration in the advancement of the Marian devotions of the Immaculate Conception and the Assumption of Mary.[54] Furthermore, both the making and practice of the Rosary, credited by pious tradition to St. Dominic via a Marian apparition in 1214, magnified in the early sixteenth century and was officially named a devotion for the Roman Catholic Church by Pope Pius V in 1569. Therefore, despite the Reformers' call for less devotion to Mary and more attention to the authority of the Bible, Roman Catholic artists, theologians and laity emphasized continuing attention to Mary as evidenced in the visual and devotional move from the *Madonna lactans* to the *Mater dolorosa*.

Nonetheless, one can infer the critical importance of Mary's role and the spirituality of her milk in the history of Christian faith from the Byzantine iconographical and liturgical tradition to the writings of medieval mystics and the art of medieval and early Renaissance painters. This role was enhanced by the transformations in cultural attitudes and Christian theology, and was reflected simultaneously in the spiritual emphasis on contemplation, devotion and image in the medieval Christian world.

## Notes

1 Margaret Yalom, *A History of the Breast* (New York: Alfred P. Knopf, 1997). For example, see any of the following selected works: Margaret R. Miles, *Carnal Knowing: Female Nakedness and Religious Meaning in the Christian West* (Boston: Beacon Press, 1998); Megan Holmes, 'Disrobing the Virgin: The *Madonna Lactans* in Fifteenth-Century Florentine Art'? in *Picturing Women in Renaissance and Baroque Italy*, ed. Geraldine A. Johnson and Sara F. Matthews Grieco (Cambridge: Cambridge University Press, 1997), 167–95; Beth Williamson, 'The Virgin *Lactans* as Second Eve: Images of the *Salvatrix*', *Studies in Iconography* 19 (1998): 105–38; Nancy Yashimoshi, 'The Virgin's Peculiar Breast: Negotiating Nudity in Devotional Painting', *Illumine* I.1 (2001–2002): 5–13; Margaret R. Miles, *A Complex Delight: The Secularization of the Breast, 1350–1750* (Berkeley: University of California Press, 2008); Vibeke Olson, 'Mystical Visions, *Maria Lactans* and the Miracle of Mary's Milk', in *Matter of Faith: An Interdisciplinary Study of Relics and Relic Veneration in the Medieval Period*, ed. James Robinson and Lloyd de Beer with Anna Hardnen (London: The British Museum, 2014), 151–58.

2 Diane Apostolos-Cappadona, 'The Space between Image and Word: The Journey from Rogier van der Weyden's *Descent from the Cross* to Walter Verdin's *Sliding Time*', *CrossCurrents* 63:1 (2013): 26–43.

3 So by ellipses in the Nativity narrative and the practical aspects of the mother–infant relationship, the concept of Mary nursing her new-born son was natural even though direct reference is not found in the canonical texts. However, *Protoevangelium of James* 14:12 reads, 'But the light gradually decreased until the infant appeared and nursed at the breast of his mother Mary.'

4 This is not a traditional theological or liturgical concept but rather my own phrase to identify this consistent attentiveness of medieval women mystics as an analogy for their understanding of the special grace dispensed by the Virgin Mary, especially as *Mater Ecclesia*, through her nursing breast.

5 The Greek word *Theotokos* is literally 'the God-Bearer'; however, it is more commonly translated into English as 'Mother of God'.

6 While originally credited to the thirteenth century Franciscan scholastic theologian and philosopher St. Bonaventure (Giovani di Fidanza), *The Meditations of the Life of Christ* (*Meditationes vitae Christi*) was written several centuries later by the individual now identified Pseudo-Bonaventura, who might have been Giovanni de Cauli. The quotations are from the edition identified as Bonaventure, *Meditations on the Life of Christ: An Illustrated Manuscript of the Fourteenth Century*. Paris, Bibliothèque naitonale, MS. Ital., 115, translated by Isa Ragua; completed from the Latin and edited by Isa Ragusa and Rosalie B. Green (Princeton: Princeton University Press, 1961), Chapter VII, 33. See also 'And the mother wiped His eyes and hers, laid her cheek on His, nursed Him, and comforted Him in every way she could', Chapter VIII, 44; and 'O Lord, with how much concern and diligence she nursed Him, that He might not have the least trouble!', and 'How readily she nursed Him, feeling a great and unknown sweetness in nursing this Child, such as could never be felt by other women!', Chapter X, 54, 55.

7 For example, see the pioneering and now classic essay by the feminist historian Susan Groag Bell, 'Medieval Women Book Owners: Arbiters of Lay Piety and Ambassadors of Culture', *Signs* 7:4 (1982): 742–68. Bell advocated for the instrumental role of

women in the initiation of another Marian motif without biblical basis—that of the Virgin reading at the Annunciation, a motif that became so popular that within a century it was depicted on altarpieces and other major works of ecclesial art.

8 The idea of the 'power of images' is most fully discussed in David Freedberg, *The Power of Images: Studies in the History and Theory of Response* (Chicago: University of Chicago Press, 1989).

9 Given both its prosaic narrative style and its history contemporary to many medieval and Renaissance artists, I employ the Douay-Rheims edition of the Bible in my iconological research. All biblical references herein are marked DR and are from the 1899 English translation now available at http://www.drbo.org.

10 See for example, Justin Martyr (d. 145), *Dialogue with Trypho*, 100; Irenaeus of Lyons (d. 202), *Against Heresies*, 3, 22; and St. Jerome (d. 420), *Tractate on Psalm 96*, 1.

11 Since 2005, art-historical scholarship unraveled the mystery behind the name of Carlo da Camerino and re-identified him as Olivuccio de Ciccaredo da Camerino, c. 1365–1439; see Andrea De Maretti, *Pittoria Camerino nel Quattrocentro* (Milan: Frederico Motta Editor, 2008 [2002]).

12 *Sacra conversazione* is Italian for 'holy conversation'. This motif for the Madonna and Child has been credited to Fra Angelico. This representation of the Enthroned Madonna and Child with saints and/or donors who, while cognizant of each other's presence and united in a common action, were also aware of the spectator. All hierarchical barriers, social and historical, were removed as all the figures within the canvas functioned within a single unified space. See Diane Apostolos-Cappadona, *Dictionary of Christian Art* (New York: Continuum, 1994), 298.

13 More often than not, Mary's exposed breast is enlarged, if not engorged, with her milk. However, the opposite breast was depicted as if flat or non-existent. Even if she had nursed the Christ Child with her other breast first, there should still be some shape or protrusion under her garment.

14 Yalom, *A History of the Breast*, 42.

15 Medievalists have identified this work as the first large-scale nude figure in European art since antiquity. Sadly, the partner panel of Adam has been destroyed.

16 For example, Masolino da Panicale, *Temptation of Adam and Eve* (1424: Cappella Brancacci, Santa Maria del Carmine, Florence); Hugo van der Goes, *The Fall of Adam and Eve* (c. 1479: Kunsthistoriches Museum, Vienna); Lucas Cranach the Elder, *Adam and Eve* (1526: Courtauld Institute of Art, London); Hans Baldung Grien, *Adam and Eve* (1531: Collezione Thyssen-Bornemisza, Madrid); Titian, *The Fall of Man* (c. 1550: Museo del Prado, Madrid); and Peter Paul Rubens, *Adam and Eve* (1626–29: Museo del Prado, Madrid).

17 This is the classical Greek term for 'nursing deities'; see note 23.

18 The classical Roman story of Cimon and Pero in which the jailed Roman senator was saved from starvation by his lactating daughter's daily visits reversed the generational exchange of sustenance from parent to child and transformed the engendered connection of female parent with male offspring to that of female offspring with male parent. This story was recorded by Valerius Maximus in Book V: 5.4.7 of his *Factorum ac dictorum memorabilium* (*Nine Books of Memorable Acts and Sayings of the Ancient Romans*) now available online at http://www.thelatinlibrary.com/valmax.html.

19 Gail Paterson Corrington, 'The Milk of Salvation: Redemption by the Mother in Late Antiquity and Early Christianity', *Harvard Theological Review* 82:4 (1989): 393–420 (401).

20 For example, the Milky Way was created when the mortal infant Herakles was suckled by Hera and was thereby granted the divine gift of immortality. However, in his hunger, Herakles sucked with such vigor that some of the goddess's divine milk sprinted across the heavens creating new celestial bodies and lilies on the earth. In a reversal of the tale of the divine mother adopting a mortal son, Amalthea as a she-goat suckled the infant Zeus while the priestess Melissa nurtured Zeus with goat's milk.

21 Yalom, *A History of the Breast*, 9.

22 For example, consider the so-called *Venus of Willendorf* (28,000–25,000 BCE: Natural History Museum, Vienna).

23 *Kourotrophos* refers to the classical Greek maternal or nursing principle manifested through suckling. Statuettes of nursing mothers were placed in tombs and sanctuaries, probably as offerings to one of the various *kourotrophos* goddesses, for example, Gaia, Hera, Aphrodite, Demeter, Persephone, and even the virgin goddesses Artemis and Athena. Other offerings included edible items, such as honey, oil and cakes, some of which were made in the form of breasts. For a discussion of the *kourotophos*, see Corrington, 'The Milk of Salvation', and also Yalom, *A History of the Breast*, 15.

24 While this direct quote is taken from Anne Baring and Jules Cashford, *The Myth of the Goddess: Evolution of an Image* (Baltimore: Penguin, 1993 [1992]), 250, there is similar referencing to these ideas in Corrington, 'The Milk of Salvation', 398–99, and throughout V. Tran Tam Tinh, *Isis lactans: Corpus des monuments gréco-romains d'Isis allaitant Harpocrate*, Études préliminaires aux religions orientales dans l'empire romain, 37 (Leiden: Brill, 1973).

25 For example, see Baring and Cashford, *The Myth of the Goddess*, 609–651, and Corrington, 'The Milk of Salvation', 397–99.

26 For example, see Nigel of Canterbury, *Miracles of the Virgin Mary, in Verse: Miracula sancte dei genitricis virginis Marie, versifice* edited from British Library MS. Cotton Vespasian D.xix by Jan Ziolkowski (Toronto: Centre for Medieval Studies, 1986); and Beverly Boyd, *The Middle English Miracles of the Virgin* (San Marino: The Huntington Library, 1964).

27 For a detailed discussion of this ritual practice and its patristic sources, see 'Milk and Honey', in Robin M. Jensen, *Baptismal Imagery in Early Christianity: Ritual, Visual, and Theological Dimensions* (Grand Rapids: Baker Academic, 2012), 122–27.

28 While my original source for this discussion was George A. Barton, 'Milk (Civilized Religions)', *Encyclopaedia of Religion and Ethics*, ed. James Hastings (New York: Charles Scribner's Sons, 1916), VIII: 637, the reader is referred to the most recent critical edition of these documents in Charles Munier (ed.), *Concilia Africae A.345–A.525,* Corpus Christianorum Series Latina 149, Turnhout: Brepols, 1974, in particular *Breviarium hipponense incipit brevis statutorum*, 40. See also *Concilium cartheginense*, Canon N of the Council of Carthage (525), for a reaffirmation in the same source, 26.

29 'Honey and milk may not be offered on the altar.' See Karl Joseph von Hefele, *A History of the Councils of the Church from the Original Documents* (Edinburgh: T. & T. Clark, 1896), II: 231.

30 *Koimesis* is the 'falling asleep' or, as it is more commonly translated into English, the Dormition.

31 Leonid Ouspensky, *Theology of the Icon* (Crestwood, NY: Saint Vladimir's Seminary Press, 1978), 73. This chant is also identified as Sixth Kontakion, Sixth Oikos of the sixth-century Akathistos Hymn dedicated to the Theotokos. In contemporary

Greek Orthodox chant, the reference is rather to the evangelist Luke and the Icon of Odigitria in Ode 9, The Heirmos of the Megalynarion of the small Paraklese: 'Άλαλα τα χείλη των ασεβών, των μη προσκυνούντων, την Εικόνα σου την σεπτήν, την ιστορηθείσαν, υπό του Αποστόλου, Λουκά ιερωτάτου, την Οδηγήτριαν.' (English reads as 'Speechless be the lips of the impious ones, those who do not reverence your great icon, the sacred one which is called Directress, and was depicted for us by one of the apostles, Luke the Evangelist.' [Directress is a title of the Theotokos Hodigetria]).

On the theme of St. Luke as the originator of the icons of the Theotokos, see Maria Vassiliki (ed.), *Mother of God: Representations of the Virgin in Byzantine Art* (Milan: Skira, 2000), especially Michele Bicci, 'With the Paintbrush of the Evangelist Luke', 79–90 (Exhibition catalogue from the Benaki Museum, Athens).

32 Christine Angelidi and Titos Papamastorakis, 'The Veneration of the Virgin Hodegetria and the Hodegon Monastery', in *Mother of God*, ed. Vassiliki, 373–424.

33 In accordance with the meaning of the Byzantine icon of the *Theotokos galaktotrophousa* as visualized through the Sixth Kontakion, Sixth Oikos of the sixth-century Akathistos Hymn dedicated to the *Theotokos*.

34 Émile Cioran, *Tears and Saints* (Chicago: University of Chicago Press, 1995), xi.

35 *The Revelations of Mechthild of Magdeburg (1210–97) or The Flowing Light of the Godhead. Translated from the Manuscript in the Library of the Monastery at Einsiedeln*, ed. Lucy Menzies (London: Longsman, Green, 1953), 13–14.

36 Otto G. von Simson, '*Compassio* and *Co-redemptio* in Roger van der Weyden's *Descent from the Cross*', *Art Bulletin* 35:1 (1953): 9–16.

37 *The Revelations of Mechthild of Magdeburg (1210–97)*, 145.

38 *The Revelations of Mechthild of Magdeburg (1210–97)*, 31.

39 '…show yourself to be a mother'.

40 This legend probably arose to Christianize a grotto that was originally a shrine to Ashtoreth or Astarte (the Canaanite/Babylonian goddess who also signified fertility and maternity including the necessary production of mother's milk and who cured infertility.).

41 There is confusion as to which of the two Paulas, St. Paula of Rome (c. 347–404) and confidante of St. Jerome, or her granddaughter Paula the Younger, was actually responsible for the building on this site. However, tradition indicates that both women were actively engaged in the devotion to the Virgin Mary at this location.

42 Susan Starr Sered, 'Rachel's Tomb and the Milk Grotto of the Virgin: Two Women's Shrines in Bethlehem', *Journal of Feminist Studies in Religion* 2:2 (1986): 193–203.

43 According to Eastern Orthodox Christian tradition, the Virgin's cincture was housed in the Ecclesia tou Theotokos Blachernitissa in Constantinople from the time of Justinian until it was transferred to the Vatopedi Monastery on Mount Athos. From about the fourteenth century, the Western Christian Church identified the *Sacra cintola* as in the care of the Cathedral of Prato in Italy. By the middle of the fourteenth century, so many pilgrims were coming to venerate this Marian relic that a special chapel (Cappella del Sacro Cingolo) had to be built for its protection and display. The Virgin's *Sancta Camisa* was reputedly kept in Constantinople until the Empress Irene sent it as a gift to the Emperor Charlemagne whose grandson Charles the Bald presented it to the Cathedral of Notre Dame, Chartres, in 876. Mary is believed to have worn the tunic now deposited and displayed in the Shrine to the Virgin in Aachen. All of these Marian relics have been associated with miracles and healings. Along with the relics of Jesus' nativity, these garments were the major Marian relics except for the vials of her miraculous milk and the icons written by St. Luke.

44 The cruciform nimbus was a specific form of the halo reserved for the Resurrected Christ as the inscribed cross in the circle of light signified that he had 'passed through his Passion and Death'. See Diane Apostolos-Cappadona, *Dictionary of Christian Art* (New York: Continuum, 1994), 182–84.

45 For a discussion of this iconography, see C. W. Kauffmann, *Biblical Imagery in Medieval England, 700–1550* (London: H. Miller, 2003), 169–70. Further, Kauffmann identified the most unusual variant of this motif in an illumination from the *Zouche Book of Hours* (c. 1350: Bodleian, Lat. Liturgy. E.41, f.50) as ill. 154, 209: *The Risen Christ and the Virgin with Bared Breast. Initial D at Vespers*. As Kauffmann described the pattern, in this incipit the Risen Christ's right hand grasped the left hand of his kneeling mother as her right hand displayed her breast. However, what Kauffmann did not note was that this positioning was almost identical – including the triumphant cross substituting for a hoe in Christ's right hand – to the motif identified as the *Noli me tangere* that I believe evolved from the earlier motif of the *Chairete* in Late Antique/Early Christian and Byzantine iconography in which both the *Theotokos* and Mary Magdalene were the first witnesses of the Resurrection; see my 'On the Visual and the Vision: The Magdalene in Early Christian and Byzantine Art and Culture', in *Mariam, the Magdalen, and the Mother*, ed. Deirdre Good (Bloomington: Indiana University Press, 2005), 123–49.

46 The two significant classical precedents for this image of Mary displaying her breasts in final appeal were the legendary tradition of the courtesan Phryne and the literary pattern established in Homer's *Iliad*. The fourth-century BCE courtesan known as Phryne had been accused by one of her lovers of the crime of blasphemy, which was then a capital offense. During her trial, when her defender, the orator Hypereides, recognized that the judges were about to condemn her despite his pleas, he had Phryne brought into the court; removing her clothing she displayed her bosom. Her lovely breasts and the lawyer's overwrought pleas aroused such compassion in the hearts of the judges that she was acquitted. Thereafter, a decree was passed stipulating that no accused person on trial could display his or her private parts, for fear of making a similar impression on the judges.

The pertinent passage in Homer's *Iliad* reads:

> And side by side with him his mother in tears was mourning and laid the fold of her bosom bare and with one hand held out a breast, and wept her tears for him and called to him in winged words: 'Hektor, my child, look upon these and obey, and take pity on me, if ever I gave you the breast to quiet your sorrow.'

See *The Iliad of Homer*, trans. by Richmond Lattimore (Chicago: University of Chicago Press, 1967), XXII: 79–83, page 437. This classical reference to Hecuba, Queen of Troy, influenced many later writers, none more so than William Shakespeare who incorporated references to her, her tears and her act of supplication in several plays including *Hamlet* (Act 2, Scene 2), *Troilus and Cressida* (Act 1, Scene, 2), *Titus Andronicus* (Act 4, Scene 1), *Coriolanus* (Act 1, Scene 3) and *Cymbeline* (Act 4, Scene 2), and in his long poem *The Rape of Lucretia*.

47 He is also identified as Ernaldus of Chartres and Arnaldus, Abbot of Bonneval even among the varied twentieth- and twenty-first-century authors writing on the iconography of the 'Double Intercession'. For Arnold's original Latin text see *Libellus de laudibus Mariae virginis* in J. P. Migne's *Patrologiae latina*, 189, col. 1725C–1726C.

48 See Chapter 72, 'The Ascension of the Lord', in *The Golden Legend: Readings on the Saints*, trans. Granger Ryan (Princeton: Princeton University Press, 2012), I: 297–298.

Readers might also consult the early fourteenth-century *Speculae humanae salvationis* (*Mirror of Human Salvation*) as another popularizing source for this devotional and iconographic motif.

49 Among the extensive published studies of this painting, the most helpful for purposes of my argument were especially Timothy Verdon, 'The *Intercession of Christ and the Virgin* from the Florence Cathedral: Iconographic and Ecclesiological Significance', in *The Fabric of Images: European Paintings on Textile Supports in the Fourteenth and Fifteenth Centuries*, ed. Caroline Villers (London: Archetype Publications, 2000), 43–54; Beth Williamson, 'The *Cloisters Double Intercession*: The Virgin as Co-Redemptrix', *Apollo* 152 (2000): 48–54; Katherine Beartjer, '*The Intercession of Christ and the Virgin* Attributed to Lorenzo Monaco', in *European Paintings in the Metropolitan Museum of Art by Artists Born before 1865* (New York: The Metropolitan Museum of Art and Harry N. Abrams, 1995), 13–14; Millard Meiss, 'An Early Altarpiece from the Cathedral of Florence', *The Metropolitan Museum of Art Bulletin* 12 (June 1954): 302–17.

50 On this significance of Monaco's presentation of the Trinity in this painting, see especially Verdon, The *Intercession of Christ and the Virgin*', 43–54.

51 The original painted texts read respectively '*DOLCIXIMIO FIGLIUOLO PELLACTE CHIO TIDIE ABBI MIA [MISERICORDIA] DI CHOSTORO*' and '*PADRE MIOSIENO SALVI CHOSTORO PEQUALI TU VOLESTI CHO PATISSI PASSIONE.*'

52 Renaissance art historians have identified one of the major compositional elements of Renaissance painting as the revival of pyramidal composition by Leonardo da Vinci, hence the significance here in the work of his predecessor Monaco.

53 Verdon, 'The *Intercession of Christ and the Virgin*', 52.

54 While present in the unfolding revelation of believers, neither the Immaculate Conception nor the Assumption of Mary was initially proclaimed as a doctrine of the church. While popular with both late medieval and early Renaissance popes as well as theologians and the Christian collective, the Immaculate Conception was not formally declared as doctrine until 1854 and the Assumption of Mary until 1950.

# 2

# IMAGES OF THE FIRST WOMAN: EVE IN ISLAMIC *FĀL-NĀMA* PAINTINGS

Zohar Hadromi-Allouche

The story of Eve and Adam and their expulsion from paradise appears in the earliest Islamic sources available to us. The Qur'an refers briefly to this story in three different chapters.[1] Other early Islamic sources add many more details to the concise Qur'anic narratives. Some of these can also be found in earlier Jewish and Christian sources (e.g. the name 'Eve' for the spouse of Adam, whom the Qur'an does not name), whereas others are unique to the Islamic sources. For example, the identification of the fruit of paradise as wheat reflects a specific Islamic interpretation of the paradise story.[2] Both Qur'anic and post-Qur'anic narratives concerning Eve and Adam are reflected, as well as interpreted, in visual representations of the couple in Islamic art, and particularly in paintings that are included in a specific literary genre of divination, known as *Fāl-Nāma*.

This chapter examines the presentation of Eve in three Islamic paintings from the sixteenth and early seventeenth centuries. These paintings describe three important moments in the lives of Eve and Adam: before, during and immediately after the expulsion from paradise. The ways in which these paintings construct the image of Eve are examined in relation to her depiction in the Islamic textual sources, particularly the Qur'an and later religious literature. A close examination of these paintings reveals, alongside similarities to the textual sources, also alternative portrayals of Eve, which are in disagreement with her depictions in the mainstream religious literature.

The first part of this chapter surveys the textual depiction of Eve in Islamic narratives of the transgression in paradise. These narratives are found in the Qur'an and later Islamic sources, such as commentaries to the Qur'an and works belonging to the Stories of the Prophets (*Qiṣaṣ al-anbiyā'*) genre. These textual sources serve as the point of departure for the second part of the chapter, which closely analyses the iconography and specific details of the portrayal of Eve in three Islamic paintings from the fifteenth and early sixteenth centuries. These paintings are taken from two pictorial *Fāl-Nāma* codices: books, images and text were used for divination. Following a short introduction to this genre, three paintings are examined. The first two were included in the Persian dispersed *Fāl-Nāma* ('Book of omens'; Qazvin, Safavid Iran, late 1550s CE or early 1560), and the third in the *Fāl-Nāma* of Ahmed I ('Book of Omens'; Istanbul, Ottoman Empire, assembled from 1614 to 1616).

The three paintings describe important moments in the lives of Eve and Adam. A close analysis of the paintings reveals both parallels and contrasts between the construction of Eve in the paintings on the one hand, and the textual tradition on the other. The paintings often reflect the narratives of the Qur'an and exegetical tradition. However, a close reading of some of the details in these paintings reveals that at the same time they also break away from the narratives. The portrayal of Eve in these paintings is, therefore, that of an ambivalent, complex image, whose story can be told in a number of ways. The textual sources relate some of these; the paintings, however, provide a glimpse into alternative narratives of Eve, about which the textual sources tend to keep quiet.

## *Eve in the Qur'an and Islamic Tradition*

### *The Expulsion from the Garden in the Qur'an*

The story of the transgression in the Garden with the resultant human descent to the earth appears three times in the Qur'an, in chapters 2, 7 and 20, always preceded by the fall of Satan (Iblīs).[3]

The narratives in Q 2:30–38 and Q 7:11–25 are highly similar, with Q 2:30–38 giving some more details on the fall of Satan, and Q 7:11–25 elaborating more on the human fall. According to Q 7:11–25, after God created and shaped the first human,[4] he commanded the angels to prostrate themselves before Adam. The angels obeyed, except for Iblīs (Satan). God instructed Adam to dwell in the Garden (*al-janna*) with his spouse and eat as they wished, but to stay away from 'this tree', lest they became wrongdoers. Nevertheless, Satan seduced them to eat from the tree, arguing that it would turn them into angels, or immortals (Q 7:19–20). Eating the forbidden fruit made Adam and his spouse realize that they were naked. As they started stitching the leaves of the Garden onto themselves, God reproached them for listening to Satan. They then asked God for forgiveness. God instructed them to descend to earth, being enemies to each other (humans and Satan? man and woman?). The narration in Q 2:30–38 adds at this point that Adam (alone) then received 'words' from God, and that God forgave Adam (Q 2:37). God also promised divine guidance (to humanity). Those who follow this guidance should be protected from fear and sadness (Q 2:38).[5] Islam, therefore, does not regard the transgression in the Garden as an 'original sin'.

The narrative in Q 20:115–123 is similar to the narratives in Q 2:30–38 and Q 7:11–25; however, it emphasizes the figure of Adam. It begins by stating that God had made a covenant with Adam before, but Adam forgot, and had no determination. The narrative then relates the divine commandment to the angels to prostrate themselves before Adam. Following the disobedience of Iblīs, God warned Adam against Satan, who was an enemy to Adam and his spouse. God also informed Adam that, while in the Garden, he would be protected from hunger, thirst, nakedness and heat of the sun (Q 20:115–19). However, Satan tempted Adam, and both Adam and his spouse ate from the tree. Their nakedness was revealed to them, and they covered themselves with the leaves of the Garden. Adam disobeyed his Lord. Then God chose Adam, forgave him and guided him (Q 20:120–22).

The Qur'anic narratives of the transgression differ from the biblical story and its Jewish and Christian interpretations on a number of levels. For the current discussion, three differences are of particular interest. First, God explicitly forgives Adam, which means that (unlike some Jewish and Christian interpretations) there is no original sin. Second, most significantly with regard to the image of the first woman, the responsibility for eating the forbidden fruit is shared between the woman and the man. According to Q 2:36 and Q 7:20–22, Satan tempts Adam and his spouse at the same time. This is in contrast to Gen. 3:1–6, where the snake is said to have first tempted the woman, who then gave the fruit to her spouse (Gen. 3:1–6). Furthermore, according to Q 20:120, initially it was Adam alone who was directly tempted by Satan. The joint consumption of the forbidden fruit by the spouse and Adam only followed later (Q 20:121). Several scholars, such as Jane Smith and Yvonne Haddad, Simonetta Calderini and Denise Spellberg, have highlighted this difference between the Bible and the Qur'an, as evidence that the Qur'an presents an egalitarian version of the paradise narrative.[6]

But whether the Qur'an indeed presents such an egalitarian version is debatable, because of a third point of interest. In the three transgression narratives, and indeed in the Qur'an as a whole, the spouse of Adam is not mentioned by name. Rather, she is called his 'spouse' (*zawj*). Furthermore, the Qur'an refers to this unnamed spouse only in relation to being tempted, eating from the forbidden tree and being expelled from the Garden. Even within this context, God does not speak directly to her (except perhaps after the transgression, when God commands all of them to descend to earth), but only to Adam. Nor is the spouse granted divine forgiveness after the transgression. In response to the couple's joint request for forgiveness (Q 7:23), no acceptance of the request is mentioned. Rather, God commands the couple to leave the Garden and descend to earth.

God does, however, grant forgiveness to Adam. According to Q 2:37, after the transgression God gave Adam words and forgave him; according to Q 20:122, God chose Adam, forgave him and guided him. Adam is also mentioned in the Qur'an in a variety of contexts, other than that of the transgression. God created Adam (Q 7:11) to be his vicegerent on earth (Q 2:30), and made a covenant with him (Q 20:115). He taught Adam the names of all creatures (Q 2:31–33) and commanded the angels to prostrate themselves before him (Q 2:34; 7:11; 20:116). Adam is a progenitor of prophets (Q 19:58), and one of the ancestors who were chosen by God (Q 3:33; 20:122). Following these highly positive characteristics of Adam in the Qur'an, later Islamic sources consider Adam a prophet.[7]

The numerous positive references to Adam are in stark contrast to the Qur'anic depiction of his spouse. Whereas the Qur'an does not regard her as particularly responsible for the Fall, it also omits all other aspects of her character that are present in the biblical story (Gen. 2–3), such as her name, in particular, but also her creation, fertility and relationship with Adam. Unlike her spouse, she is mentioned in the Qur'an only as an illustration to the story of the expulsion. This treatment of Eve is particularly notable when comparing the Qur'anic depiction of Adam's spouse with those of some other women. Although the Qur'an mentions only one woman figure by name (Mary; e.g. Q Maryam 19), there are several other women to whom it refers, including, for example, the (positive) figures of the wife of Abraham, queen of Sheba and wife of Pharaoh; as well as the (negative) seductive wife of the Egyptian man who bought Joseph.[8] The Qur'an relates the independent, direct speech and actions of all these women. Adam's spouse, on the other hand, speaks or acts only as part of Adam's actions, such as eating the fruit (Q 7:122; 20:121) or approaching God (7:23). The minor but distinctively negative role of Eve does not, therefore, comply with the 'egalitarian' image that has been suggested by Smith and Haddad, Calderini or Spellberg: while not considered as particularly blameworthy for the transgression, Eve is hardly considered at all. As a person she is nearly eliminated from the Qur'anic narrative.

### *Eve in the Islamic Tradition*

An ambivalent depiction of the first woman emerges also from post-Qur'anic literature, such as Qur'anic exegesis, collections of prophetic reports that are meant to document the sayings and deeds of the prophet Muḥammad, Stories of the Prophets literature (*Qiṣaṣ al-anbiyā'*) and historiographical sources.

Unlike the Qur'an, all these sources refer to the spouse of Adam by the name 'Eve' (Ḥawā').[9] At the same time, however, in the six most authoritative compilations of prophetic reports in Sunnī Islam, which contain thousands of such reports, the name 'Eve' only appears four times. This further demonstrates the enduring tension in the Islamic tradition between acknowledging Adam's spouse and ignoring her.

An ambivalent approach towards Eve further emerges through the diverse portrayal of her image in the sources. Some reports, which can be found in exegetical, historiographical and *Qiṣaṣ al-anbiyā'* sources, present a rather positive, even egalitarian, image of Eve. For example, some Shī'ite sources, such as al-Rāwandī's (d. 1178 CE) and al-Jazā'irī's (d. 1100 CE) *Stories of the Prophets* works argue that God created Eve from earth, as he created Adam.[10] In terms of physicality, both al-Kisā'ī (d. eleventh century CE) and al-Rāwandī narrate that Eve was created as a good (*ḥasan*) creation, similar in shape to Adam; but feminine. Al-Kisā'ī adds that Eve was created equal to Adam in every way, however more delicate and more beautiful (in contrast to the *Babylonian Talmud*, where it is said that compared to Adam Eve seemed like a monkey).[11] Regarding the transgression, some reports follow the Qur'anic narrative and describe Eve and Adam as being concurrently tempted by Satan to eat the forbidden fruit.[12] Such positive depictions of Eve are particularly typical of Shī'ite sources, possibly because of the significant role of Fāṭima, the daughter of Muḥammad, in Shī'a Islam. In Shī'ite tradition, Fāṭima holds a venerated status herself, in addition to her portrayal as the wife of an imam

(ʿAlī, d. 661 CE) and the mother of imams (Ḥasan, d. 669 CE; and Ḥusayn, d. 680 CE). She thus serves as a positive paradigm of a feminine role model, which parallels Eve, and implies a more positive view of women in general.[13]

Other reports, however, portray Eve in a rather negative manner. These depictions are more similar to the image of Eve in Rabbinical and Christian sources. For example, many sources relate, similarly to Genesis 2, that Eve was created from Adam's rib—a secondary, inferior creation.[14] In explicit contrast to the Qur'an, various sources—historiographical as well as exegetical—record traditions that depict Eve as tempting Adam to eat the forbidden fruit.[15] Similarly, reports relating that the transgression resulted in punishments in addition to the expulsion (echoing Gen. 3:14–19) either count more punishments as being bestowed on Eve than on Adam or Satan, or else mention only the punishments of Eve, while Adam is completely excluded.[16]

This ambivalence continues further into later centuries and other forms of cultural expression, such as Islamic paintings from sixteenth and early seventeenth-century Safavid Iran and Ottoman Turkey.

## *Eve in Islamic* Fāl-Nāma *Paintings*

### *The Pictorial* Fāl-Nāma

The sixteenth century, which marks the beginning of the early modern period (1500–1800), was in the Islamic world a time of political instability. The approaching end of the first Islamic millennium (1591–1592) inspired millenarian worldviews and messianic expectations throughout the Safavid, Ottoman and Mughal empires, among Muslims and non-Muslims alike.[17] The messianic Jewish movement of David Reubeni and Solomon Molcho is one example of such a movement;[18] the rise of the Safavid dynasty (1501–1722), which conquered Iran, is another. The rise to power of Shah Ismāʿīl (ruled 1501–1524), the first Safavid ruler, was supported by a Turkmen Sufi brotherhood turned into a millenarian political movement. Shah Ismāʿīl then declared his son, Shah Ṭahmāsp (ruled 1524–1576), the Messiah; however, Shah Ṭahmāsp himself abandoned these utopian promises. Rather, he adopted doctrinal Shīʿism, thus breaking with his father's antinomian spirituality.[19]

These messianic worldviews and political and religious developments also influenced the cultural systems in the Islamic world. Millenarianism and messianic movements inspired a manifest interest in divination, the occult and eschatology, on the one hand, and didactic, often religious, paintings on the other. Several groups of illustrated manuscripts emerged in the Islamic world during the sixteenth century. Their main themes were hagiography and divination. Hagiographical art was mainly manifested through illustrations of *Qiṣaṣ al-anbiyāʾ* works. Divination was manifested through works of pictorial *Fāl-Nāma*s.[20]

*Fāl-Nāma* was a genre of large-scale works, which were used for the art of bibliomancy (divination through text). Bibliomancy had been popular among ruling elites in the Islamic world since late Umayyad period (661–750). Over time, pictorial *Fāl-Nāma*s emerged as well. These were popular in the Islamic world in the sixteenth century, particularly in Iran and Turkey. Four such volumes, dating from between the mid-sixteenth and early seventeenth centuries, are known today. Unlike other *Fāl-Nāma*s, these monumental *Fāl-Nāma*s also included the textual divinatory interpretation of the images. Together, image and text represented the augury. Notably, the pictorial *Fāl-Nāma*s had a considerable iconographical influence on other works, both contemporaneous and later.[21]

The *Fāl-Nāma*s codices also represent the political and religious transformations in the early modern Persianate world. The paintings combine both symbolic and religious meanings. They offer seekers access to concealed knowledge, but also include religious figures, and prompt the seeker to perform religious practices (e.g. ritual prayers). The *Fāl-Nāma*s, therefore, reflect the middle way between messianism and structured religion, similar to Shah Ṭahmāsp's position.[22]

The themes around which the *Fāl-Nāma*s revolve are resurrection, apocalypse and the battle between divine and evil powers. The second most frequent subject in these codices is Islamic and Abrahamic prophets, which serve as the bracket between creation and apocalypse, as well as being principal agents of divination. Their presentation is hagiographic, focussing on iconic scenes from their lives. While the Abrahamic prophets helped with the legitimization of the practice of divination, Massumeh Farhad and Serpil Bağcı emphasize that the paintings were also given further allegorical meanings.[23] The paintings in which Eve is portrayed are part of this group.

### *Eve in the Pictorial Fāl-Nāma*

The discussion below focuses on the representation of Eve at three different moments of her life, according to the Islamic tradition: before, during and immediately after the expulsion from paradise. The paintings to be examined are part of the dispersed *Fāl-Nāma* (Figures 2.1 and 2.2), and the Ottoman *Fāl-Nāma* of Ahmed I (2.3).

The methodology used in this chapter combines an iconographic approach, with special attention to the details of the images, in particular those details that do not conform with the religious pre-text that the image presumably depicts. A close attention to such details reveals additional meanings in the images, and sometimes a contra-narrative, which can serve as an alternative to the main narrative of the pre-text. This approach is similar to the 'close reading' of images, which Begüm Özden Firat applies in her analysis of Ottoman miniatures (see Figure 2.3).[24]

Firat notes that iconography, which is a prominent methodology for 'traditional art-historical analysis of narrative images',[25] reads the visual in relation to the verbal. It seeks to identify pictorial elements within the image that comply with the pre-text that the image is meant to illustrate. An informed iconographical reading therefore depends on pre-existent motifs. It results in a conservative reading of the image, and prevents the emergence of alternative interpretations that might unnerve the main narrative, to which the iconographical approach is subordinated.

**Figure 2.1** Artist unknown, *Angels Bow before Adam and Eve in Paradise*. The Dispersed *Fāl-Nāma*: Qazvin, Iran, Safavid period. Opaque watercolour and gold on paper; 59.3 × 44.5 cm. Freer Gallery of Art and Arthur M. Sackler Gallery, Smithsonian Institution, Washington, DC: Purchase: Smithsonian Unrestricted Trust Funds, Smithsonian Collections Acquisition Program, and Dr Arthur M. Sackler, S1986.254, late 1550s or early 1560s.

In order to overcome these shortcomings, Firat draws on the work of Mieke Bal and Naomi Schor in proposing to complete the iconographical reading with a close reading of the details in the image.[26] Such a reading begins where the iconographical reading stops, since it focuses on those details that do not agree with the textual sources and are therefore iconographically dysfunctional. By turning the detail from a marginal element into the prism through which the entire image is interpreted, such a reading emphasizes the differences between the image and the text. It can therefore change the conventional interpretation of an image, by allowing the meaning of the image to develop in alternative directions.

Such a reading is particularly suitable for the *Fāl-Nāma* paintings, which are meant to be read for divination purposes. As Bağcı has noted, these paintings do not interpret a narrative. Rather, each *Fāl-Nāma* painting has an adjoining

**Figure 2.2** *Eve and Adam expelled from Paradise.* The Dispersed *Fāl-Nāma*: Freer Gallery of Art and Arthur M. Sackler Gallery, Smithsonian Institution, Washington, DC: Purchase – Smithsonian Unrestricted Trust Funds, Smithsonian Collections Acquisition Program, and Dr. Arthur M. Sackler, S1986.251a, late 1550s or early 1560s. Qazvin, Iran, Safavid period. Opaque watercolour and gold on paper; 59.7 × 44.9 cm.

narrative, which interprets the painting by elaborating its divinatory meaning. Within the *Fāl-Nāma* codices, the image is always on the right-hand page, and the related text follows on the left-hand page. The order of the images within each volume is random (regardless of the historiographical chronology of the depicted episodes), to increase chance when consulting them. Both formally and conceptually, therefore, the paintings precede their corresponding texts, and stand in their own right as the major mode of communication in this genre.[27]

### *Angels Bow before Eve and Adam in Paradise*

The so-called dispersed *Fāl-Nāma* (Book of Omens) is one of the most notable works, which combine images and texts, of sixteenth-century Iran. Of the group of monumental *Fāl-Nāma* manuscripts, it is the earliest, and the one most frequently

**Figure 2.3** *Adam and Eve Leaving Paradise*. The *Fāl-Nāma* of Ahmed I: Topkapı Palace Museum, Istanbul, Turkey, H.1703, f.7b, c. 1610–15. Attributed to Nakkaş Hasan Pasha. Opaque watercolour and gold on paper; 49 x 36.4 cm.

published. Thirty leaves of this *Fāl-Nāma* are known today. The artistic and historical circumstances of its creation are uncertain. Modern scholars, such as Farhad, as well as Rachel Milstein, Karin Ruhrdanz and Barbara Schmitz (Milstein et al.), maintain the view of Edgar Blochet from 1929 (later repeated by Stuart Cary Welch) that it was probably completed in Qazvin for Shah Ṭahmāsp (ruled 1524–1576), himself a painter and a calligrapher, and a distinguished patron of illustrated books.[28]

The style of paintings in the dispersed *Fāl-Nāma* is, according to Bağci and Farhad, the most homogeneous of the existing *Fāl-Nāma* copies. Their style can be related to the court milieu of Qazvin, where they were probably made by a number of artists. Welch attributed these paintings to the court painters Āqā Mīrak and 'Abd al-'Azīz.[29] The divinatory texts of this *Fāl-Nāma* are commonly attributed to the sixth Shī'ite Imam, Ja'far al-Ṣādiq (d. 765); Farhad and Bağcı, however, note that it is more likely that the text emerged from later oral and written hagiographical sources.[30]

Figure 2.1, *Angels Bow before Adam and Eve in Paradise*, was probably the first painting (fol. 1b) in the dispersed *Fāl-Nāma* when the work was in its complete form.[31] It depicts Eve and Adam in paradise, surrounded by adoring angels. Although the adjoining text for this painting is missing, this identification of the subject is supported through a similar painting from the Dresden *Fāl-Nāma* (E445; f. 13b), probably inspired by Figure 2.1, which the adjoining text (f. 14a) identifies as 'the sign of the paradise of Adam and Eve'.[32]

The dispersed *Fāl-Nāma* painting (Figure 2.1) is the first instance in Islamic art of an illustration of Eve and Adam in the Garden, and its iconographic influence was substantial. In addition to the Dresden *Fāl-Nāma*, this subject appears also in two later *Qiṣaṣ al-anbiyā'* works; and nine works of *Qiṣaṣ al-anbiyā'* include illustrations of the angels adoring Adam alone. Furthermore, this painting also influenced the composition and iconography of two paintings of Solomon and the queen of Sheba (Bilqīs). Similarly to Eve and Adam, Bilqīs and Solomon are depicted as sitting on a dais, and surrounded by angels (as well as demons, animals and humans). The close stylistic similarity made Binyon, Wilkinson and Gray (1933) mistake Eve and Adam in Figure 2.1 for Bilqīs and Solomon.[33]

The painting shows Eve (to the left) and Adam on a dais, against a flowery background of abundant vegetation. They are surrounded by angels, who fly above them, prostrate themselves before them, or serve them with food, drink or presents. At the top left side, the darkened figure of Iblīs can be spotted. Unlike many Christian paintings of the couple, here Eve and Adam are portrayed as fully clothed. This concurrently reflects the scarcity of unclothed figures in Islamic paintings (see below), as well as the textual Islamic tradition concerning Eve and Adam. Whereas Gen. 2:25 relates that the woman and man were unclothed in the Garden prior to the transgression, in Q 20:118–19 the couple is assured that while in the Garden they will neither be naked nor suffer the heat of the sun.

The composition of this painting is unique in that it depicts the angels as prostrating themselves before Eve and Adam alike. In the Qur'an (e.g. Q 2:34) God specifically commands the angels to prostrate themselves before Adam; Eve is not mentioned in this context. The Qur'anic text introduces her only at a later point in the narrative, when God instructs Adam that both he and his spouse should dwell in the Garden (Q 7:19). The inclusion of Eve in the prostration scene is, therefore, an expansion of the Qur'anic narrative. The result gives Eve an elevated status, equal to that of Adam.

For Milstein *et al.* the apparent discrepancy between the painting and the Qur'anic text suggests that this painting, to which they refer as 'the enthronement of Adam and Eve',[34] does not depict the Qur'anic episode. In the Qur'an as well as the *Qiṣaṣ al-anbiyā'* narratives, the angels prostrate themselves before Adam. According to most *Qiṣaṣ al-anbiyā'* narratives, Eve was created only later. Bağcı also indicates that the Qur'an (Q 7:11–25 in particular) 'mentions the angels' veneration of the newly created Adam, but this takes place before God has fashioned Eve (who is not mentioned by name in the Qur'an) from one of Adam's ribs'.[35] Milstein *et al.* further add that the angelic prostration is said to have occurred before Eve and Adam entered paradise, whereas the painting depicts Eve and Adam inside the Garden. Finally, they point out that the Dresden *Fāl-Nāma* manuscript, which also contains a painting of this episode (fol. 13b), includes an additional, separate painting (fol. 4b) of the angels prostrating themselves before Adam alone. Milstein *et al.* thus conclude that the painting from the dispersed *Fāl-Nāma* (Figure 2.1) does not represent the angels' prostration before Adam, but rather a different, unidentified event.[36]

It would, however, seem rather unlikely that this painting relates to an unknown episode. The *Fāl-Nāma* paintings tend to depict iconic scenes from the lives of the prophets and, according to Milstein *et al.*, are often self-explanatory.[37] The setting of the scene inside paradise is, curiously, typical also of later illustrations, which specifically depict the Qur'anic scene of the angels prostrating themselves before Adam (alone). For example, in H.1227, fol. 11a, Adam is portrayed (alone) on a dais in the Garden, with the angels prostrating themselves before him and showering him with light.[38] Presumably, the linkage between the pre-Fall Adam (and Eve) and paradise superseded the Qur'anic chronology. Milstein *et al.* also mention additional cases of discrepancies between texts and images, such as illustrations of the expulsion from paradise in which Adam has no halo, although according to the text he maintained his halo.[39] That is, such discrepancies are not unheard of. Rather, they enable us to consider alternatives to the mainstream narrative.

Notably, God's command to the angels to prostrate themselves before the newly created Adam is indeed quite specific. However, the Qur'an does not mention at all the creation of Eve (or Adam's spouse), and the creation from his rib is a biblical theme, which is absent from the Qur'an, and appears in Islamic exegetical and historiographical traditions only. Rather, in the Qur'an the existence of Adam's spouse is a given. She is first introduced through God's words to Adam, 'Dwell you and your spouse in the Garden' (Q 7:19). Furthermore, the verses that precede the commandment to the angels relate to the creation of humanity, rather than to Adam. This becomes evident as the Qur'an uses here the plural form: 'We have created you (pl.: *khalaqnā**kum***), then shaped you (pl.: *ṣawwarnā**kum***)' (Q 7:11). Therefore, an assumption (by the artist or oral tradition) that Eve already existed at the time of the angelic prostration does not contradict the explicit Qur'anic text, and would not necessarily seem inconceivable.

Rather than an unknown scene, the discrepancies with the Qur'anic text probably reflect a combination of the angelic prostration with another episode from the biography of Eve and Adam. According to Milstein *et al.*, such combinations are typical of religious iconographic styles.[40] This additional episode might be Eve's and Adam's glorious entry into paradise, which is also suggested by Bağcı, or else their wedding. According to al-Kisāʾī, upon the creation of Eve, God gave her in marriage to Adam. Although the wedding took place outside the Garden, the description of it recalls the scene in the painting: Eve and Adam were put on a throne of pearls, surrounded by the angels, who were showering paradisiacal candies (or coins) over them. In the painting, the two angels on the top right-hand side are showering the couple with light. Alternatively, al-Kisāʾī's narrative relates that once inside the Garden, Eve and Adam were 'crowned, diademed and honored'. They then sat on a splendid dais, and were offered the fruit of paradise. All these elements are present in the painting.[41]

Finally, the distinction in the Dresden *Fāl-Nāma* between the two prostrations might be a later reaction to the notion of angelic prostration before Eve. For one, the dispersed *Fāl-Nāma* does not (as far as we know) include an additional prostration scene. Furthermore, Milstein *et al.* indicate that two later *Qiṣaṣ* works also include illustrations of Eve and Adam on a dais, surrounded by angels in the Garden.[42] These manuscripts do not include separate illustrations of the angels prostrating themselves before Adam. Moreover, one of them depicts Eve and Adam on the dais inside the Garden, with the angels serving them with fruit; however, it completely omits the angelic prostration, and only Adam is portrayed with a halo.[43] It would thus seem that the emphasis of these paintings was not so much on the chronology of events, but rather on questioning the highly positive portrayal of Eve in Figure 2.1 from the dispersed *Fāl-Nāma*. Their response was either to omit the elevating motifs, such as the halo and angelic prostration, or to omit Eve herself.

Indeed, the presentation of Eve in this painting as the subject (together with Adam) of prostration by the angels is evident of a highly positive, inclusive and elevating perception of her character. Seeing that the *Fāl-Nāma* was created in Iran, it might reflect the aforementioned generally more positive attitude of Shīʿa Islam towards women characters, following the adoration of Fāṭima, daughter of Muḥammad. This might also reflect earlier discussions in Islam, regarding the possibility of there having been (usually four or six) women prophets, among whom Eve is also mentioned.[44] That Eve is depicted here as a prophetic figure is also suggested through her halo.

Both Eve and Adam are depicted as having golden-green, flaming halos (although Eve's halo is smaller). According to Milstein *et al.*, a flame-shaped halo signifies a prophetic status.[45] The fiery edge of this halo is typical of angels and prophets, and the fire represents the notion of light: according to Shīʿa Islam, there exists a universal line of divine light, which begins with Adam and thereafter continues through the chain of prophets to Muḥammad and the Shīʿite imams.[46] That the halo in this painting is significant becomes evident through other paintings of the angelic prostration to Eve and Adam in the Garden, where only Adam has a halo.[47] Likewise, also Mary, for whom the claim for a prophetic status was more popular,[48] is sometimes portrayed with a (fiery) halo,[49] but not always; whereas Bilqīs, who features (together with Solomon) in enthronement scenes that are closely related to this painting, is not portrayed with a halo.[50]

An inclusive approach towards Eve in this painting emerges also through the blackened character of Iblīs. Milstein *et al.* interpret his dark skin as representing his being the embodiment of evil.[51] In this particular context, however, the colour black seems to have an additional significance. The Arabic expression 'to darken', or blacken someone's face means 'to humiliate'. According to some Islamic traditions, when God intended to create Adam, he sent angels to bring some earth for this purpose. But the earth refused to give of itself for the creation of a sinful creature, and sought refuge in God against them. Eventually God sent Iblīs, who ignored the pleas of the earth and brought some of it to God. God therefore informed Iblīs that he would create from this earth a creature that would 'blacken your face', that is, humiliate Iblīs.[52] The portrayal of Iblīs in the painting recalls this story. By so doing, it again extends this pre-Creation episode to include Eve as well, similar to the angelic prostration and prophetic halo. The image of Eve that emerges from this painting is, therefore, highly positive and inclusive. At this pre-Fall moment, she is provided with prophetic traits, and in many aspects is equal to Adam, to the extent that later illustrators of this scene, while influenced by this painting, felt it necessary to omit some of these traits. A rather different scene is presented in Figure 2.2, which relates to the moment of the expulsion.

### *Adam and Eve Expelled from Paradise*

Another painting of Eve and Adam in the dispersed *Fāl-Nāma* depicts the expulsion of Eve and Adam from paradise. This painting probably belonged between the twentieth and thirtieth pages of this *Fāl-Nāma* before it became dispersed. Dating from the second half of the sixteenth century, it is the first illustration of the expulsion from paradise in Islamic art, which was soon repeated in several works of *Qiṣaṣ al-anbiyā'* later in the sixteenth century. Of the twenty-one full *Qiṣaṣ* manuscripts examined by Milstein *et al.*, eleven include paintings of the expulsion. The expulsion also appears as an omen in the Topkapı Persian *Fāl-Nāma* (H.1702), and the Ahmed I copy in the Topkapı Palace Library H.1703 (see Figure 2.3). It is therefore evident that the *Fāl-Nāma* was indeed 'forging new visual language for illustrations of religious manuscripts'.[53]

The illustration in the dispersed *Fāl-Nāma* depicts the expulsion as a turbulent and dramatic event. The transgressors are located in the centre, between two rows of observing angels, many of whom seem astonished and grieved. At the bottom left the blackened-yet-satisfied character of Iblīs can be spotted.

Notably, the angels, who bowed before Eve and Adam upon their entrance into the Garden (Figure 2.1), now observe their expulsion from it. The location of the angels in two rows, from above and below, is somewhat reminiscent of the Israelites crossing the Red Sea upon leaving Egypt (Exod. 14:15–30; Q 26:63–68), partly due to the curved line (yellow above, pink below), which resembles river curves, and which delineates between the transgressors and the angels. Both the Bible and the Qur'an depict how, in order to save the Israelites, God split the sea in two, so that the Israelites could pass over in the middle. The passage of Eve, Adam and their company between the angelic rows counter-parallels this scene, but also highlights that the expulsion (like the Exodus) concurrently signifies both an end and a new beginning.

The company of transgressors includes four figures: Eve, Adam and their respective riding beasts: a peacock and a dragon-like snake. All of them are literally being driven out of paradise, as a character holding a long rod and dressed in a Safavid court dress and a turban prods the snake to hurry her.[54]

Adam, riding the snake, is at the front, with Eve close behind him, on a smaller-size peacock. The riding motif is unknown from textual descriptions of the expulsion, and appears here for the first time; it recurs in illustrations of this scene in later *Qiṣaṣ al-anbiyā'* works.[55] Milstein *et al.* suggest that the meaning of this motif might be symbolic. Jalāl al-Dīn al-Rūmī (d. 1273) describes the carnal nature as a peacock, who tempts one towards vanity. The riding could thus be a metaphor of either an attempt to control carnal passions, or riding evil inclination towards sin.[56]

More inclined towards the latter explanation, the riding motif can also be a counter-parallel to Eve's and Adam's entrance parade into paradise, according to Islamic traditions. Al-Kisāʾī records a report that describes how, upon introducing them into the Garden, God honoured Adam with mounting him on a magnificent horse, and Eve followed behind him on a wonderful she-camel, with the angels surrounding them.[57] Their riding out of the Garden is thus an inverted parade of shame. Contrary to Bağcı's view of them as 'sitting tall on their mounts and conversing with cheery animation',[58] it rather seems more likely that this apparent high position only emphasizes their shame, not the least because they are presented naked in public.

Hoffman notes the rarity of unclothed figures in Islamic art, arguing that such figures are generally limited to scientific, astronomical and magical texts, and to beings 'derived from scientific and mythological personifications of late antiquity'.[59] Possibly as part of the boldness of the *Fāl-Nāma* genre, both the dispersed *Fāl-Nāma* (Figure 2.2) and the *Fāl-Nāma* of Ahmed I (Figure 2.3) portray Eve and Adam as naked. According to the Qur'an, while in the Garden Eve and Adam were protected from being naked. However, following the consumption of the forbidden fruit, their private parts became apparent to them, and they attempted to cover themselves with leaves (Q 20:118–21).[60]

Eve's nakedness reflects the physical transformation she has undergone following the transgression. Some of her body is darkened, in particular her hands (which picked the fruit and gave it to Adam) and belly (which consumed the fruit). Although Adam, too, consumed the forbidden fruit, and despite a literary tradition that describes his complexion as blackened following the transgression (see below), in this painting the darkened limbs are those of Eve alone. This distinction between Eve and Adam represents the view that she has an increased responsibility for the transgression. An active participant in the temptation of Adam, she is depicted as physically resembling Iblīs, who is also painted here with dark face, neck and hands. This sinister, demon-like characterization of Eve is reminiscent of the biblical narrative (Gen. 3:6), and of post-Qur'anic traditions, which often depict Eve as actively tempting Adam into eating the forbidden fruit. In contrast, the Qur'an describes Satan as either tempting both Adam and his spouse together at the same time (Q 2:30–38; 7:11–25), or as tempting Adam alone (Q 20:115–23).

Nevertheless, and despite the loss of their clothes, both Eve and Adam still have their halos. Some other illustrations of the expulsion also depict them with halos; however, this is not always the case. In some *Qiṣaṣ al-anbiyāʾ* works neither of them has a halo. In other works only Adam has one, again suggesting a differentiation between Eve and Adam with regard to the transgression. In the present context (Figure 2.2) both maintain their halos, which could imply a more egalitarian view. However, it should also be noted in this painting that the halos have specific flaming edges. The colour of these edges is fiery orange, and they are distinctly separated (by lines) from the main halo. For comparison, the halos in Figure 2.1

above and Figure 2.3 below are clearly more homogeneous. Another unusual detail concerning the halos in Figure 2.2 is that the halo of Eve is larger than that of Adam; in other paintings this is often the other way around.[61] It is possible that in this painting the halos serve to symbolize the transformation that the couple has gone through following the transgression, with the flames signifying fire rather than light; in that case, Eve would here be presented as more blameworthy than Adam.

Eve's increased fault (which is completely absent from the Qur'an) is further demonstrated through the composition of the characters. Adam turns his body back towards Eve, his hands pointing at her, as if saying, 'This is all your fault'. This motif reappears in later *Qiṣaṣ al-anbiyā'* manuscripts.[62] The location of Adam in the painting is higher than that of Eve, so that he literally speaks down to her. This element, too, can be found in later paintings of the expulsion.[63] It expresses a perception of presumed masculine supremacy over women. Similarly, the depiction of Eve as riding behind Adam represents a patriarchal social norm of masculine priority over the female. This motif is present not only in Figure 2.2, which depicts the expulsion, but also in the aforementioned narratives concerning Eve's and Adam's ride into the Garden. Furthermore, according to al-Kisā'ī, during their walks in the Garden, Eve used to walk behind Adam.[64] The presentation of this patriarchal norm as a primordial divine ruling further supports and legitimizes it, in the same way that Gen. 3:16 has God say to the woman, 'And your desire is to your man, and he shall govern over you'.

Whereas Adam looks at Eve, Eve and the peacock gaze accusingly at the snake. Like Adam, also the head of the snake is turned back, towards both Eve and Adam; her mouth, in which Iblīs hid himself in order to enter paradise (see below),[65] is wide open, as if ridiculing them; notably, also the horse on which Adam rode into the Garden was, according to al-Kisā'ī, talking to Adam.[66] The peacock, on the other hand, seems rather gloomy, with his tail and colours being reminiscent of (hell) fire. This game of gazing recalls the biblical narrative in Gen. 3:11–13, where Adam blames Eve, and Eve blames the snake. Indeed, the presence in this painting of the snake and peacock (as well as in illustrations of the expulsion in later *Fāl-Nāma* works)[67] reflects biblical, Qur'anic exegetical and *Qiṣaṣ al-anbiyā'* traditions. Although the Qur'an mentions only Satan as tempting the couple, many narratives in the Islamic tradition also include the snake and peacock as helping him in this. Since, according to the Qur'an, God expelled Iblīs from heaven before he let Adam and his spouse into the Garden, the question emerges, how did Iblīs get into the Garden in order to tempt the primordial couple? One proposal is that, using flattery, and promising that the fruit of paradise would grant them eternal youth, beauty and immortality, Iblīs convinced the peacock to let him into the Garden, and the snake to hide him in her mouth and lead him to Eve, with whom she had a close relationship. Iblīs then convinced Eve to consume the forbidden fruit, and later Eve gave it to Adam as well.[68]

An interesting parallel can be drawn between the two animals and Eve, all of whom are portrayed in the textual sources as actively helping Iblīs. Both the Islamic tradition and the painting to an extent depict the snake and the peacock as fanciful,[69] vain, naïve and treacherous. The snake (*ḥayya*), in particular, is a grammatical feminine in Arabic, and the Islamic sources treat this snake as a feminine being, which is beautiful, adorned and treacherous.[70] These characteristics are often used as derogative stereotypical feminine traits. Also the person in the painting who prods the she-snake with the rod appears in another illustration of the expulsion, which is included in a *Qiṣaṣ al-anbiyā'* manuscript. There, he hurries Eve herself out of the Garden.[71] As will be demonstrated below, Eve's reluctance to leave the Garden is a reoccurring motif in illustrations of the expulsion scene.

The different portrayals of Eve in Figure 2.1 and Figure 2.2, both of which were originally included in the currently dispersed *Fāl-Nāma*, possibly reflect the transformation that Eve went through following the transgression. Unlike Figure 2.1 above, which portrays the pre-transgression Eve in a highly positive way, Figure 2.2 represents a mixed image of Eve. On the one hand, she is depicted as inferior to Adam and bearing a greater responsibility than him for the transgression; on the other, she still maintains her halo. Notably, Eve is not depicted in a completely negative manner, perhaps thanks to the positive image of Fāṭima in Shī'ite Islam. The public expulsion still bears some remnants of Eve and Adam's glorious entry into the Garden, and allows for hope of a new beginning, leading to a potentially positive future. A similarly composite view is reflected through the symbolic meaning of the expulsion in the dispersed *Fāl-Nāma*. The adjoining text interprets this painting as a sign of great misfortune, which will then be superseded by a greater good outcome.[72]

Figure 2.3, which presents Eve and Adam at the moment right after the expulsion, again portrays Eve in a new, different light.

### *Eve and Adam Leaving the Garden*

The *Fāl-Nāma* of Ahmed I (TSM H.1703) is the only extant pictorial *Fāl-Nāma* with text in Ottoman Turkish. It is also the only one with a detailed preface. The preface states that it was compiled as a gift for Sultan Ahmed I (ruled 1603–1617) by Kalender, a high Ottoman courtier, probably during 1614–16, when he served as the vizier of the Sultan.[73] This *Fāl-Nāma* resembles earlier works assembled by Kalender, which reflect Safavid thematic influence, with an emphasis on Abrahamic prophets, who were meant to serve as lessons for the readers. Of the thirty-five paintings in this *Fāl-Nāma*, most were earlier existent images, to which Kalender added relevant text.[74]

The painting of Eve and Adam leaving paradise (Figure 2.3), however, was probably commissioned especially for this volume. It is attributed to Nakkaş Hasan Pasha (d. after 1620), a notable government official and artist who had a considerable influence on book illustrations from 1580 to 1620. Whereas most other paintings in this volume combine a synthesis of Ottoman and Safavid themes, the style of this particular painting is, according to Bağcı, 'more Ottoman'.[75]

Similar to Figure 2.2 from the dispersed *Fāl-Nāma*, this painting depicts the expulsion of Eve and Adam from the Garden. However, the Ottoman painting depicts a slightly later moment: here, Eve and Adam are already outside the

Garden. Their transition from the celestial sphere to the earthly one is emphasized through their location on the dark land, beyond the area of vegetation. Firat considers this empty land as barren;[76] however, black soil is usually highly fertile. It is still empty because Eve and Adam are yet to fulfil this potential.

Bağcı notes that, since this painting focuses on the results of disobedience (post-paradise existence), it highlights the moral dimension of the Fall.[77] While it can be argued that human moral responsibility is further emphasized through the absence of Iblīs from this painting, Milstein *et al.* interpret this absence as highlighting the prophetic (rather than fallen) aspect of Adam [and Eve].[78] This motif, therefore, offers ambivalence; which is also evident from other aspects of the painting.

Unlike the dramatic setting of the expulsion scene in the dispersed *Fāl-Nāma* (Figure 2.3), this painting seems almost tranquil, 'the calm after the storm'. A crowned angel, possibly Riḍwān the gate keeper, stands at the doorway of paradise, watching, surprised (as indicated by his finger) as Eve and Adam, followed by the snake and peacock, slowly walk away from the Garden (which arcade walls resemble the archways of the Topkapı Palace).[79]

Like in Figure 2.2 above, here too, Eve and Adam both have halos. Different from those in the dispersed *Fāl-Nāma* paintings, the halos here are not fiery, but rather green-coloured (green being the colour associated with the Prophet Muḥammad).[80] The halo of Adam is bigger. At the same time, the complexion of Adam is significantly darker than that of Eve, possibly representing the narrative in some of the *Qiṣaṣ al-anbiyā'* works that counts a dark complexion as one of Adam's punishments for the transgression.[81] Notably, Eve is portrayed with a pale skin, like that of the angel. Firat notes that these different complexions are also found in illustrations of the poem *Ḥadīqat al-su'adā'* (The Garden of the Happy) by the Ottoman poet Fuḍūlī (d. 1556), which retells the story of the expulsion. The angelic association creates a role reversal between Eve and Adam. Whereas in the dispersed *Fāl-Nāma* (Figure 2.2) Eve is depicted with blackened limbs, similar to Iblīs, in Figure 2.3 she is located higher than Adam in the celestial hierarchy, thanks to her angelic pale features.[82] Possibly, this higher location also made it more difficult for Eve to accept the expulsion.

Contrarily Adam, who is portrayed as being in the midst of stepping away from the Garden, seems to fully accept the divine decree. He firmly holds in his hand the hand of Eve, who stands in one place, somewhat leaning backwards, while Adam seems almost to be pulling her forward. They face each other, but their gazes do not meet. Adam's right foot firmly turns forward, whereas Eve's left (sinister) foot expresses doubt (a satanic feature). Following Na'ama Brosh and Milstein, Firat notes that the holding hands motif probably reflects Fuḍūlī's poem, which includes this motif. Firat further suggests that Eve is reluctant to follow Adam, and considers taking her own independent journey (thus reflecting the Islamic tradition about Adam falling in India and Eve in Jeddah).[83] However, Eve does not seem to be going anywhere. Even her halo turns backwards, with the pointed tip towards the gate of the Garden, whereas Adam's clearly bends forward, directing him further away from the Garden. Apparently, she again fails to obey the divine command, and refuses to leave the Garden and its vicinity. Her reluctance to leave is apparent also in other illustrations of the expulsion in *Qiṣaṣ al-anbiyā'* works.[84]

This difference in the couple's coming to terms with the new conditions is also reflected in more ways in the painting. Eve and Adam are portrayed as leaving the Garden wearing only a girdle of fig leaves (echoing Gen. 3:7). Following their consumption of the forbidden fruit, they both now realize their nakedness. However, only Adam attempts to cover his bare breast with his hand; Eve stands shamelessly, her hands spread to the sides of her exposed body. This is particularly remarkable considering that even the animals seem ashamed – the snake hides behind the leaves of the bush next to the door, and the peacock hides his head in his tail. Similar to the dispersed *Fāl-Nāma* image (Figure 2.2), a parallel between Eve and the peacock is evident here as well. Like Eve, he too is adorned (with a fancy tail), and seems reluctant to leave, still standing at the threshold of paradise.[85]

Notably, while Eve and Adam lose all their garments, Eve does not leave with nothing. She still maintains her earring. According to the *Qiṣaṣ* work of al-Kisā'ī, when God created Eve and gave her in marriage to Adam, he adorned Eve with all kinds of jewellery.[86] The golden earring is the only remnant of these – possibly a reminder to *listen* better next time, but also a symbol of materialism, vanity, sensuality and subordination. Restrained sexuality is also reflected through the clips that hold her long hair, whereas Adam's remains loose. Furthermore, in her left (sinister) hand Eve still holds six stalks. The stalks represent a prevalent Islamic view, that the forbidden fruit of paradise was wheat. According to a report recorded by al-Kisā'ī, Eve picked seven stalks from the paradise tree.[87] The image portrays her as carrying the six remaining stalks (one would have been consumed) down to earth. Eve is thus portrayed as a trickster figure: shameless and remorseless, she destroyed the existing divine order by causing the expulsion from paradise. But at the same time she also creates the beginning of a new order (life on earth), by bringing new knowledge: the use of wheat (previously unavailable to humans). Wheat being a symbol of civilization and sedentary life, Eve holds the seeds for earthly nutrition, and symbolizes the transformation from a paradisiacal gatherer community into an agricultural civilization. Her disobedience is thus Promethean, rather than demonic.

Finally, a significant detail that further emphasizes the differentiation between Eve and Adam in this painting is that Adam has a navel, which indicates that Adam is a human, who was born from his mother's womb. Firat notes that the concurrent absence of a navel from Eve's body (since she was created, rather than born) allows us to speculate that she was Adam's mother.[88] The biblical and Islamic tradition narrative about Eve being created from Adam is thus reversed, as Eve becomes the mother of *all* living. Firat concludes that the four features, of the wheat, Eve's autonomy over against Adam's position, her angelic complexion and Adam's navel, create an image of Eve that is very different from that of the mainstream cultural tradition. For Firat this episode is to be read for the 'victim' (Eve), rather than for the 'main character'.[89]

But it is exactly these details that make the term 'victim' unsuitable in this context. Firat, while recognizing that this painting offers an alternative image of Eve, chooses to stop at this point. However, the characteristics of Eve – land fertility, procreation, primordial motherhood, celestial qualities and autonomy – create the image of an exiled fertility goddess, who is understandably reluctant to leave the divine realm.

## *Summary*

A combined approach of informed iconography and close reading of the portrayals of Eve in the *Fāl-Nāma* paintings reveals that these paintings complete the Islamic textual tradition about Eve, by revealing aspects of this tradition, which otherwise are difficult to trace in the literary sources. Similar to the religious Islamic tradition, these paintings portray Eve as a complex and ambivalent character. The spouse of a prophet, potentially a prophet in her own right and the primordial mother of humanity, she is also held blameworthy for the transgression in paradise. The paintings seem to push these contrasts even further: like Adam, Eve too has a prophetic halo; nevertheless, at the same time she is portrayed as not only disobedient but physically demonic.

But a close reading of the details in the paintings reveals that the *Fāl-Nāma* paintings also break with the textual tradition about Eve, by suggesting alternative narratives of her story, which the textual sources could not, or would not, relate. Figure 2.1 depicts Eve within the divine realm, so to speak, before the transgression, that is, still obedient. However, already here she is characterized in a way that does not coincide with her mainstream textual depictions: she has a prophetic halo; the angels prostrate themselves before her; her existence is expanded beyond and before the event of the transgression; and in many ways she is portrayed as equal to Adam. The level of subversion of this portrayal of Eve becomes evident through later illustrations of the same episode. Many such illustrations were influenced by Figure 2.1; however, they omit those motifs, which elevate Eve, such as the halo and angelic prostration.

Of the three paintings, Figure 2.2 appears to be most in line with the textual tradition. An iconographic reading of this painting presents Eve as inferior to Adam, bearing the main responsibility for the transgression, and physically related to the demonic realm. Nevertheless, here, too, Eve still maintains some of her elevating characteristics, such as the halo (although an ambivalent one). A close reading discloses a promise of a new beginning. Eve is thus portrayed as a trickster figure, partly demonic, but also Promethean, in her contribution towards the fulfilment of a potentially better future, which the expulsion embodies. Her middle position, which is characteristic of such figures, is evident through the combination of the blackened limbs with the prophetic halo. Notably, the adjoining text of this image within the dispersed *Fāl-Nāma* interprets this painting as predicting a great misfortune, to be followed by a greater good outcome.

Figure 2.3 is probably the most subversive of the three paintings. Outside the Garden, Eve is portrayed as an active, independent figure. A manifest trickster, she has destroyed the old paradisiacal order, and carries in her hand the wheat, which is the key for the emergence of a new one. A close reading characterizes Eve as a primordial goddess of earth and fertility. Contrary to the textual tradition, she is the progenitor of Adam, and humanity as a whole. Sent out from the divine realm, she maintains her nurturing quality by carrying the celestial wheat to the mundane, barren land. The black land, which is reminiscent of the blackened body of Eve in Figure 2.2, following her consumption of the celestial wheat, contrasts with Eve's angelic white hand, now carrying this wheat. By bringing the wheat to earth, Eve integrates her celestial (Figure 2.1) and earthly (Figure 2.2) nature, and fulfills her fertility potential (Figure 2.3). Eve's celestial nature, which is revealed through these *Fāl-Nāma* paintings, thus completes, as well as breaks with, her image in the Islamic textual tradition.

## Notes

1 Q 2:30–38; 7:11–25; 20:115–23.

2 Zohar Hadromi-Allouche, 'The Wheat and the Barley: Feminine (In)fertility in Eve and Adam Narratives in Islam', in *Texts in Transit in the Medieval Mediterranean*, ed. Y. Tzvi Langermann and Robert G. Morrison (Pennsylvania: Pennsylvania State University Press, 2016), 116–27.

3 The fall of Iblīs also appears independently in the Qur'an: Q 15:26–44; 17:61–65; 18:50; 38:71–85.

4 Literally, 'We have created you, then shaped you' (Q 7:11).

5 Q 2:30–38 adds some details concerning the general angelic objection to the divine intention of creating Adam. See also Leigh Chipman, 'Adam and the Angels: An Examination of Mythic Elements in Islamic Sources', *Arabica* 49 (2002): 429–55; Haim Schwartzbaum, 'Jewish and Moslem Sources of a Falasha Creation Myth', in *Studies in Biblical and Jewish Folklore*, ed. Raphael Patai, Francis Lee Utley and Dov Noy (Bloomington: University of Indiana Press, 1960), 48.

6 Jane I. Smith and Yvonne Y. Haddad, 'Eve: Islamic Image of Woman', *Women's Studies International Forum* 5 (1982): 135–44; D.A. Spellberg, 'Writing the Unwritten Life of the Islamic Eve: Menstruation and the Demonization of Motherhood', *International Journal of Middle East Studies* 28 (1996): 305–24.

7 See, for example, Roberto Tottoli, 'Adam', in *Encyclopaedia of Islam THREE*, ed. Kate Fleet, Gudrun Krämer, Denis Matringe, John Nawas and Everett Rowson, Consulted online on 14 June 2016.

8 Q 11:71; 29: 51 (wife of Abraham); 27:29–44 (Queen of Sheba); 9:28, 11:66 (wife of Pharaoh); 12:23–32 (seductive Egyptian).

9 The name 'Eve' (Ḥawā') for Adam's spouse appears already in one of the earliest Islamic sources available to us: Muḥammad Ibn Isḥāq (d. 150 AH/ 767 CE), *Al-Mubtada' fī qiṣaṣ al-anbiyyā'*, ed. Muḥammad Karīm al-Kawwāz (Beirut: Arab Diffusion Company, 2006), 58.

10 Niʿmatallāh al-Jazā'irī (d. 1112 AH/1701 CE), *Al-Nūr al-mubīn fī qiṣaṣ al-anbiyā' wa'l-mursilīn* (Beirut: Dār al-Andalus, n.d.), 28,52–53; Quṭb al-Dīn Sa'd bin Hibatallāh

al-Rāwandī (d. 573 AH/1178 CE), *Qiṣaṣ al-anbiyā'*, ed. Ghulām Riḍā 'Irfanyān al-Yazdī (Beirut: Mu'assasat al-Mufīd, 1989), 57–58.

11 Muḥammad b. 'Abdallāh al-Kisā'ī (d. sixth century AH/ eleventh century CE), *Qiṣaṣ alanbiyā'*, ed. Isaac Eisenberg (Leiden: Brill, 1922), 31; Babylonian Talmud, B.Bat. 58a.

12 Muqātil Ibn Sulaymān (d. 150 AH/767 CE), *Tafsīr Muqātil Ibn Sulaymān*, ed. Ahmad Farid (Beirut: Dār al-Kutub al-'Ilmiyya, 2003), 1:42 (sūra 2), 1:386 (sūra 7:20–21); Abū Ja'far Muḥammad b. Jarīr al-Ṭabarī (d. 310 AH/923 CE), *Tafsīr al-Ṭabarī* (Beirut: Dār al-Fikr, 1405 A.H. [1984 C.E.]), 12:347–349, 351 (sūra 7:20–21); Abū Ja'far Muḥammad b. Jarīr al-Ṭabarī (d. 310 AH/923 CE), *Ta'rīkh al-Ṭabarī*, ed. Ṣadīq Jamīl al-'Aṭṭār (Beirut: Dār al-Fikr, 1998), 1:77.

13 Kohlberg, however, notes some contradictory views of Eve in Shī'ite sources; for example, that she and Adam were jealous of Fāṭima and the imams, and this jealousy led them into temptation. See Etan Kohlberg, 'Some Shī'ī Views of the Antediluvian World', *Studia islamica* 52 (1980): 41–66. Serpil Bağcı, 'Abrahamic Traditions', in *Falnama: The Book of Omens*, by Massumeh Farhad and Serpil Bağcı, with contributions by Maria Mavroudi, Kathryn Babayan, Cornell H. Fleischer, Julia Bailey, Wheeler M. Thackson, Jr. and Sergei Tourkin (London: Thames & Hudson, 2009), 97–115.

14 Ibn Isḥāq, *Al-Mubtada'*, 58. Abū Isḥāq Aḥmad b. Muḥammad b. Ibrāhīm al-Naysābūrī al-Tha'labī (d. 427 AH/1035 CE), *Qiṣaṣ al-anbiyā' al-musammā 'arā'is al-majālis*, ed. Muḥammad Sayd (Cairo: Dār al-Fajr li'l-turāth, 2001), 45. Muḥammad b. Manī' al-Hāshimī al-Baṣrī Ibn Sa'd (d. 230 AH/845 CE), *Al-Ṭabaqāt al-kubrā* (Beirut: Dār al-kutub al-'ilmiya, 1997), 1:34. Al-Ṭabarī, *Ta'rīkh*, 1:75. Al-Ṭabarī, *Tafsīr*, 1:514 (sūra 2:35). Muḥammad Fakhr al-Dīn b. Ḍiyā' al-Dīn 'Umar al-Rāzī (d. 606 AH/1209 CE), *Tafsīr al-Fakhr al-Rāzī* (Beirut: Dār al-Fikr, 2005), 13:88 (sūra 6).

15 Ibn Isḥāq, *Al-Mubtada'*, 61–62. Al-Tha'labī, *Qiṣaṣ*, 47; Abū al-Fidā' Ismā'īl Ibn Kathīr, *Qiṣaṣ al-anbiyā'* (Beirut: Dār al-Fikr, 1992), 27; Al-Ṭabarī, *Ta'rīkh*, 1:78; Al-Ṭabarī, *Tafsīr*, 1:530 (sūra 2:36); Al-Rāzī, *Tafsīr*, 3:14 (sūra 2).

16 According to a tradition that is recorded by al-Tha'labī, Adam was punished with five curses, Satan with ten curses and Eve received fifteen curses. (*Qiṣaṣ*, 48–52). Other reports only mention the punishments of Eve and the earth, or Eve and the snake — but not of Adam or Satan; see Al-Ṭabarī, *Ta'rīkh*, 1:76–77. Al-Ṭabarī, *Tafsīr*, 1:526 (sūra 2:36), 12:355–356 (sūra 7:22).

17 Rachel Milstein, Karin Ruhrdanz and Barbara Schmitz, *Stories of the Prophets: Illustrated Manuscripts of Qiṣaṣ al-anbiyā'*, Islamic art and architecture series, 8 (Costa Mesa, California: Mazda Publishers, 1999), 4. Kathryn Babayan, 'The Cosmological Order of Things in Early Modern Safavid Iran', in *Falnama*, by Farhad and Bağcı, 245–55.

18 See for example, Moti Benmelech, 'History, Politics, and Messianism: David Ha-Reuveni's Origin and Mission', *AJS Review* 35 (2011): 35–60.

19 Babayan, 'Cosmological order', 246–54.

20 Babayan, 'Cosmological order', 248. Serpil Bağcı, 'The *Falnama* of Ahmed I (TSM H.1703)', in *Falnama*, by Farhad and Bağcı, 68–76. Milstein *et al.*, *Stories of the Prophets*, VII, 1–5.

21 Massumeh Farhad and Serpil Bağcı, 'The Falnama in the Sixteenth and Seventeenth Centuries', in *Falnama*, by Farhad and Bağci, 27–40. Milstein *et al.*, *Stories of the Prophets*, 4, 95.

22 Milstein *et al.*, *Stories of the Prophets*, 33. Babayan, 'Cosmological order', 246–51. Massumeh Farhad, 'Between the Past and the Future: The *Fālnāma* (book

of omens) in the Sixteenth and early Seventeenth Centuries', in *People of the Prophet's House: Artistic Ritual Expressions of Shi'i Islam*, ed. Fahmida Suleman (London: Azimuth Editions in association with the Institute of Ismaili Studies [and] in collaboration with the British Museum's Department of the Middle East, 2015), 137–45.

23 Serpil Bağcı and Massumeh Farhad, 'The Art of Bibliomancy', in *Falnama*, by Farhad and Bağcı, 19–25. Farhad and Bağcı, 'The Falnama in the Sixteenth and Seventeenth centuries', 35–37. Babayan, 'Cosmological order', 246–25. Roger Savory, *Iran Under the Safavids* (Cambridge: Cambridge University Press, 1980), 50–75, 129. Īraj Afšār, 'Fāl-nāma', *Encyclopædia Iranica*, IX/2: 172–76, available online at http://www.iranicaonline.org/articles/fal-nama (accessed on 20 January 2012). H. Massé, 'Fāl-Nāma', in *Encyclopaedia of Islam*, 2nd edn, ed. P. Bearman, Th. Bianquis, C.E. Bosworth, E. van Donzel and W. P. Heinrichs, consulted online on 5 November 2016, <http://dx.doi.org/10.1163/1573-3912_islam_SIM_2256>.

24 Begüm Özden Firat, *Encounters with the Ottoman Miniature: Contemporary Readings of an Imperial Art* (London: I.B. Tauris, 2015), Kindle edition, 'Introduction' and Chap. 1.

25 Firat, *Encounters*, location 709.

26 Mieke Bal, *Reading 'Rembrandt': Beyond the Word/Image Opposition* (Cambridge: Cambridge University Press, 1991); Naomi Schor, *Reading in Detail: Aesthetics and the Feminine* (New York: Methuen, 1987).

27 Babayan, 'Cosmological Order', 246–51. Farhad and Bağcı, 'The Falnama in the Sixteenth and Seventeenth Centuries', 27–40. Firat, *Encounters*, 'Introduction' and Chap. 1.

28 Milstein *et al.*, *Stories of the Prophets*, 7, 66; Farhad, 'Between the Past and the Future', 137.

29 Farhad and Bağcı, 'The Falnama in the Sixteenth and Seventeenth Centuries', 38. Massumeh Farhad, 'The Manuscripts: The Dispersed Falnama', in *Falnama*, by Farhad and Bağci, 41–51. Farhad, 'Between the Past and the Future', 144, 145, n. 28. Milstein *et al.*, *Stories of the Prophets*, 66.

30 Farhad and Bağcı, 'The Falnama in the Sixteenth and Seventeenth Centuries', 31.

31 Milstein *et al.*, *Stories of the Prophets*, 83; Farhad, 'The Manuscripts: The Dispersed Falnama', 43.

32 Bağcı, 'Abrahamic Traditions', 97.

33 *Idem*, 97–115; Laurence Binyon, Wilkinson and Gray, *Persian Miniature Painting: A Descriptive Catalogue of the Miniatures Exhibited at Burlington House, January–March 1931* (Oxford: Oxford University Press, 1933); Milstein *et al.*, *Stories of the Prophets*, 107–108. Wheeler M. Thackston, Jr., trans., 'The Dispersed Falnama', in *Falnama*, by Farhad and Bağcī, 257–64. Sergei Tourkin, trans., 'The Falnama of Ahmed I (TSM H.1703)', in *Falnama*, by Farhad and Bağci, 295–305.

34 Milstein *et al.*, *Stories of the Prophets*, 83.

35 Bağcı, 'Abrahamic Traditions', 97.

36 Milstein *et al.*, *Stories of the Prophets*, 70, 83.

37 Milstein *et al.*, *Stories of the Prophets*, 33.

38 Istanbul, Topkapı Sarayı Müzesi, H.1227, text by Naysābūrī, 1574–75 or 1575–76, fol. 11a; Istanbul, Topkapı Sarayı Müzesi, B.249, text by Naysābūrī, fol. 6b; Milstein *et al.*, *Stories of the Prophets*, 33, 205 (Ms. T–1), 213 (Ms. T–7); figs. 25, 57.

39 Milstein *et al.*, *Stories of the Prophets*, 27.

40 *Idem*, 29.

41 Al-Kisā'ī, *Qiṣaṣ*, 31–35. Bağcı, 'Abrahamic Traditions', 97; Muḥammad ibn 'Abd Allah al-Kisā'ī, *Tales of the Prophets (Qiṣaṣ al-anbiyā')*, trans. Wheeler M. Thackston, Jr. (Chicago: Great Books of the Islamic World, 1997), 35–36.

42 Paris, Bibliothèque Nationale de France, persan 54, text by Naysābūrī, calligraphy by Kujī Mīr b. Muḥibb 'Alī Rashīdī, 1581, fol. 6a; New York Public Library, Spencer Collection, Persian Ms. 46, text by Naysābūrī, 34.7x22.5, fol. 9a. Milstein *et al.*, *Stories of the Prophets*, 70, 199–201 (mss. N–2 and P–1); plate XIII.

43 New York Public Library, Spencer Collection, Persian Ms. 46, fol. 9a.

44 E.g., Aḥmad bin 'Alī Abū al-Faḍl Ibn Ḥajar al-'Asqalānī (d. 852 AH/ 1449 CE), *Fatḥ al-bārī: Sharḥ Ṣaḥīḥ al-Bukhārī*, ed. Muḥammad Fu'ād 'Abd al-Bāqī and Muḥibb al-Dīn al-Khaṭīb (Cairo: Al-Maktaba al-Salafiyya, n.d.), 6:473–74. Ibn Ḥajar quotes the views of a number of scholars, such as al-Ash'arī (d. 324 AH/ 935 CE) and al-Qurṭubī (d. 671 AH/1273 CE), who supported this view. On the controversy in Islam regarding the prophecy of women see Maribel Fierro, 'Women as Prophets in Islam', in *Writing the Feminine: Women in Arab Sources*, ed. Manuela Marín and Randi Deguilhem (London: L.B. Tauris, 2002), 183–98.

45 Milstein *et al.*, *Stories of the Prophets*, 106.

46 Uri Rubin, 'More Light on Muhammad's Pre-existence: Qur'anic and Post-Qur'anic Perspectives', in *Books and Written Culture of the Islamic World: Studies Presented to Claude Gilliot on the Occasion of his 75th birthday*, ed. Andrew Rippin and Roberto Tottoli, Brill, Islamic History and Civilization, 113 (Leiden: Boston, 2015), 288–311.

47 E.g., New York Public Library, Spencer Collection, Persian Ms. 46, fol. 9a; Milstein *et al.*, *Stories of the Prophets*, 109, 199–200 (ms. N–2).

48 Fierro, 'Women as Prophets in Islam', 183–98.

49 London, Keir Collection, text by Naysābūrī, fol. 244a. Istanbul, Topkapı Sarayı Müzesi, H. 1225, text by Naysābūrī, fol. 209b; Milstein *et al.*, *Stories of the Prophets*, 194–96 (ms. K; plate XXXV), 210–11 (ms. T–5; fig. 18); Istanbul, Topkapi Palace Museum, H.1703, c. 1570s–1580s, fol. 32b. Bağcı, 'Abrahamic Traditions', 110.

50 Thackston, 'The Dispersed Falnama', 257.

51 Milstein *et al.*, *Stories of the Prophets*, 28, 106, 109.

52 'Abdallāh bin Muḥammad bin Ja'far, Abū Muḥammad al-Iṣbahānī (d. 274 AH/979 CE), *Kitāb al-'aẓama*, ed. Riḍā'allāh bin Muḥammad Idrīs al-Mubārakfūrī (Riyad: Dār al-'Āṣima, 1408 AH [1987 CE]), 5:1563–1564. 'Abd al-Raḥmān bin Abī Bakr Jalāl al-Dīn al-Suyūṭī (d. 910 AH/1505 CE, *Al-Durr al-manthūr fī 'l-tafsīr al-ma'thūr* (Beirut: Dār al-Fikr, 1993), 1:119–120. See also Leigh Chipman, 'Mythical Aspects of the Process of Adam's Creation in Judaism and Islam', *Studia islamica* 93 (2001): 5–25.

53 Massumeh Farhad and Serpil Bağci, 'Beyond the Falnama', in *Falnama*, by Farhad and Bağcı, 198–217; Massumeh Farhad, 'The Manuscripts: The Dispersed Falnama', 44; Bağcı, 'Abrahamic Traditions', 98; Milstein *et al.*, *Stories of the Prophets*, 70, 108.

54 Bağcı, 'Abrahamic Traditions', 98.

55 Istanbul, Bezayet Devlet Kütüphanesi, ms. 5275, text by Daydūzamī, fol. 47a; Istanbul, Topkapı Sarayı Müzesi, H.1225, fol. 14b; Istanbul, Topkapı Sarayı Müzesi, H.1228, text by Naysābūrī, fol. 8a. Milstein *et al.*, *Stories of the Prophets*, 190–91 (ms. I–1), 210 (ms. T–5), 214 (ms. T–8).

56 Bağcı, 'Abrahamic Traditions', 98; Milstein *et al.*, *Stories of the Prophets*, 70, 109.

57 Al-Kisā'ī, *Qiṣaṣ*, 33–34.

58 Bağcı, 'Abrahamic Traditions', 98.

59 Eva R. Hoffman, 'The Beginnings of the Illustrated Arabic Book: An Intersection between Art and Scholarship', *Muqarnas* 17 (2000): 37–52. A portrayal of biblical

(or pre-Islamic) unclothed personages is Found in the Morgan ms. of *Manāfiʿ al-ḥayawān* (1297–1300). There is disagreement with regard to whether the characters in this painting represent Adam and Eve or the Persian Mashī and Mashyānī. Hoffman further notes that unclothed characters in Umayyad desert palaces were probably 'adaptations of the pre-Islamic indigenous Greco-Roman visual vocabulary of mythological personifications', and served for private purposes (Hoffman, 'The Beginnings', 50, n. 38).

60 Bağcı, 'Abrahamic Traditions', 98.

61 Berlin, Staatsbibliothek zu Berlin, Preussicher Kulturbesitz, Orientabteilung, Diez A fol. 3, text by Naysābūrī (1577), fol. 13b. Istanbul, Bezayet Devlet Kütüphanesi, ms. 5275, fol. 47a. Istanbul, Topkapı Sarayı Müzesi, text by Naysābūrī, 8a. Istanbul, Topkapı Sarayı Müzesi, H.1228, R. 1536, text by Naysābūrī, fol. 16b. Istanbul, Topkapı Sarayı Müzesi, H.1225, fol. 14b. Milstein *et al.*, *Stories of the Prophets*, 109, 185 (ms. B; fig. 2), 190–91 (ms. I–1), 208 (ms. T–3; fig. 40), 210 (ms. T–5; fig.48).

62 E.g. Istanbul, Topkapı Sarayı Müzesi, fol. 16b; Milstein *et al.*, *Stories of the Prophets*, 208 (ms. T–3; fig. 40).

63 E.g. Istanbul, Topkapı Sarayı Müzesi, H.1225, fol. 14b; Milstein *et al.*, *Stories of the Prophets*, 210 (ms. T–5; fig. 48).

64 Kisāʾī, *Qiṣaṣ*, 35.

65 *Idem*, 37–38.

66 *Idem*, 34.

67 The Topkapi Persian *Fāl-Nāma* [H.1702] and the Ahmed I *Fāl-Nāma* [H.1703]); Bağcı, 'Abrahamic Traditions', 98.

68 Al-Kisāʾī, *Qiṣaṣ*, 36–39; Milstein *et al.*, *Stories of the Prophets*, 108.

69 Bağcı, 'Abrahamic Traditions', 98.

70 Al-Kisāʾī, *Qiṣaṣ*, 37; Al-Thaʿlabī, *Qiṣaṣ*, 45–47.

71 Berlin, Staatsbibliothek zu Berlin, Preussischer Kulturbesitz, Orientabteilung, Diez A fol. 3, fol. 13b. Milstein *et al.*, *Stories of the Prophets*, 185 (ms. B; fig. 2).

72 Thackston, 'The Dispersed Falnama', 262.

73 Serpil Bağcı, 'The Falnama of Ahmed I (TSM H.1703)', 68–76. Farhad and Bağcı, 'The Falnama in the Sixteenth and Seventeenth Centuries', 28.

74 Bağcı, 'The Falnama of Ahmed I', 69–75; Farhad, 'Between the Past and the Future', 145 n. 29.

75 Bağcı, 'Abrahamic Traditions', 100; Bağcı, 'The Falnama of Ahmed I', 69, 317 (n. 16). For the differences see Michael Rogers, 'Safavids versus Ottomans: The Origins of the Decorative Repertoire of the Aleppo-Zimmer', in *Angels, Peonies, and Fabulous Creatures: The Aleppo Room in Berlin: International Symposium of the Museum für Islamische Kunst* (Staatliche Museen zu Berlin 12–14 April 2002), 127–31.

76 Firat, *Encounters*, location 814.

77 Bağcı, 'Abrahamic Traditions', 100.

78 Firat, *Encounters*, location 871; Milstein *et al.*, *Stories of the Prophets*, 108.

79 Al-Kisāʾī, *Qiṣaṣ*, 33; Bağcı, 'Abrahamic Traditions', 100.

80 John Renard, *Islam and the Heroic Image: Themes in Literature and the Visual Arts* (Macon, Georgia: Mercer University Press, 1999), 144.

81 Bağcı, 'Abrahamic Traditions', 100.

82 Firat, *Encounters*, location 864.

83 Firat, *Encounters*, locations 765, 828; Naʿama Brosh and Rachel Milstein, *Biblical Stories in Islamic Painting* (Jerusalem: Israel Museum, 1991), 26–29.

84 Berlin, Staatsbibliothek zu Berlin, Preussischer Kulturbesitz, Orientabteilung, Diez A fol. 3, fol. 13b; Milstein *et al.*, *Stories of the Prophets*, 185 (ms. B; fig. 2).
85 Bağcı, 'Abrahamic Traditions', 100.
86 Al-Kisā'ī, *Qiṣaṣ*, 31–32.
87 Al-Kisā'ī, *Qiṣaṣ*, 39; Hadromi-Allouche, 'The Wheat and the Barley', 118.
88 Firat, *Encounters*, location 911.
89 Firat, *Encounters*, locations 374, 953, 958.

# 3

# BEAUTY AND ITS BEHOLDERS: ENVISIONING SARAH AND ESTHER

Ori Z. Soltes

## *The Shaping of Two Heroines*

In the narrative of the Hebrew Bible, there is a good number of important female figures, some of them – like Potiphar's wife or Jephthah's daughter – not even named, many more of them presented as adjuncts to their central-focus husbands. Some of them are noted for their beauty, but in promoting an unconventional God-concept relative to that embraced by the ancient peoples among whom the text's adherents dwelled and moved, one of the remarkable aspects of its females is that they are not valued for their offspring-producing capabilities. On the contrary, Sara, Rebekah and Rachel, most obviously – three of the four matriarchs – are depicted as loved and valued by their husbands in spite of a decided inability to provide them with sons.[1] In the case of Esther, the story never even arrives at the question of her progeny.

All of these characters have been visually portrayed in the vast array of art that has focused on figures and events in the Bible. For the most part, the artists until two centuries ago were Christian, for reasons beyond this discussion, so that the sensibilities they have brought to the subject are Christian. There are some exceptions to this but even within the realm of Hebrew illuminated manuscripts, often the illuminator is Christian. Conversely, in the world of the mid-nineteenth through early twenty-first centuries, Jewish artists are increasingly notable, as if making up for lost time, and with their arrival in the art world, some of the more interesting depictions of Hebrew biblical heroines appear.

Sarah and Esther offer a particularly interesting pairing, both conceptually and visually. They mark the beginning and the end of the Hebrew biblical narrative with respect to the chronology of events and with them, the evolution of the biblical God-concept as well as the evolution of the group that defines itself in relation to that concept.[2] Thus for those Hebrews – a term with socio-economic connotations (of being itinerant), rather than with ethnic or spiritual meaning – referred to as the patriarchs and matriarchs, God can be seen to have been viewed as personal and localized; their descendants, the Israelites (a term with both ethnic and spiritual connotations), viewed God in ethnocentric, national terms. Eventually, the Judaean remnant of Israel, carried into exile by the Babylonians and returning from exile thanks to the Medo-Persians, forges a fuller-fledged universalist understanding of God that will be yet further refined as the Jewish and Christian sensibilities.

Sarah, to repeat, falls at the beginning of this evolutionary story, Esther at its end. As bookend figures they stand apart from other biblical heroines, even as all share in common attributes that, in part, derive from the unique agenda of the text and in part, paradoxically, from being women in a narrative shaped by men. Sarah and Esther also play – sometimes obliquely – parallel and very important kinds of roles in the storylines of which they are part. Both of them are particularly noted for their physical beauty, but where in Esther's case her looks are a centrepiece of her story – an instrument essential to her people's survival – in Sarah's case that feature is used more to present an aspect of Abraham's personality, either his cleverness or his cowardice or both: her beauty is used to emphasize Abraham's fear of a royal prerogative similar to but different from that which pushes the Book of Esther forward – to whom her physical looks offer a potential threat to his own survival.

The two figures share crucial moments of assertiveness, Sarah preserving the future of the people that will be saved in the future by Esther. Sarah pushes Abraham to find another source (Hagar) through which to produce an offspring when she herself seems incapable of reproduction, but she is also the prime mover in convincing Abraham to drive Hagar and Ishmael away when her son, Isaac, is threatened: she both protects her son as a mother and perhaps also recognizes (where Abraham is oblivious to this) the greater spiritual appropriateness of Isaac, rather than Ishmael, as the inheritor and future conveyor of the Covenant.[3] Ironically, when the consummate moment of covenantal transmission arrives – the *Akedah* (Binding) and near-killing of Isaac – she is left in the background.

Does she even know of the experience from which she was directly excluded? For she seems never to have seen Abraham again. That same Abraham who is non-heroic vis-à-vis the pharaoh (Gen. 12) and King Abimelech of Gerar (Gen. 20), returns, after the *Akedah*, to Beersheba and only 'comes to' Hebron to mourn for and bury Sarah (Gen. 23:2). That detail, suggesting that he remained separate from her until her death perhaps speaks of his fear of her anger as a mother after what he almost did to their only son.[4]

Esther is pushed into a heroic role by her uncle Mordecai and by her own courage, risking her life to save the Judaeans from destruction.[5] Where Sarah demanded that Hagar be pushed aside, Esther's accession to a royal position is facilitated by the pushing aside of Vashti, without which action Esther would never have entered the scene and been in a position to play her salvational role. Her understated power leads to her success before the king and against her people's enemy. If the end of Sarah's story is filled with lonely loss, that of Esther is crowded with family, friends and triumph.[6]

Moreover, Esther's redemptive role for the Judaeans of Persia helped assure her place within the biblical canon, and enabled her to assume a larger role as a symbol of salvation, within both the Jewish and Christian traditions.[7] As she intercedes on behalf of the Judaeans with Ahasuerus, she prefigures the Virgin who intercedes on behalf of Christians with God during the Last Judgment. She entered the Christian canon by way of the Septuagint's Greek rendering, through St Jerome's vulgate translation and the arrival at an official Bible by c. 393–97 CE at the Council of Hippo. There, perhaps not by accident, the book is placed after the Book of Judith – another Judaean heroine, who saves Jerusalem by beheading its besieging general, Holofernes the Assyrian, and thus another, more oblique precursor of the Virgin Mary – which is not found in the Jewish canon, in the order of which Esther follows Ecclesiastes.[8]

Esther's role expands beyond that of Sarah. In the seventeenth century – in part connected to the surge in the Jewish false messianic Sabbatean Movement and in part to the discovery of Jews in Kai Feng Fu, China, by the Jesuit missionary, Matteo Ricci, as well as to the further exploration of the interior of the Amazon River valley in South America and the false assumption that the Yanoama Indians were speaking Hebrew – there evolved a conviction on the part of various European groups that the Lost Ten Tribes of Israel were to be found among the indigenous inhabitants of the New World and, therefore, that the messianic advent was imminent.[9] A notion emerged that Esther the intercessor for endangered Judaeans had a distinctive relevance for endangered Indians. Thus the terms used by Friar Bernardino Cardenas in petitioning the Spanish King Philip IV (ruled 1621–1665) in 1629 for funds with which to educate indigenous Peruvians included the assertion that 'just as it was when King Ahasuerus, for love of Esther, exalted the humble and the scorned, giving them favors and mercy', so ought the king to help, 'for the love of Esther, who is the Virgin Mary, …[for] the salvation of these poor Indian people'.[10]

During the seventeenth and eighteenth centuries, Esther in her capacity as the prefiguration of the Virgin also assumes a popular position as St Esther, particularly in the Coptic, Greek Orthodox and Catholic traditions.[11] The first offers a Feast of St Esther on December 20, the second no particular feast day and the third a feast day on 1 July first celebrated in eighteenth-century Venice. The Catholic tradition assumes a noticeable focus in the Spanish Church that flourished in the Americas.[12]

## *Sarah's Ageless Beauty*

Not surprisingly, visual directions with regard to the two heroines differ. The physical, even seductive youthful beauty of Esther is a consistent emphasis, underscoring that feature as essential to her redemptive accomplishment; Sarah is more often depicted in old age, underscoring the miracle of the birth of Isaac that will lead to the salvation of the Covenantal future – although all of this noticeably changes in the twentieth century.

One early example is a lush mosaic cycle created for the Church of San Vitale in Ravenna (528–43 CE). In one of the lunettes, the story in Gen. 18:1–15 is depicted, in which Abraham looks up at noon, sees three anthropomorphic beings approaching his tent by a tree at Mamre, and invites them in for a meal. Events are shown taking place against a rich greenery, as Abraham bows towards the angels with his platter of meat, as they sit behind a table already laden with three cruciform-incised loaves of bread. Sarah observes from behind her husband, standing in a small aedicule. Across from Sarah and Abraham on the left and the angels in the centre, the right-hand side of the composition depicts the binding of Isaac (Gen. 22), without Sarah, naturally – compositionally, her place is taken by Isaac, lying on the altar of sacrifice – and with an Abraham much older than he is when shown waiting on the angels.

The scene at Mamre is repeatedly offered through the centuries – and often with anticipatory Christological symbols (like the three cruciform loaves in the San Vitale mosaic). In Russian icons, sometimes a goblet in Abraham's hand and in Sarah's a cloth suggest aspects of the Eucharist. Sometimes the Christological language is stylistic. An oil panel by the Flemish master Jan Provost (1465–1529) depicts Abraham and Sarah with only one angel. Sarah listens from behind the door to the conversation between her husband – who looks at the angel but gestures back towards his wife – and his gesticulating visitor (Figure 3.1). That the latter is announcing extraordinary news is reinforced by the manner in which his position and gestures recall Annunciation images; if one were to move the seated Abraham to the right, and eliminate the figure of Sarah (or remove the figure of Abraham, leaving only the angel and Sarah), one would have a distinctly Annunciation-inspired scene. Sarah, only partially visible, is on the other hand attired in the same bright red that Abraham wears and the same white that the angel wears: she is the coloristic centring point between the two, even as she is compositionally to the side and half obscured by the doorway. She is also swathed in the green of spring and rebirth, not only anticipating Isaac's birth, but, given his Christian role as a forerunner of Jesus, the symbolism of the green may be said to look all the way forward to the birth of Christ by way of a different sort of miraculous birth.

The Jewish visual tradition follows a similar course of not often making Sarah the centre of the action in the Mamre scene, albeit for centuries that tradition was limited to manuscript illuminations, most often in either *haggadot* to guide the festive Passover meal – the *Seder* – or in Scrolls of Esther (*Megillot Esther*) read during the lesser holiday of Purim. These often reflect Christian stylistic and symbolic ideas. The *Golden Haggadah* (c. 1300–20) – so called due to the exquisite gold-leaf-tooled background for its illustrations – offers the moment within the Mamre narrative when the patriarch is receiving the great news delivered by the divine messengers. He looks intently at his three visitors, while gesturing back to his right (the viewer's left), pointing towards Sarah, who stands within an aedicule in a manner reminiscent of the Virgin Mary in an Annunciation: one hand is raised, *orans* style, to receive the news, and the other rests on her belly.

An interesting attempt to accord Sarah a more central visual place in this narrative moment is that by the Italian Baroque painter Bartolomeo Guidobono

**Figure 3.1** Jan Provost, *Abraham, Sarah and the Angel*, c. 1520. Oil on wood panel. Musée du Louvre.

(1654–1705), in which both she and Abraham lean in from the upper left to the three angels, listening intently as the middle one delivers the extraordinary news and gestures dramatically heavenward. Abraham is more to the front, but Sarah's face marks the compositional centre.

Images that focus on the triangle of Abraham, Sarah and Hagar – or the pent-angle that includes both sons in this problematic, dysfunctional family story – seem to emerge frequently as one moves from the late sixteenth century forward – and tend to underscore Sarah's elderly state, although offering her a central place in the composition. Flemish painter and sculptor Bartholomeus Spranger (1564–1611) depicts Sarah presenting Hagar to Abraham (Gen. 16:2–3) in an oil on canvas (1600;

Dulwich Gallery), in which the matriarch is in the centre, her left hand placed encouragingly on her husband's shoulder, to the viewer's right – he is virtually naked, sitting up among the bedclothes, with bright red drapery as his backdrop and a green-and-white strip of cloth strategically covering his private parts – while gesturing towards a young, luscious Hagar to Sarah's right (the viewer's left) whom we see, almost entirely naked, from the rear, lightly holding Abraham's right hand in her own right hand at the very centre of the composition. If we could turn her from a vertically to a horizontally placed figure, we would be looking at a Venus or Odalisque image from a slightly different time and place. As for Sarah, she looks like an old procuress (Figure 3.2).[13]

**Figure 3.2** Bartholomeus Spanger, *Sarah Presents Hagar to Abraham,*1600. Oil on canvas. Dulwich Gallery.

One does see Sarah as a young, beautiful woman in the less commonly depicted engagement of the pharaoh in Egypt of Abimelech, in both of which passages Abraham represents his wife as his sister.[14] The pharaoh takes a strong interest in the young beauty, but God intervenes so that nothing untoward takes place between the monarch and the matriarch, and he, disgruntled, returns her to Abraham's custody. It is this act, 'Pharaoh Returns Sarah to Abraham' (oil on canvas, 1640; Rijksmuseum), that the Dutch painter Isaac Isaacsz captured. Just to the left of the centre stands the beautiful Sarai,[15] attired in scintillating white, and counterbalanced by a second, more shadowed female figure behind her to the right of centre – perhaps the not-yet-involved Egyptian, Hagar. Sarai is moving towards the viewer's left, where the red-robed Abraham is starting to envelope her with his outstretched arms; behind her the luxuriously attired pharaoh is separated from her by the sceptre reaching towards her from his extended right hand. Our heroine remains surrounded by males (Figure 3.3).

Towards modernity, as the Bible becomes an object of academic study and as the colonial and archaeological devouring of the Middle East by Europe and the West expands exponentially, a growing array of artists seeks to systematically depict key biblical scenes and personages. One of the more prolific of these is the French painter, James (Jacques) Tissot (1836–1902). One of Tissot's Sarah images offers the moment when the matriarch is first taken *to* the pharaoh's palace, in a

**Figure 3.3** Isaac Isaacsz, *Pharaoh Returns Sarah to Abraham*, 1640. Oil on canvas. Rijksmuseum.

water colour from his 1896–1902 biblical series (Jewish Museum, New York). He presents her seated to the left, enveloped, almost drowning, in luxurious robes and jewellery – we can barely make out her face, buried as she is in all that material, but we can see enough to note that her expression is distinctly unhappy – associating these trappings with a would-be wife of the pharaoh (in any case, her garments are exotic and 'other', although they suggest Central Asia more than Egypt). Two similarly clad handmaidens are seated behind her and an array of Egyptians, identified by their hair and their garments, assess her, from the right. Behind her is what we can also recognize as a kind of Egyptian wall-painting that helps set the visual context as 'Egyptian' (Figure 3.4). What she dominates compositionally – our eyes, like those of the Egyptians, are drawn to her – dominates her psychologically, her visible body parts limited to stiffly held lower arms and a face with eyes staring grumpily into space.

In the twentieth century Sarah eventually assumes a fuller role as the centre of her own narrative. Marc Chagall (1887–1985) – one of many Jewish artists who become an increasingly frequent part of the world of painting and sculpture by the early twentieth century – was influenced, among other things, by the rich colouristic values of the icons in the world of Belarus in the East where he was born and grew up. His images uniquely echo the medieval penchant for erasing the secular norms of time and space in sacred images. A 1956 colour lithograph of Abraham and Sarah is one of the earliest within the visual repertoire to place the matriarch literally front and centre. The entire ground is swathed in shades of blue

**Figure 3.4** James Tissot, *Sarah in the Pharaoh's Palace*, c. 1900. Watercolour. Jewish Museum, New York.

and celadon green. Sarah is depicted as a beautiful young woman – no doubt modelled on the artist's first wife and life-long muse, Bela, who perished in America of appendicitis, in 1943 – in profile, as the dominating, central figure. Abraham occupies the middle ground, off to the upper right, reaching towards her; their itinerant life (somewhat like that of Marc and Bela during their years together) is symbolized by the camel in the upper left background corner.[16]

A 1960 Chagall lithograph offers Sarah alone, receiving the annunciation from the three angels. Seen from the neck up in profile, her eyes closed in ecstasy, she raises her hands in thanksgiving – or joyous clapping as the angelic figures are entirely drenched in birth-blood red, one of them proclaiming the news by blowing on a shofar (a ram's horn that perhaps anticipates the *Akedah*).

Mordecai Ardon (1896–1992), one of Israel's most important artists, turns the issue in a still more dramatic direction in his 1947 oil, 'Sarah' (Figure 3.5). She fills the image, a gigantic, blood-red centre between past and future, her arms raised towards her open-mouthed face in a gesture of grief. Before her, to the viewer's right, a completely white figure of Isaac lies as if dead – it is as if she is *present* not at his *binding* but at his actual *sacrifice* – and tiny in the background to the viewer's left is the hunched-over figure of Abraham, his sleeves covered in the red of bloody sacrifice. Lying on the ground just behind him is a ladder that alludes to the future, first significant dream of Isaac's son, Jacob. Will that future not happen if this past is transformed? Was it Sarah's presence in Abraham's mind that took the form of the voice of God commanding him to desist? Is this Sarah not every mother, who

**Figure 3.5** Mordecai Ardon, *Sarah*, 1947. Oil on canvas. Private Collection.

feels the pain of her child even if he is away from her – who feels the moment of the *Akedah* not as the mind-blinding transcendent Abrahamic experience, but as a cold-blooded betrayal of the fundamental parenting ethic: to protect? Is she not every Israeli mother whose son is raised to fight in the army of survival, particularly in the aftermath of the destruction of so many Jews by the Nazis, and of the faith of many survivors – this work conceived and birthed in the shadow of the Holocaust even before the state had fully coalesced?

American artist Janet Shafner (1931–2011) turns us back to Mamre in her 1998 oil on canvas 'Sarah' – part of an extensive series on biblical figures. Sarah sits meditatively in profile, raked by the intense light and shadow that pierce her tent; the three bearded figures lounge outside in the middle distance, awaiting the repast that Abraham, nowhere to be seen, is presumably off preparing for them – while Sarah seems to be waiting, intuiting the extraordinary news that will change her old age dramatically (Figure 3.6).[17]

Siona Benjamin (b. 1961) – a Jew who grew up in the Hindu and Muslim community of Mumbai, attending Zoroastrian and Catholic schools and eventually immigrating to the United States – has produced an extraordinary series called *Finding Home*, that resonates with interfaith, multicultural and international

**Figure 3.6** Janet Shafner, *Sarah,* 1998. Oil on canvas. Private Collection.

elements. In *Finding Home* #61: *Beloved*, Siona unites Sarah and Hagar, defying the traditional texts that cast them as antagonists protecting their sons (Figure 3.7). They are wrapped together as one being with two, virtually identical, haloed visages. They are their own descendants: one wears a Jewish skullcap (*kippah*); the other a *kafiyah*. The danger of separation is updated – not only because their unibody is broken four times, with large drops of blood filling the space where the breaks occur and pooling below them. The yellow background presents in silent outline a triple figure with a bomb wrapped around his chest, on the side of Hagar; and two soldiers – looking away from the suicide bomber(s) – as well as a camera, focused on them, on Sarah's side. The frame, overrun with vegetal motifs and with 'Sarah' and 'Hagar' inscribed in Hebrew along the bottom edge, is punctuated by images of grenades and guns. Sarah and Hagar have become a rhetorical question: can we defuse what threatens to blow us apart and come to truly embrace what binds us together, as Muslims and Jews – as humans?

**Figure 3.7** Siona Benjamin, *Finding Home #61: Beloved.* Gouache on paper, 2004. Courtesy of the Artist.

**Figure 3.8** Richard McBee, *Sarah and the Three Angels*, 1998. Acrylic on canvas. Courtesy of the Artist.

No contemporary artist has devoted more attention to Sarah than American painter Richard McBee (b. 1947). In the last quarter-century, he has followed an extended series of paintings focused on the problematic relationship between Abraham and Isaac in the aftermath of the *Akedah* with a diverse series with Sarah as the focus, called *Sarah's Trials*. One image, 'Sarah and the Three Angels' (1998), does the opposite of what we have observed again and again in art history: he eliminates the figure of Abraham altogether, leaving the three angels – as a semi-abstract trio of faceless figures in brilliant shades of blue – to the right, and Sarah, moving in a hurry away through a doorway, on the left (Figure 3.8). She casts a long shadow as she moves through a gold-yellow field of colour, as if rushing off to be alone to think over the extraordinary news that she has just received. That yellow hue is, after all, associated in the history of Christian art with betrayal: does Sarah see beyond the unexpected angelic annunciation the near-disaster of the *Akedah* and its aftermath for her?

A second, very moving image from the series, called 'The Death of Sarah' (2010), shows the heroine wrapped up in a plain white shroud and lying on a sort of bier to the lower right. Against a variegated backdrop – a flat, perspectiveless space of blues and some greys, parts of it broken up into myriad mosaic-like tesserae – the lone, bereaved figure of Abraham stands and looks over the corpse of his long-loved and long-lost wife, so completely wrapped that he cannot even get a last look into her face. He has returned to bury her, never having dared to face her after the faith experiment that involved their only son.[18] The artist has done what artists have done throughout history: sartorially updated his figures, so that Abraham is attired as a contemporary Hassid, who might have come in from a street in Brooklyn – a man of piety, as the empty space and inaccessible visage of his wife reverberate with silent grief. Sarah is what the dead are expected to be in the Jewish tradition: unremarkable, plainly attired, about to return to the dust from which we all come.

## *The Beauty of Esther*

By contrast to Sarah, Esther is frequently – but not always – a central figure across the narrative of visual history. Not surprisingly, she is among the characters depicted in the earliest extant visual cycle in the Jewish tradition, the wall paintings (c. 244–45 CE) in the synagogue at Dura Europas on the banks of the Euphrates River – the border between the Roman and Sassanian Persian empires. Esther appears on the western wall, enthroned, next to but just behind King Ahasuerus – in counterpoint to Mordecai, who is mounted on a white steed, the two scenes separated within the larger frame by a small crowd cheering Mordecai on – taking her place among characters and events associated with Hebrew biblical moments of salvation and/or future redemption. Indeed, she is just to the left of the Torah niche that occupies the centre of the Jerusalem-oriented wall; a young David is shown being anointed by the prophet Samuel on the opposite side of the niche.[19]

For centuries we possess no evidence of Jewish visual activity – between the time of the mosaic-decorated synagogues of the sixth and seventh centuries and the emergence of synagogues in Worms, Prague and Toledo in the late eleventh through early thirteenth centuries. Soon thereafter, visual activity re-emerges in the Jewish world, in the form of manuscript illuminations and illustrations. Among these, Esther scrolls typically offer all of the major characters and events within the narrative, and so the heroine rarely stands out; she is typically attired, as others are, consistently with the style of the time and place, in colour or in sepia, in a variety of settings.

Occasionally, a different sort of image makes its appearance. Thus an anonymous Dutch illustration of a *Purimspiel* from 1657 presents the central figure, presumably Esther, wearing a high, conical hat and holding a handkerchief to her face, while a second dances before her and the viewer. For the most part, however, the Jewish images of Esther in this and the following two centuries continue to be found in *megillot*.[20]

In the centuries during which we possess no evidence of Jewish visual activity and those in which that recorded activity is limited to illuminations, Esther is found in a number of Christian art and architectural contexts. She appears in the ninth-century wall-paintings of St Clemente in Rome, and again, carved in relief by Master Mateo, over the western portal (1168–88) of the pilgrimage church of Santiago de Compostela. She is also portrayed over the north portal (c. 1215) of the Chartres Cathedral, as the most beauteous among Christ's 'ancestors'.[21]

Such sculptural/architectural examples present Esther in the company of diverse significant biblical figures, rather than within her own story. Conversely, at the other end of the scale and medium spectrum, one of the more charming panels in an anonymously devised manuscript from late twelfth-century Alsace, known as the *Hortus deliciarum* (Garden of Delicacies – a gastronomic compendium), presents her in a definitive handling of the denouement of the story. Esther and Ahasuerus dine on fish and a large pretzel (this is arguably the first image of a pretzel in art). They are flanked at the table by Mordecai and Haman, so that the anonymous artist has taken a slight liberty with what we might suppose was one of the two banquets to which Esther initially invited the king and his anti-Judaean adviser (Esth 5:4, 7–8). Mordecai has been added, no doubt in the interest of presenting all *four* major characters as enjoying the fateful – ultimately salvational (albeit fatal for Haman) – meal (Figure 3.9).

The gestural language is simple and straightforward. As Mordecai (wearing the horned hat shortly required of Jews in many Christian communities after the Lateran Council of 1215) looks to his right while pointing to his left (the viewer's right); Esther gesticulates to her left, to the king and beyond him, to Haman; Ahasuerus emphatically points to Haman, who gestures, his right hand on his heart, as if to say, 'who? me?' She has obviously just accused him of the intended genocide against her people – and therefore against her (Esth 7:3–5). It looks like a slice of a relatively benign 'Last Supper' painting, with Haman as a Judas (the only one without a head cover, like Judas without a halo or placed in shadow)

**Figure 3.9** Anonymous, *Hortus deliciarum*. 'Esther's Feast' Book Illumination, twelfth-century, Hohenburg Abbey.

professing innocence of his imminent crime, and the rouge-cheeked but modest, wimple-wearing Esther as the centre of the composition.

The heroine and her story seem to recede into the background in the next few centuries, but a number of interesting depictions of different sorts appear again as we arrive into the Renaissance. She is often seen in the act of being chosen as queen – or presented simply as a beauty for the (male) viewer to admire as if he were Ahasuerus (Esth 2:15–17). She is depicted in conversation with Mordecai or dealing with Mordecai's warning (Esth 4:8–13) – risking an uninvited audience with King Ahasuerus, entertaining Haman and the king (Esth 5:5–6; 7:1–2), or pleading with him for her people (Esth 7:3–5) – or being pleaded *to* by Haman (Esth 7:7–8) – and most frequently, she is shown approaching the king with trepidation to invite him to the dinner at which she will eventually plead for the salvation of her people (Esth 5:2).

Illuminations by barely known miniaturists, like the so-called Masters of Azor (one or more Dutch masters working in Utrecht, c. 1430) offer various moments in the narrative. That in which the king acknowledges Esther's approach is set in a walled courtyard outside the palace. The image offers the enthroned, white-bearded Ahasuerus extending an extraordinarily long, fleur-de-lis-tipped sceptre from his lap to the mouth of his heavily clad, kneeling queen – ostensibly to symbolize his granting her the right to speak – who grasps the shaft in her right hand. A modernist would wonder what level of consciousness impelled the artist towards such an inordinately, if somewhat subtly, sexually charged moment (Figure 3.10).[22]

**Figure 3.10** Masters of Azor, *Esther before Ahasuerus*. Illumination, c. 1430. Royal Library, The Hague.

North of the Alps, a 1435 work (in St Leonards Church, Basel) by German-born Konrad Witz (1400/10–1446; active mainly in Basel, Switzerland) presents the king inclining towards her and touching her head with his sceptre. This rendition in particular suggests the conceptual relationship between Esther and the Virgin Mary: the manner in which Esther inclines her head, kneels, closes her eyes and throws up her hands, as the king turns smiling towards her with his sceptre, formally recalls many depictions of the Annunciation (one thinks of the Van Eyck Annunciation in the National Gallery of Art, Washington, DC, for instance, painted at virtually the same time – with the figure placement reversed and the role of the angel here taken up by the king). The artist, consciously or not, has underscored this earlier moment as anticipatory of the later moment: both are the beginning of a step-by-step narrative leading to redemption (Figure 3.11).

The Florentine Renaissance master Sandro Botticelli (1445–1510) composed, c. 1470–75 – apparently leaving much of the actual tempera painting to his younger colleague, Filippino Lippi (1459–1504) – a series of scenes commissioned for what we know to have been a pair of wedding chests. One panel (in the Louvre) sets three scenes in the same register, almost as a triptych, with columns separating the central scene from those on the sides. That central image shows Esther swooning and held up by two handmaidens as she approaches the king – high on his throne

**Figure 3.11** Konrad Witz, *Esther before the King,* 1435. Oil on wood panel. St Leonard's Church, Basel.

he gestures with his sceptre towards her – to make her request. The artist has captured the moment described in the Septuagint version (but not in the Hebrew version): 'But as she was speaking, she fell fainting. And the king was agitated, and all his servants sought to comfort her'.

Her swoon has a visual and conceptual ripple effect, left/right and past/future. For Esther's emotional moment is flanked, to the viewer's left, by a Mordecai partially sprawled (not quite swooning) on the ground (just prior to Esther's royal audience) in mourning for his people's possible fate (Esth 4:1); and to the right, the same Haman who in the central scene dispassionately watches Esther collapsing while leaning on his sword, is shown on his knees, beseeching Esther for mercy (Esth 7:7–8; he also is not quite swooning) – as the king hurries in from the rear just in time to misinterpret the moment between his vizier and his wife (Figure 3.12).

Other artists of the fifteenth century, both Italian and Northern, depicted Esther and diverse scenes from her story. However, with the arrival of Martin Luther onto the stage of history, in the 1520s the Additions to the Book of Esther ended up outside the Protestant Bible, along with several other books still found in the Catholic Bible. In the Counter-Reformation that followed, the latter was re-confirmed by the Council of Trent (1546–65) – which was the time when Esther's role as a Marian precursor was also re-affirmed or perhaps first distinctly declared. During and after the trauma of Reformation/Counter-Reformation, images of the narrative and its heroine become both more frequent and often more luxurious. Baroque Venetian painters such as Paolo Veronese (1528–1588) were drawn to the potential for pomp in the feasting scenes that were often their focus – almost more than to the characters.

The moments when Esther comes before the king offer ambiguous artistic possibilities. Sometimes, as for example in the 1645–50 oil painting by the Neapolitan Baroque painter Bernardo Cavallino (1616–1656), where she kneels, gesturing

**Figure 3.12** Sandro Botticelli/Fra Filippino Lippi, *Three Scenes from the Story of Esther*, c. 1470–75. Oil on wood panel. Musée du Louvre.

**Figure 3.13** Bernardo Cavallino, *Esther and Ahasuerus,* 1645–50. Oil on canvas. Ufizzi Gallery.

with her arms, and Ahasuerus – portrayed with a very Christ-like face, and surrounded by a rich, blood-red textile backdrop – inclines towards her with an arm gesture that obliquely echoes hers, it is not clear whether she is approaching him with trepidation to plead on behalf of her people, or whether this is the earlier moment when she is being chosen by the king to be his queen (Figure 3.13).

There is a similar ambiguity in the oil of 'Esther before Ahasuerus' (1623; Metropolitan Museum of Art, New York), by Neapolitan Baroque genius Artemisia Gentileschi (1593–1651/53) – one of the few pre-modern paintings of Esther done by a woman. As the king leans forward with interest – or perhaps concern – almost pushing up from his throne, Esther is swooning in the arms of two handmaidens. No other figures encumber the image, with a large space between the two protagonists that accentuates the separateness of the worlds they inhabit, rather than the reconciliation between them that, to the viewer familiar with the text, is imminent (Figure 3.14).

One might even imagine this *not* as the familiar pre-redemptive moment. For there is no sceptre in the king's hand, so it *feels* like the moment when she, like so many other women from throughout his vast empire, has been brought before him to be examined with regard to her fitness to be his new queen (Esth 2:15). Small-town girl in the big city of Shushan, in the palace of the king, before his majesty, no less, she swoons. And the king's look seems directed towards the pale flesh of her décolletage, rather than the face of this beautiful, distressed woman before him.

**Figure 3.14** Artemisia Gentileschi, *Esther before Ahasuerus*, 1623. Oil on Canvas, 82 x 107¾ in. (208.3 x 273.7 cm). Gift of Elinor Dorrance Ingersoll, 1969. The Metropolitan Museum of Art, New York, 69.281.

Indeed, these details duly observed, it must also be noted that Esther's solid figure is a substantial column, while the king is hardly more than an overly luxurious, effete adolescent (it was, after all, a drinking party that led to the demise of Esther's predecessor). So Artemisia may be said to have offered a distinct equation between the Judaeans and the female as ostensibly weaker but morally superior, and the Persians and the male as ostensibly stronger but morally inferior, through the paradox of an Esther as physically powerful albeit passively losing consciousness and an Ahasuerus somehow smaller albeit actively alert.

Rembrandt's 1633 painting of 'Esther Preparing to Intercede with Ahasuerus', as, so often in his work, featuring his young wife, Saskia, as the subject, offers her as a pool of golden light within an undefined shadowy background. Even with her handmaiden assisting her – but nearly enveloped by the darkness – the awful solitude of the Judaean Queen of Persia, who is faced with such a serious and dangerous task in which nobody can help her, is emphasized.

The somewhat later, less renowned Dutch artist, Aert de Gelder (1645–1727), further underscores that condition and connects Esther to his own era in offering a 1684 work with a double title: 'The Jewish Bride' or 'Esther Bedecked'. Is this the moment after she has been chosen by Ahasuerus to be his new wife or is it the moment before she seeks his audience? She is being dressed, as recent or

**Figure 3.15** Aert de Gelder, *The Jewish Bride/Esther Bedecked*, 1684. Oil on canvas. Alte Pinakothek, Munich.

risk-taking queen, surrounded by handmaidens in an almost claustrophobic manner, suggesting the burden that is slowly being placed upon her shoulders – in a second piece from the same year the artist added an ermine collar, symbolizing royalty and thus her position as queen but, more obliquely, the reality that that collar is also a yoke (Figure 3.15).

By the late nineteenth century, as the socio-cultural world was becoming more open to Jews and even, somewhat, to women, a work signed by the otherwise unknown Jewish artist Sara Eydel Weissberg (fl. c. 1875–1900), made of perforated paper embroidered with wool and silk and created in Jerusalem, was intended to be hung on the wall. On it, brief texts in block-shaped Hebrew letters quote passages that identify the primitivist, folk-style scenes with figures that include Esther before Ahasuerus, acknowledging her presence with his sceptre. Figures – solid and stiff – are labelled and narrative passages are added for clarification, in Hebrew, while the middle text passage is in Yiddish, identifying the artist.

By this era, as Jews began to make their way more definitively into mainstream visual art – including genre painters such as Moritz Oppenheim (in Germany) and Mauricy Gottlieb (in Poland) on the one hand and impressionists such as Camille Pissarro (in France) and Josef Israels (in Holland) on the other – the figure of Esther was beginning to assume a place in 'modern' art with representations reflecting sensibilities not limited to the sacred. Indeed, sensual beauty is clearly the import of Dominican-born French painter Théodore Chassériau's 1841 oil on canvas – 'Toilette of Esther' (Louvre) – with her naked torso and arms upraised to fix her remarkably blond hair (Figure 3.16). Chassériau (1819–1856) was already the prized pupil of Ingres at age 11, and later, after Ingres left Paris for Rome, he came under the influence of Delacroix, so that his style is sometimes spoken of as an attempt to mediate between the rigorous and chilly classicism of the former and the more colouristically fiery romanticism of the latter. This painting surely follows that path within art history intended to capture the eye and imagination of lustful male viewers. It is designed to offer a strident answer to the implicit question: 'What exactly would have made the king raise his sceptre in her direction so readily when she arrived, unannounced, in his throne room?'

Style and subject variation continue into recent times, from Marc Chagall's c. 1958–59 ink, wash and brush on paper – whose Esther dominates the frame that reduces the king and his retinue to small background figures – to Salvador Dali's (1904–89) surreal, psychoanalytic lithograph, 'Ahasuerus Falls in Love with

**Figure 3.16** Theodore Chassériau, *Toilette of Esther*, 1841. Oil on canvas. Musée du Louvre.

**Figure 3.17** Leonard Baskin, *Esther*, c. 1975. Coloured lithograph.

Esther' (1964), in which the face of the maiden floats within the bald head of the king, his flowing beard and intense expression reminiscent of Leonardo da Vinci.

American Leonard Baskin's (1922–2000) very different, coloured lithograph 'Esther' (c. 1975), stands gigantically within colourless, empty, contextless space (Figure 3.17). She is identified in large Hebrew letters, and holds her right hand on her heart, suggesting either protest or plea. Her garment is plain, as she herself is. Baskin has thus deliberately eschewed the idea that her beauty was physical, implying that it was her charm and intellect that captured the king's attention. Moreover, since nothing identifies her ethno-religiously, then as a paragon of female heroism she is neither Jewish (despite her name written in Hebrew) nor from some far-away exotic time and land: she symbolizes universal moral victory.

The other side of the text-image coin, as well as the rabbinic tradition's reflection on Esther's beauty as other than physical, is explored more recently in J. T. Waldman's (b. 1977) graphic novel, *Megillat Esther* (2005). Art, calligraphy and bi-lingual text offer spectacular contemporary visual richness – both serious story and comic-book amusement, reflecting the simultaneously light-hearted and heavy approach to Esther in the Jewish tradition. Our first view of the future queen suggests Bette Midler rather than Marilyn Monroe (Figure 3.18).[23] She is, after all, regardless of how physically beautiful or not – and the rabbinic tradition discusses her being as young as 14 and as old as 74, 75 or even 80 – a heroine who conquered Ahasuerus and undid Haman with her wits – a character worthy of the admiration of everyman and everywoman.[24] Like Sarah, her actions – for the sake

**Figure 3.18** J. T. Waldman, *Megillat Esther* (detail). 'Esther' graphic novel 2005.

of others, rather than herself – make her age irrelevant to her place as a woman of valour worthy of the wide range of depictions to which she has been subject over the centuries.

The accounts woven around Sarah and Esther have inspired artists over time to imagine these heroines at the signal moments of their narratives. They have offered Christian and, more recently, Jewish artists the opportunity to add visual interpretations to the textual interpretations found in the rabbinic and patristic and later traditions. Like the figures themselves, these artists have enhanced our understanding of the complex issues of human–human and divine–human interaction that are repeatedly explored in the Bible.

## *Notes*

1 One might further note, in the matter of unconventionality, that rarely is the son who inherits the primary covenant and its responsibilities the older son – i.e., primogeniture is ignored. Thus Abraham, Isaac, Jacob, Joseph, Moses, Saul, David and Solomon, to name the most obvious figures, are all younger (even youngest) sons.

2 I do not mean that they are at the beginning and the end of the Hebrew Bible as its books are sequenced.

3 I mean by this her anticipation of God's comment to Abraham in Gen. 20:12 regarding Isaac – and perhaps the blind faith that he, and not only Abraham, exhibits in Gen. 22. Needless to say, this Judaeo-Christian perspective is not shared by Islam.
4 As for that son, Isaac, no explicit reference is made to where he went after the *Akedah*. Gen. 22:19 states that Abraham and the young men whom he had brought along went (back?) to Beersheba, 'and Abraham dwelt at Beersheba'. That Isaac went back to Sarah and that they moved on to Hebron might be inferred from Gen. 24:67 when he receives Rebekah as his wife 'and brought her into his mother Sarah's tent'. But the typically laconic text is not explicit.
5 Note that I consistently use the term 'Judaean' where it is more common to read 'Jew/ish'. Both of these English-language terms are conveyed by the identical term in Hebrew, Aramaic, Greek and Latin – the languages most important just prior to and following the time of Jesus in the eastern corner of the Mediterranean that is today Israel/Palestine/Jordan. I believe that it is historically important, since we can make the distinction in English, to do so, since what we understand as Judaism – including the Bible that Jews read and the rabbinic tradition of understanding it – was not yet shaped at the time of Esther. Both Judaism and Christianity are shaped out of a common Judaean parent as twins each claiming to be the legitimate offspring of that parent.
6 Where Gen. 20 culminates with the successful denouement of the Abimelech story, and Gen. 21 begins with Sarah's joy at the miraculous birth of Isaac, by 21:10–11 she has demanded the expulsion of Hagar and Ishmael, mightily displeasing Abraham – and, even if God tells Abraham not to be displeased (Gen. 21:12–13), the next time we find a reference to her, after Gen. 22 and the *Akedah* in which she plays no active part, she is dead and Abraham has come to mourn for her (Gen. 23:2). So either her last years were spent in the company of her son but not her husband, or in the company of neither of them. Loneliness seeps out of the text.
7 The Book of Esther, rather than, per se, the character for whom it is named, raised rabbinic discomfort – due to the absence of God's name or mention of the Land of Israel within it – leading to hesitation regarding the text's inclusion in the canon of the Hebrew Bible (arrived at by 140 CE). The desire to embrace it perhaps reflected the need for an uplifting narrative in the aftermath of the failed Bar Kokhba Revolt (132–35 CE), the uncharacteristic Roman oppression of Judaism that followed thereafter for several years, and because the entirety of the story takes place in a diasporic context that would have resonated for the dispersed Jewish community of the mid-second century. So it ended up in the Bible, albeit in a half-hearted way: at the time of Purim it is read from a separate scroll – *megillah* – rather than by opening the Bible to the appropriate pages.

The visual advantage of that semi-exclusionary position is that, historically, there was far less discomfort with embellishing those scrolls with visual imagery than with any other book in the Hebrew Bible. To whatever extent Jews have understood the Second Commandment to preclude illustrating and illuminating the Word of God – an understanding reinforced by a desire to emphasize the differences between Judaism and Christianity, which is articulated by such a rich visual tradition – they very often relaxed that sensibility where the Book of Esther was concerned.

The book is unique in another fundamental way, offering as it does a woman as its central heroic figure. Unlike Sarah and the pre-modern images of her, Esther plays the central dramatic role. She and her uncle and co-hero, Mordecai, as well as her foils, Vashti (her deposed predecessor as queen of Persia), Ahasuerus the King and Haman the Villain – each very different in what he or she represents – could not fail to inspire rabbinic discussion and raise important hermeneutical questions. The Book of Esther is one of only five biblical books besides the Torah that receive extended interpretive treatment in the Midrash Rabbah.

It is also a book to which several significant additions were made in the Greek-language Septuagint translation typically read by Christians and not found in the Hebrew version read by Jews, most notably the insertion of God's name and presence at a number of appropriate places in the narrative, thus solving that most vexing of problems where the rabbis had been concerned. Esther clearly captures the imagination, visual and otherwise.

8 In some codices, Lamentations falls between Ecclesiastes and Esther, rather than before Ecclesiastes.

9 Since the coming – or return – of the Messiah is associated, among other things, with 'the ingathering of the exiles' then the idea that the Lost Tribes of Israel had been located in China or the New World in turn yielded the idea that, if they could be brought back to the Holy Land, the great event would occur.

10 Bernardino Cardenas, *Miscelanea de Ayala* (Manuscritos de America, Signatum II/ 2849.XXXVI (Madrid: Biblioteca Nacional del Palacio Real, 1629).

11 See Judith Neulander, 'The Ecumenical Esther: Queen and Saint in Three Western Beliefs', in *The Book of Esther in Modern Research*, ed. L. Greenspoon and S. W. Crawford (London and New York: T&T Clark International: 2003), 181–83.

12 She is listed as a saint in any number of compendia, from the Pontifical Lateran University's *Bibliotheca sanctorum* to H. G. Holweck's *Biographical Dictionary of the Saints* and Omer Engelbert's *Lives of the Saints*. Nonetheless, as Judith Neulander points out, strictly speaking, she is beatified rather than canonized, so that what evolves visually reflects more of a folk tradition allied to Marian folk movements than a more formal Church-sanctioned idea. Her veneration, particularly in the New World, expanded during the colonial period the early part of which coincided with the Council of Trent's reaffirmation of the Book of Esther in the canon of the Catholic Bible – a development in part made possible by the greater religiosity exhibited in the Septuagint version of her story than in the Hebrew version, as noted above.

Although beyond the scope of this discussion, it might be noted that the increasing popularity of Esther in the Spanish Catholic New and Old Worlds, in conjunction with the Counter-Reformation use of Baroque theatricality in the visual arts, also led to an expansion of written dramas focused on her story (and inevitably, its Christian allegorical significance), as well as an expanding array of oral, usually rhymed, anonymous folk poetry. Much of the latter, together with a *Fiesta de Santa Ester* and its accompanying pageantry in some places, took shape in America – most interestingly, for the purposes of our discussion, in New Mexico, concerning which there has been an excited debate in the past two and a half decades as to whether the basis of the Hispanic community there evolving in the sixteenth and seventeenth centuries was Old Christian/Catholic or Crypto-Jewish, and thus which religious identity was ultimately reflected by such a *fiesta*. As Neulander points out, the Crypto-Jews elsewhere in the Spanish and Portuguese worlds celebrated a serious *fast* of Esther – focused on a figure with whom they could certainly identify, given her decision not really to reveal her Judaeanism to Ahasuerus until that critical Haman-accusing feast – whereas Catholics celebrated a festive *feast* of Esther. So the New Mexico event would seem to be more consistent with an Old Christian than Crypto-Jewish sensibility.

There are still *Santa Ester* celebrations in Spain itself that underscore the connection between Esther and the Virgin Mary – and with elements that parallel the Purim parties celebrated in the Jewish community, including costumed children parading in the streets. Aside from stylized images of a red-cheeked Saint Esther with her hands held up in an *orans*/petitionary position that not long ago served as part of the décor for such a pageant, the figures costumed as Esther (and other characters) marching in the procession may be seen as *living* visual images of the heroine, who ends up tied to diverse celebrations. Neulander offers photographs of such costumed characters in her article – specifically, a Christianized Esther holding a sceptre crowned by a cross, from a Holy Week procession in Valencia in 1999.

13 There is also a particularly odd element in the image: in the lower right foreground there is the front part of a sphinx – a naked woman from the waist up, with wings sprouting from her shoulders, and a lion body from the waist down – as if observing the rest of the scene. Is the sphinx's role to underscore that this moment which will solve one problem – creating an heir for Abraham – will lead to others, just as Oedipus' solution to the sphinx's riddle had done in a different tradition? Or is it to be associated with Egypt and, therefore, used as a symbol of anticipation regarding the future movements of Abraham's descendants?

14 Interestingly, given that Abraham and Sarah come to Canaan from Haran, Sarah may have been legally understood to be his sister – and therefore was in charge of his household – following the Hurrian custom. Neither the pharaoh nor Abimelech in the narrative (nor the later biblical redactors) would have understood the legal or cultural nuance. See E. A. Speiser, 'The Wife–Sister Motif in the Patriarchal Narratives', in *Biblical and Other Studies*, ed. A. Altman (Cambridge: Harvard University Press, 1963), 15–28. Not everyone embraces this theory, of course. Some simply see Abraham as a liar.

15 Sarai is the original name in Genesis, until the moment (Gen. 17:5, 17) when both she and Abram experience the nominal transformation that yields 'Abraham' and 'Sarah', respectively.

16 See M. Chagall, *The Bible* (Paris: Teriade, 1958).

17 J. Shafner, *Women of Mystery, Men of Prophecy* (New York: Jewish Heritage Project, Inc., 2002).

18 This notion is from a discussion with the artist, in fall, 2016.

19 See E. R. Goodenough, *Jewish Symbols in the Greco-Roman World*, vols 9–11 (New York: Pantheon Books, 1964).

20 For some details on Esther Scrolls and their décor, see O. Z. Soltes, 'Images and the Book of Esther: From Manuscript Illumination to Midrash', in *The Book of Esther in Modern Research,* ed. L. Greenspoon and S. W. Crawford (London and New York: T&T Clark International, 2003) 137–75.

21 See A. Katzenellenbogen, *The Sculptural Programs of Chartres Cathedral* (Baltimore, MD: Johns Hopkins Press, 1959).

22 For more details see the *History Bible of Utrecht* (Royal Library, The Hague: Ms Den Haag KB, 78 d 38 I).

23 See J. T. Waldman, *Megillat Esther* (Philadelphia: The Jewish Publication Society, 2005).

24 See *Gen. Rabbah* 39:13; and *Midrash Abba Gurion*, para. 20.

# 4

# RE-VISIONING WOMEN IN MARK'S GOSPEL THROUGH ART

Christine E. Joynes

## *Introduction*

From coins to canvas, stained-glass windows to sarcophagi, reception history of the Bible encompasses a vast amount of diverse material, extending far beyond the sermons and treatises produced by influential commentators of the Jewish and Christian traditions.[1] Indeed a significant contribution of reception history has been its emphasis on broadening the definition of 'biblical interpreter' to include artists, writers and musicians.[2] Why, for example, should one assume that George Caird (to take an Oxford example) is a better biblical interpreter than Artemisia Gentileschi (1593–1653), the much-neglected female Italian Baroque artist? By expanding the borders of biblical interpretation to include the visual arts, scholars have begun to discover valuable information and insights as to how particular people in particular places have interpreted the Bible.

A problematic approach in many emerging definitions of reception history is their tendency to treat 'reception history' simply as equivalent to the 'history of interpretation', namely as a magisterial treatment of classic (male) commentators.[3] Therefore, this chapter aims to show that there are other ways to do biblical reception history beyond tracing the literary tradition of the text among the fathers of the church. More specifically, this chapter seeks to illustrate how encounters with artistic representations of some female characters in Mark's Gospel can provide fresh perspectives on the biblical text. It offers snapshots from different historical periods, focusing on three particular Markan texts: the haemorrhaging woman (Mk 5:25–34); pushy mothers who bring their children to Jesus (Mk 10:13–16); and the women at the empty tomb (Mk 16:1–8).[4] I have chosen these examples primarily because the art discussed includes explicit citation of Markan texts. The artistic examples also illustrate the diverse media in which biblical art occurs – ranging from magical amulets to oil paintings and reliquary covers. Furthermore, these case studies offer contrasting perspectives on the place and significance of women in Mark's narrative: the haemorrhaging woman's bold risk-taking action, often obscured in subsequent tradition, is found to be an empowering narrative, used by women in the ancient world. The pushy mothers to emerge from Cranach's paintings of Mark 10 make visible hitherto invisible female characters in the Markan narrative. And the women disciples at the Markan empty tomb are regarded – at least in some contexts – as responding to a divine epiphany, rather than manifesting character failings. I have written about these passages in three independent articles previously, and here seek to bring together my findings in order to reflect more broadly on how artistic representations of women in Mark are significant.[5] Most importantly I argue that, by surveying the reception histories of Markan female characters in biblical art, one becomes acutely aware that 'women' cannot be defined as a single category whose experiences of patriarchy in different times and places are necessarily similar. Therefore, a more nuanced approach is required.

Before exploring further the 'afterlives' of these Markan female characters,[6] some additional explanatory comments concerning my methodological approach are required. This chapter does not seek to offer a developmental account of visual motifs; hence it does not adopt a chronological approach but rather focuses on unrelated artistic examples, bringing these into dialogue with the Markan text. Nor is my aim to provide a comprehensive discussion of all passages pertaining to women in Mark's Gospel; rather through some select examples I aim to illustrate the wider benefits resulting from encounters with the reception of Mark's Gospel in art.

## *Part 1: Encountering Some Artistic Representations of Women in Mark's Gospel*

### *A Bleeding Woman Seizes Healing (Mk 5:25–34)*

In contrast to Mark's significant textual interweaving of Jairus's daughter with the haemorrhaging woman, the visual afterlife of the *haemorrhoissa* (or woman with the flow of blood) is more often alone than in the company of her narrative partner (as Elizabeth Struthers Malbon has pointed out).[7] The frequency with which the haemorrhaging woman appears in early Christian art (more so than Jairus's daughter) is particularly noteworthy. In a range of contexts – from magical amulets to sarcophagi – she becomes a conventional figure in miracle cycles, grasping Jesus' garment in a prostrate posture.

The earliest known image of the *haemorrhoissa*, dating from the early third century, can be found in the Catacomb of St Marcellinus and St Peter in Rome (Figure 4.1). It depicts Jesus turning to bless the woman at the same time as she grasps the hem of his garment. This portrayal of the woman receiving a blessing from Jesus as she touches his garment became a standard feature of iconographic representations *but it reverses the dramatic import of the Markan text.*[8] For according to the biblical narrative, the woman gains healing anonymously from among the crowd, so that Jesus is unable to identify her. Visual representations of Jesus blessing the woman as she grasps his hem direct the viewer to focus on Jesus' action

**Figure 4.1** *Christ Healing the Woman with an Issue of Blood*, c. 200 CE. Catacomb of St Marcellinus and St Peter, Rome, Italy. Photo credit: © Robin Jensen.

rather than that of the woman. Indeed sometimes Jesus is even portrayed touching the woman's head.[9] Thus what becomes the established iconographic convention changes Mark's radical emphasis on the woman's bold, risk-taking action.

A striking feature of the Markan account is that the haemorrhaging woman's healing takes place without Jesus' knowledge. He appears to know nothing about her intentions, and only speaks to confirm the healing after it has happened (5:34); she is healed at the moment she touches his garment (5:29). Although elsewhere in Mark's Gospel Jesus appears to resist some requests for healing (e.g. 7:27), nowhere else in the Gospel does a miracle take place without his prior knowledge or consent.[10] This detail, therefore, increases the significance of the haemorrhaging woman's initiative, without which the miracle would not have taken place.[11] It is also a significant cause of embarrassment with which later interpreters grapple.[12]

Barbara Baert's investigation of the haemorrhaging woman's healing in early visual culture draws attention to the relevance of physical context when assessing the *haemorrhoissa* catacomb image. In particular, she suggests a connection between the *haemorrhoissa* image and the Agape image, in which a woman ministers the sacrificial meal.[13] Baert's proposed visual association between the woman's flow of blood and the blood of the Eucharist here can be further supported by linguistic occurrences of the term 'blood' in Mark's Gospel, which appears only at 5:25, 5:29 and 14:24.[14]

Notably, as Baert has highlighted, there were ongoing debates in the early church (which continued into the fourteenth century) about whether menstruating women should participate in the Eucharist.[15] The *haemorrhoissa*'s story is appealed to on both sides of the debate. Some figures – such as Dionysius of Alexandria (d. 264) and Hippolytus of Rome (170–236) – clearly sought to enforce barriers to participation in the Eucharist, explicitly excluding menstruating women, despite the inclusivity towards such women implied by Mark's narrative. This debate, therefore, suggests that visual representations of the *haemorrhoissa* within sacred spaces could be deeply subversive, especially when her image appears in close proximity to the altar space.

A different perspective on the haemorrhaging woman emerges when we include further material evidence of her reception, specifically on magical amulets designed as aids for women with 'reproductive health and menstrual problems'. On the example in Figure 4.2, a corrupted version of the Markan text is cited.[16]

**Figure 4.2** *Amulet Carved in Intaglio (Incised)*, sixth to seventh century CE, Byzantine. 5 x 3.7 x 1 cm. The Metropolitan Museum of Art, New York. Photo credit: © The Metropolitan Museum of Art, New York.

On one side of the amulet reference is made to a woman with a flow of blood suffering much, having spent her money to no benefit, getting not better but worse; the reverse side details that her haemorrhage stopped on account of her faith. To my knowledge, this is the only amulet to cite a Markan text, although other amulets depicting the haemorrhaging woman - arguably based on Mark but without any inscriptions - do exist.[17] The apotropaic use of the biblical text on magical amulets is an important reminder of the perhaps uncomfortable 'magical' elements in the Markan narrative (where Jesus perceives power 'going out of him' without his prior knowledge). Here then we find rare evidence that biblical texts *about* women were used *by* women in the ancient world.

A third example of the *haemorrhoissa* in art can be found preserved among the mosaics of the Chora Monastery (Kariye Camii), Istanbul. Commissioned by Theodore Metochites and produced between 1310 and 1321 by a metropolitan workshop, the mosaic is located in one of the squinches of the south eastern dome in the inner narthrex (Figure 4.3). As David Knipp has argued persuasively, the scene is prominently positioned probably because of its significant juxtaposition with the Deesis mosaic next to it, in which the Chora benefactor Maria Palaiologina (who after 1307 became the nun Melania) appears.[18]

Melania's donor portrait is positioned directly beneath the mosaic depicting the healing of the *haemorrhoissa*, and her kneeling posture links her to the crouching position of the biblical character. Knipp's identification of the haemorrhaging woman with Melania is convincing, and highlights that women sometimes played important roles as patrons in the production of biblical art.

**Figure 4.3** *Christ Healing the Woman with the Flow of Blood*, c. 1310–21. Mosaic, Chora Monastery (Kariye Camii), Istanbul. Photo credit: © Artstor.

These three examples of visual interpretations of Mk 5:25–34 illustrate the fascinating variety of contexts in which the Markan narrative was used. This diversity, both inside and outside sacred spaces, alerts the viewer to the important breadth of extant interpretations.

*Pushy Mothers Bring their Children to Jesus*

Our explorations thus far have illustrated the multifaceted contributions of biblical art to the task of exegesis, including some instances where it functions in ways that contrast with the biblical text (as in the catacomb image where the focus is on Jesus blessing the woman). Sometimes, however, the opposite situation is the case, and biblical art can *reveal* aspects of the text that have otherwise been missed. A notable example is found in the painting *Christ Blessing the Children*, by Lucas Cranach the Elder (1472–1553) and his workshop, which produced more than twenty versions of the narrative based on Mk 10:13–16.[19] The example in Figure 4.4 dates from the mid-1530s and is now held in the Städel Museum in Frankfurt. Despite the episode's familiarity through later stained-glass window and panel design, prior to Cranach the story was rarely depicted. Its sudden rise in popularity is often associated with Martin Luther's use of this biblical text in his controversy with the Anabaptists. However, this context provides only a partial explanation for the narrative's broader appeal.[20]

**Figure 4.4** Lucas Cranach the Elder, *Christ Blessing the Children*, 1535–40. 83.8 x 121.5 cm. Städel Museum, Frankfurt. Photo credit: © Wikimedia Commons.

The image shows Christ surrounded by a crowd of women, densely grouped together against a black background. As Kibish notes, 'the frame cuts very low above the heads of the figures thus increasing the effect of closeness and density'.[21] In his left hand Christ, somewhat precariously, holds a child (presumably belonging to the woman with praying hands). Simultaneously he stretches out his right hand to bless a child lying on a cushion. Its mother, however, is distracted by her other child, to whom her gaze is directed. All the babies in the picture are portrayed naked, in contrast to the older (clothed) children present.[22] On the right, a baby suckles at its mother's breast, while behind Jesus another baby attempts to clamber onto his back. One of the less pushy mothers (at the back) draws the viewer into the picture by looking straight at us. Meanwhile, the woman on the left of the picture touches Jesus' garment, evoking the image of the haemorrhaging woman discussed above. Her child clutches an apple, symbolizing fallen humanity.

The image engages the viewer with its agitated movements and gestures. Steven Ozment's assessment that the 'scene depicts a throng of infants and their older siblings *as they wait patiently in line* to be taken from the arms of their mothers and placed in those of their Savior (my italics)' does not provide a particularly apt description of the painting.[23] Rather the scene is considerably more chaotic, with figures clamouring to get near to Jesus for him to touch their children, as they encircle him.

Observe how the male disciples are marginalized in the image, confined to the left-hand corner in contrast to the women and children who dominate the painting. The apostles are physically squeezed out of the picture, with only three faces being visible. Along the top of the picture (though not visible in the photographic reproduction), the text from the Gospel of Mark (10:14) is inscribed in German: *Lasset die kindlin zu mir kommen und weret inen nicht / denn solcher ist das reich Gottes (Let the children come to me and do not refuse them; for of such is the kingdom of God).* The use of the vernacular, rather than Latin, for the biblical inscription is worth noting.

Maybe the densely crowded nature of the image, with its prominent gaggle of women, is what brought to my mind the label 'pushy mothers'. The artist certainly succeeded in drawing my attention as viewer to the identity of those who brought the children to Jesus. In contrast, the Markan text does not specify who brought the children to Jesus, using the impersonal third person plural verb – *prosepheron* – to simply state 'they were bringing children to him'. Later visual representations of the text have variations in the audience depicted: some include many women; others only one or two. The visual impact of Cranach's image suggests a stark contrast between the women as models of discipleship and their male counterparts. His painting, therefore, suggests that 'pushy mothers' deserve a place in any discussion of women disciples in Mark's Gospel.[24] The dominant visual presence of the 'pushy mothers' in Cranach's paintings prompts the viewer to return to the biblical text and reconsider the role of those who brought their children to Jesus.

*Women at the Empty Tomb*

Further comparison between women disciples and their male counterparts is suggested at the conclusion to Mark's Gospel, where reference is made to some female disciples fleeing from the tomb and saying nothing to anyone because of their fear (16:8).[25] Opinion is divided about how this conclusion is to be interpreted. Are the women ultimately to be regarded as failures (even they let Jesus down in the end) or simply as fallible followers (with the narrator implying that despite their initial silence, the message was passed on in the end)? The women's flight at 16:8 is set against the backdrop of Mark's earlier account detailing the flight of Jesus' male disciples at the point of Jesus' arrest (Mk 14:50–51).

Visual interpretations of Mk 16:1–8 offer some distinctive contributions to the discussion about how to interpret the narrative. Of particular interest is the connection that emerged between Mark 16 and baptism, with the women portrayed as symbols of dying and rising with Christ. Hence the women at the tomb frequently appear on baptismal fonts, as illustrated by the numerous examples included in the *Baptisteria Sacra Index*.[26] Furthermore, as Robin Jensen argues, the baptismal font was frequently regarded as a womb by early church writers, symbolizing the converts' birth from the fertile womb of the mother church.[27] It is worth noting at this point that the earliest imagery of the resurrection was not of Jesus emerging from the tomb, but rather of the women finding the empty tomb.[28] Typically the women are portrayed encountering an angel and clutching spices; their demeanour is apprehensive or fearful. The women's flight from the tomb is depicted less frequently.

Visual interpretations of Mark 16 often interpret the text canonically, that is placing it alongside other biblical texts. This clearly affects how the Markan narrative is regarded. So for example, a ninth-century silver container from the Vatican represents the women running away from the angel at the tomb. Their feet are turned in flight as they respond in fear and trembling to the angel's message.[29] However, since the depiction of Mk 16:8 is juxtaposed with representations of the road to Emmaus and John's and Peter's visit to the empty tomb, fear and silence is clearly not regarded as the end of the story on this artefact.[30] Other episodes with which the narrative is visually juxtaposed include the crucifixion,[31] different resurrection appearances, such as the appearance to Thomas,[32] and also the birth of Christ.[33] This latter juxtaposition is particularly noteworthy, since it highlights a striking parallelism between the women bringing spices and the magi bearing gifts (in both instances clutching jars), and again emphasizes the close connections between death and life.

Further light is shed on the Markan narrative when we consider the evidence offered by an eleventh- or twelfth-century silver reliquary cover (Figure 4.5). One woman's foot turns outwards, as she looks back towards the angel, in her anxiety clinging to her companion. Citations from the Gospels are distributed on the surface of the silver cover: over the angel it reads, 'Come and see (*Deute ide*) the place where they laid the Lord' and above the women is written, 'They were overcome with trembling and shock (*tromos kai ekstasis*)', peculiarly Markan terms (Mk 16:8). On the edge of the cover stands the text of a Greek hymn:

**Figure 4.5** *Women at the Empty Tomb*, eleventh/twelfth century. Silver reliquary cover. St-Denis, Paris. Photo credit: © Hirmer Verlag, München.

> In what glory appeared the angel to the women;
> From far away one sees the splendour of his innate dignity
> And the purity of his immaterial transcendence.
> His beauty proclaims the splendour of the resurrection;
> He calls loudly: the Lord is risen.[34]

This example demonstrates the impact of combining text and image, with the words of the Greek hymn influencing how the viewer interprets the visual depiction of the women. It clearly suggests that the Markan references to the women's trembling and astonishment are to be understood in response to epiphany, an encounter with the divine. This interpretation of the Markan narrative has occasionally been suggested by scholarly commentators but has not gained widespread acceptance.[35]

## Part Two: Reflections

What conclusions can we draw from these brief encounters with artistic representations of women in Mark's Gospel? Three areas in particular deserve further consideration.

### *Destabilizing the Gender Debate*

It has come to be widely acknowledged that the New Testament texts are the products of a male elite, presenting the male as normative, with the female defined in relation to the male as 'other', and indeed portrayed from a male perspective. There are multiple possible responses to this situation. My decision to focus on the reception history of Mark's female characters, thereby highlighting the impact of some marginal figures in the Gospel, could be challenged for conforming to a binary gender distinction that should instead be destabilized. Thus for example, Deborah Sawyer proposes that instead of understanding identity categories by adopting a binary masculine and feminine gender approach, underpinned with compulsory heterosexuality, one should recognize that these categories are, in fact, the products of particular socio-political contexts.[36] She follows contemporary philosopher Judith Butler in pointing out that the institutions, practices and discourses constructing identity are themselves multiple and diffuse with their own histories. Or as Jorunn Økland puts it, 'Ideas that the text presents as obvious, natural or divinely ordained are the results of long processes and struggles during which other possibilities … were open.'[37]

I have, however, opted to highlight the female characters in Mark, in the belief that the reception histories of these marginal figures in art can be illuminating.[38] Indeed, I have adopted this approach precisely to underline the *diversity* in the reception of these female figures in biblical art. By demonstrating how gender structures vary according to place and situation, the reception histories of Gospel women in many ways support the position advocated by Sawyer, highlighting that gender structures are neither stable nor eternally given.

### *Reinscribing Patriarchy?*

According to Cheryl Exum, 'Art can enhance our understanding and appreciation of the biblical text, but it can also bring a critical dimension; it can point to problematic aspects of the text and help us "see" things about the text we might have overlooked, or enable us to see things differently'.[39] While this is indeed the case, I would add a note of caution to my otherwise enthusiastic embrace of biblical reception history at this point, to question whether it has sometimes, perhaps unconsciously, exchanged one form of patriarchy for another. In the course of this chapter, I have pinpointed some occasions where the bold, risk-taking actions of women in the Markan narrative have been obscured or downplayed in later artistic representations. This highlights that biblical art can sometimes serve to distort or exceed the gender biases of the biblical texts themselves.

It is important to question the extent to which interpreting Mark's Gospel through art heightens the separation between masculine and feminine. How far is the text's hierarchy, where the masculine is the norm, endorsed? Here one might include further reflection on the gendered division of labour, where the female is characterized as mother and birth-giver. Some female characters are identified in the Markan narrative only in relation to their parents (such as Herodias's daughter and Jairus's daughter).[40] Similarly, the aforementioned 'pushy mothers' feature only because of their parental responsibilities. Does then the encounter with these characters through art conform to the practice of 'redeeming women from the biblical text' as practised by some feminists (such as Elizabeth Schüssler Fiorenza)? Or are we rather reinscribing problematic gendered categories in a different medium – in art rather than text?

On the one hand, I would argue that biblical art can indeed function to 'redeem' women from the text, by giving unnamed figures in the narrative an identity. Representing the biblical narrative visually means that figures such as Cranach's pushy mothers, who were once invisible, can now become visible. However, a cursory glance at the reception history of female characters in Mark highlights that 'women' should not be categorized as a single group whose experiences of patriarchy are comparable across the centuries. Hence, experiencing artistic representations of biblical women alerts one to the complexities of a gender agenda, and the varying roles that women play, both in the biblical text and in their afterlives.

To put it another way, the universalizing and essentializing tendencies of Western biblical interpreters need to be resisted. As Deborah Sawyer points out, this is imperative to avoid being blind to basic differences of experience, where from a twenty-first-century standpoint, the 'minority experience of white, colonial, educated and comparatively affluent women [has] become the given norm for women's experience'.[41] To extend this critique still further, one must also be alert to the temptation of presenting biblical art simply as the art produced by Italian Renaissance masters, rather than reflecting its diversity both geographically and temporally.

### *Contextualizing our Biblical Interpretation*

Reception history clearly demonstrates that our situatedness affects the way we read; it also has the potential to re-open options that have been closed off. So contra Nancy Klancher's dismissive remark that 'The best reception histories today have moved beyond the recuperation of long-lost readings and the rectification of exegetical amnesia', I prefer to follow Linda Nochlin's approach, highlighting that the unquestioned domination of white male subjectivity is an intellectual distortion that needs to be corrected.[42] There is, I contend, much work still to be done to bridge the knowledge gap and provide a more balanced view.

Not only can biblical art function to expose the privileging of the male point of view in the recounting of biblical stories about women but juxtaposing different versions of the same biblical narrative can also serve the additional purpose of alerting us to our own social and cultural assumptions. As Martin O'Kane puts it, 'By appreciating a range of visual expressions of the same biblical subject in many different art traditions, we free ourselves from the limits of our present horizon and recognize that no single expression of the theme is ever complete or definitive, since the subject addressed is simply inexhaustible and therefore always more than any individual expression.'[43] One corollary of this is that biblical scholars should surrender their claims to control the biblical text. Rather their role is to offer interpretations as possibilities, instead of trying to identify a single right meaning of the Bible.

## *Conclusion*

In this chapter, I have argued that significant new insights emerge when New Testament scholars pay attention to artistic interpretations of female characters in the Gospel of Mark. This is a much neglected and potentially fruitful area to explore. I have also pointed to the importance of material evidence – such as magical amulets and reliquary covers – some of which originates at the same time as textual sources from the early church, which New Testament scholars are more than happy to engage with.

But beyond this, I have highlighted more particularly the reception histories of certain female characters in Mark's Gospel, to illustrate their potentially liberating and empowering potential. As Jorunn Økland reminds us (citing Adrienne Rich), 'Re-Vision – the act of looking back, of seeing with fresh eyes, of entering an old text from a new critical direction – is for women more than a chapter in cultural history: it is an act of survival.'[44] Some reception history approaches – such as those focussed on a Jaussian summit of 'classic thinkers from across the centuries' have yet to take on board the significant theoretical challenges posed by the broader demands of *Wirkungsgeschichte*. Focusing on white, male, Western interpretations of the Bible obscures the wider spectrum of interpretative possibilities offered by this newly emerging field of study. Reception history offers the potential to enlarge our interpretative horizons and in so doing to facilitate a commitment to those who have often been marginalized.

My juxtaposition of a number of Markan female figures in art brings into association images that are completely unrelated. Nevertheless, by so doing one sees clearly how the imaginative spaces provided by the biblical text are vividly filled in with gender constructions. Not only do these images testify to the cultural impact of the Gospel and the different contexts in which it was used but through the reception history of these female characters in art, our interpretative horizon is significantly enlarged.

## *Notes*

1 Examples of such 'classic' interpreters might include Rashi, Augustine, Aquinas, Luther, Calvin *et al.*

2 See for example, Heidi J. Hornik and Mikeal C. Parsons, *The Acts of the Apostles through the Centuries* (Malden, MA and Chichester, UK: Wiley, 2017), and other contributions to the Wiley-Blackwell Bible Commentary series.

3 The terminological differences between reception history (*Wirkungsgeschichte*) and history of interpretation (*Auslegungsgeschichte*) have been widely noted. The scholarly tendency to engage in reception history as if it is synonymous with history of interpretation has been generally overlooked, however. See further, Christine E. Joynes, 'Reception History', in *The Oxford Encyclopedia of the Bible and Gender Studies*, ed. Julia O'Brien (New York and Oxford: OUP, 2017, http://www.oxfordbiblicalstudies.com/article/opr/t998/e27).

4 I assume Markan priority with regard to the relationship between the Synoptics. Although some of the female figures discussed here appear also in Matthew and Luke, my purpose is to discuss only the Markan text.

5 See Christine E. Joynes, 'Wombs and Tombs: The Reception History of Mark 16:1–20', in *From the Margins II: Women of the New Testament and their Afterlives*, ed. Christine E. Joynes and Christopher C. Rowland (Sheffield: Sheffield Phoenix, 2009), 226–43; Christine E. Joynes, 'Still at the Margins? Gospel Women and their Afterlives', in *Radical Christian Voices and Practice: Essays in Honour of Christopher Rowland*, ed. Z. Bennett and D. Gowler (Oxford: OUP, 2012), 117–35; Christine E. Joynes, 'A Place for Pushy Mothers? Visualizations of Christ Blessing the Children', *Biblical Reception* 2 (2013): 117–33.

6 The term 'afterlife' is not here used to imply that somehow the real life of the text ceased prior to its reception. I use the term in the sense adopted by Jonathan Z. Smith in his SBL Presidential address, where he applies it in the sense of 'continuing life'. See J. Z. Smith, 'Religion and the Bible', *JBL* 128 (2009): 23, n. 27.

7 Elizabeth Struthers Malbon, 'The Healing of the Haemorrhaging Woman on Fourth-Century Sarcophagi from Rome', in *The Woman with the Blood Flow (Mark 5:24–34): Narrative, Iconic, and Anthropological Spaces*, ed. B. Baert (Leuven: Peeters, 2014), 109–42. Some examples of the pairing can be found though, as for example in the miniature from the tenth-century Gospel of Otto III, Reichenau where Jairus's daughter and the haemorrhaging woman appear together.

8 Other similar images are illustrated in Gertrud Schiller, *Iconography of Christian Art*, vol. 1 (London: Lund Humphries, 1971). See for example plate 464.

9 See, for example, the sarcophagus fragment from the St Callixtus catacomb, reproduced in T. F. Mathews, *The Clash of Gods: A Reinterpretation of Early Christian Art* (Princeton, NJ: Princeton University Press, 1993), 64.

10 The summarizing passages of Mk 3:10 and 6:56 should, however, be noted at this point, since through these the evangelist may intimate that similar healings took place on other occasions, which he has chosen not to narrate.

11 Barbara Baert, '"Who touched my clothes?": The Healing of the Woman with the Haemorrhage (Mark 5:24–34; Luke 8:42–48 and Matthew 9:19–22) in Early Medieval Visual Culture', *Konsthistorisk tidskrift: Journal of Art History* 79.2 (2010): 66, refers to the woman's 'stolen' healing to express this sentiment.

12 For example, Matthew removes this uncomfortable Markan feature by presenting the woman's healing only *after* Jesus turns to address her (9:22).

13 See Baert, '"Who touched my clothes?"', 80–81.

14 Also of relevance here is Malbon's study, 'The Healing of the Haemorrhaging Woman on Fourth-Century Sarcophagi from Rome', 109–42. Here Malbon illustrates how the haemorrhaging woman functioned as a metaphor for salvation on fourth-century Roman sarcophagi and convincingly identifies a five-fold pattern of scenes that frequently occur together. Of particular note is the juxtaposition in this pattern of the

*haemorrhoissa*'s healing with a miracle involving food and drink (i.e. with Eucharistic overtones).

15 See Baert, '"Who touched my clothes?"', 79.

16 As acknowledged by Jeffrey Spier, 'Medieval Byzantine Magical Amulets and their Traditions', *Journal of the Warburg and Courtauld Institutes* 56 (1993): 44, n. 111.

17 See further, Spier, 'Medieval Byzantine Magical Amulets and their Traditions', 25–62; Baert, '"Who touched my clothes?"', 65–90.

18 David Knipp, 'Narrative and Symbol. The Early Christian Image of the Haemorrhoissa and the Mosaics in the Narthrex of the Kariye Camii', in *The Woman with the Blood Flow (Mark 5:24–34): Narrative, Iconic, and Anthropological Spaces*, ed. B. Baert (Leuven: Peeters, 2014), 143–63.

19 The Cranach images explicitly cite the Markan text, though the blessing of the children narrative also appears in Matthew and Luke (cf. Mt. 19:13–15; Lk. 18:15–17).

20 See further, Christine E. Joynes, 'A Place for Pushy Mothers? Visualizations of Christ Blessing the Children', *Biblical Reception* 2 (2013): 118.

21 C. Kibish, 'Lucas Cranach's *Christ Blessing the Children*: A Problem of Lutheran Iconography', *The Art Bulletin*, 37.3 (1955): 197.

22 The babies are not naked in all the Cranach versions. A version currently in a private collection but available online at www.wga.hu portrays a mother carrying a clothed baby on her back and gazing directly at the viewer.

23 Steven Ozment, *The Serpent and the Lamb: Cranach, Luther and the Making of the Reformation* (New Haven and London: Yale University Press, 2011), 171.

24 Despite extensive research on female characters in Mark's Gospel, the women who brought their children to be blessed have been overlooked. See for example, Susan Miller, *Women in the Gospel of Mark* (London: T. & T. Clark, 2004).

25 Mk 16:1 mentions Mary Magdalene; Mary, mother of James; Salome.

26 I am grateful to Harriet Sonne de Torrens for this observation.

27 See Robin Jensen, *Understanding Early Christian Art* (London and New York: Routledge, 2000), 173; Robin Jensen, *Baptismal Imagery in Early Christianity: Ritual, Visual and Theological Dimensions* (Grand Rapids, MI: Baker Academic Press, 2012), 138.

28 See Gertrud Schiller, *Iconography of Christian Art*, vol. 1 (London: Lund Humphries, 1971), 17.

29 See Schiller, *Iconography of Christian Art*, 22.

30 Equally, it might also be argued that this artefact elevates the significance of the women's encounter with the angel at the tomb to the same level as the resurrection appearances with which it is juxtaposed.

31 See, for example, the Rabbula Gospels.

32 Schiller, *Iconography of Christian Art*, 325, pl. 41.

33 Schiller, *Iconography of Christian Art*, 324, pl. 40.

34 Schiller, *Iconography of Christian Art*, 28. My translation.

35 Cf. A. Yarbro Collins, *Mark* (Minneapolis, MN: Fortress, 2007), 800, who interprets the women's flight in fear and trembling as a response to epiphany. This interpretation was suggested previously (e.g. D. Catchpole, 'The Fearful Silence of the Women at the Tomb', *Journal of Theology for Southern Africa* 18 [1977], 3–10) but has not been widely adopted. See for example, Andrew Lincoln, 'The Promise and the Failure: Mark 16:7, 8,' *JBL* 108.2 (1989), 286, who rejects this reading of the text.

36 Deborah F. Sawyer, 'Biblical Gender Strategies: The Case of Abraham's Masculinity', in *Gender, Religion and Diversity: Cross-cultural Perspectives* (ed. Ursula King and Tina Beattie; London: Routledge, 2005), 162–75.

37 Jorunn Økland, 'Men Are from Mars and Women Are from Venus: On the Relationship between Religion, Gender and Space', in *Gender, Religion and Diversity: Cross-cultural Perspectives*, ed. Ursula King and Tina Beattie (London: Routledge, 2005), 157.

38 In some instances surprising interpretations emerge, such as the identification of Jesus with ritually unclean women, which is particularly striking. Here we find biblical women functioning as models of empowerment against the forces of death.

39 J. Cheryl Exum, 'Toward a Genuine Dialogue between the Bible and Art', in *Congress Volume Helsinki 2010*, ed. Martti Nissinen (VT Sup, 148; Leiden: Brill, 2012), 474.

40 Discussed further in Joynes, 'Still at the Margins? Gospel Women and their Afterlives', 117–35.

41 Sawyer, 'Biblical Gender Strategies: The Case of Abraham's Masculinity', 162.

42 Nancy Klancher, 'A Genealogy for Reception History', *Biblical Interpretation* 21:1 (2013), 129; Linda Nochlin, 'Why Have There Been No Great Women Artists?' in *Women, Art, and Power and Other Essays* (London: Thames and Hudson, 1991), 146.

43 Martin O'Kane, 'Wirkungsgeschichte and Visual Exegesis: The Contribution of Hans-Georg Gadamer,' *JSNT* 33.2 (2010): 152.

44 Jorunn Økland, 'Feminist Readings of the Bible', in *The New Cambridge History of the Bible*, vol. 4, ed. John Riches (Cambridge: CUP, 2015), 262.

# 5

# How Salomé Fell for the Baptist, or John the Baptist as *L'Homme Fatal*: Artistic Interpretations of a Biblical Narrative

Ela Nutu

According to the Bible, John the Baptist is executed by decapitation at the request of a little girl.[1] Matthew (14:1–12) and Mark (6:14–29) recount that during one of King Herod's birthday banquets, Salomé[2] dances so pleasingly in front of her stepfather and his guests that Herod promises to give his wife's daughter anything she may desire, 'even half of his kingdom' (Mk 6:23). Salomé asks her mother for advice and at her suggestion declares her wish to be the head of John the Baptist on a charger. Though seemingly disconcerted by the request, Herod follows through on his promise and orders John's execution. When she is presented with John's head, Salomé offers it to her mother. The biblical account is very brief, yet Salomé has become for many the quintessential *femme fatale*, 'the symbolic incarnation of undying Lust, the Goddess of immortal Hysteria, the accursed Beauty exalted above all other beauties'.[3] Her metamorphosis is largely due to Salomé's power to inspire artists, whose sensory interpretations of the biblical narrative have in turn left an indelible mark on the readers' imagination.

There is an undeniable dialogue between the Bible and Art that has led to what one could describe as creative co-dependency. This is something that both biblical scholars and art historians should be able to acknowledge. While in the past both disciplines placed a great emphasis on modern, scientific, unified approaches to knowledge and to truth (an attitude predicated perhaps on the feeling that we perceived ourselves to be curators of sacred objects and sacred texts), present-day scholarship allows for many dissonant voices to emerge and challenge such structuralist approaches. Without dispensing with the past, present-day criticism explores diverse approaches to interpretation – from feminist to queer, from semiotic to poststructuralist, from ideological to postcolonial. This change of course is due, in part, to the realization that identity – of objects, ideas as well as individuals – is the result of both inner and outer forces, negotiated on the threshold between the summoning law of society and its subversions; and that identity influences knowledge, and thus 'objective scholarship' may be a bit of a chimaera. The aim of this chapter is to explore some of the journeys that the biblical woman now known as Salomé has undertaken through different social and individual histories, traced through works of biblical art, with a focus on late-nineteenth- and early-twentieth-century European artistic interpretations of the biblical narrative.

Many *fin de siècle* European artists were enthralled with Salomé, and she emerged at that time as the *femme fatale par excellence*. As representative of the way some of Picasso's contemporaries saw her, one can consider Henri Regnault's *Salomé* (Figure 5.1) celebrated at the time as one of the most accomplished portrayals of Salomé. Some might say Salomé here is terribly exotic. Positively Oriental. Hot. Oscar Wilde, however, thought that Regnault's Salomé looked like

**Figure 5.1** Henri Regnault, *Salome*, 1870. Oil on canvas, 63 x 40½ in. (160 x 102.9 cm). The Metropolitan Museum of Art, 16.95. Gift of George F. Baker, 1916.

a 'mere gypsy'.[4] Wilde was instead completely taken by Gustave Moreau's *Salomé* (Figure 5.2), who truly lived up to Wilde's own interpretation of the biblical woman. In the words of the Dutch novelist, Joris-Karl Huysmans, who like Wilde focussed on Moreau's interpretation and also borrowed the French language as the best medium for Salomé:

> Neither St Matthew, nor St Mark … nor any of the sacred writers had enlarged on the maddening charm and potent depravity of the dancer. She had always remained … beyond the reach of punctilious, pedestrian minds, and accessible

**Figure 5.2** Gustave Moreau, *Salomé Dancing before Herod* (Detail of Salomé), 1876. Oil on canvas. 156½ x 41 1/16 inches (143.5 x 104.3 cm). The Armand Hammer Collection, Gift of the Armand Hammer Collection. Hammer Museum, Los Angeles.

> only to brains shaken and sharpened and rendered almost clairvoyant by neurosis … In Gustave Moreau's work, which in conception went far beyond the data supplied by the New Testament … [Salomé] had become, as it were, the symbolic incarnation of undying Lust, the Goddess of immortal Hysteria, the accursed Beauty exalted above all other beauties … the monstrous Beast, indifferent, irresponsible, insensible, poisoning …[5]

In Wilde's 1896 eponymous play, Salomé is enamoured with but rejected by John the Baptist and she commits the most nauseating act in biblical dramatics: she kisses the decapitated head of John, or Jokanaan in the play.

Richard Strauss had Wilde's play translated into German as a libretto for his 1905 opera *Salomé*. A natural transition perhaps, for even Wilde referred to his play as a 'beautiful coloured musical thing'.[6] However, in the German opera the kiss is no longer aesthetic, as it is in the French play, but rather erotic and thus deeply disturbing. While in Wilde's text Salomé's monstrosity always threatens to regress into adolescent naughtiness, Strauss's dramatic soprano is a creature of power and steely invincibility. Even her dance, meant as a *tableau* of sensuality, is performed with the strong determination of an Amazonian general, behind her a 'brazen, convulsive orchestra'.[7] Strauss composed the music for Salomé's infamous 'dance of the seven veils' last, and he also wrote clear instructions about its choreography, much of it relating back to Moreau's painting and indeed to Gustav Klimt's *Judith II (Salomé)* (Figure 5.3).[8] In the latter, the woman is captured in a mobile moment. She disregards the viewer, intent on pursuing her goal. Her stance is purposeful, her presence elaborately adorned and the exposing of her breasts deliberate. The disturbing element here resides with the woman's hands. While richly bejewelled and otherwise elegantly formed, Judith/Salomé's hands are frozen in a claw-like gesture, her left hand's fingers entangled in John's/Holofernes's hair, his decapitated head swinging in her grip. The woman's bag (another indication that this is Judith, not Salomé, who would have portrayed with a charger instead), in which she carries her kosher food, here awaits carnivorously for the unclean, disembodied head – a *vagina dentata*, ready to devour the man. In Klimt's work Strauss saw, in his words, 'much of my own music, particularly *Salomé*'.[9] The score for the 'dance of the seven veils' is somewhat different from the rest of the opera, for Strauss purposely tried to introduce nuances of the Orient into it, perhaps not surprisingly, since the fascination with everything Oriental in late-nineteenth- and early-twentieth-century art is quite evident. As Rana Kabbani aptly notes, 'Oriental dance was for Europeans a metaphor for the whole East, a trope for Oriental abandon.'[10] Perhaps that is why Salomé is frequently depicted at this time as dancing, often bare-breasted and surrounded by the exotic: sometimes African slaves, whose ethnic features are exaggerated to the point of caricature; at others, sheiks, Scheherazadian tents, carpets and oil lamps; or luscious silks and leopard's skins – for example, in *Salomé* works by Pierre Bonnaud (c. 1900), Franz von Stuck (1906), Robert Henri (c. 1909) and Gaston Bussière (1914).

Lovis Corinth, a founding member of the Munich *Sezession*, who had studied under Regnault in Paris and who designed the costumes for the first performance

**Figure 5.3** Gustav Klimt, *Judith II (Salome)*, 1909. Photo courtesy of Imagno/Getty Images.

of Wilde's play in Germany in 1902,[11] follows the Orientalist trend when producing his interpretation of Salomé (Figure 5.4). Richly adorned – for she has jewellery on every finger and more on her hair and around her neck, dangling above her naked breasts – Corinth's Salomé is exotic, erotic and obviously deadly. Corinth's Salomé is not merely perverse, but also an object of desire. Corinth himself looks at her from within the painting (he positions himself in the work as the executioner) with admiration, if not gallantry, his left hand tucked behind his back. She is the *femme fatale par excellence*. Her interest in the decapitated head of John is personal, for she gets extremely close to it, and her golden skirts get caught in the

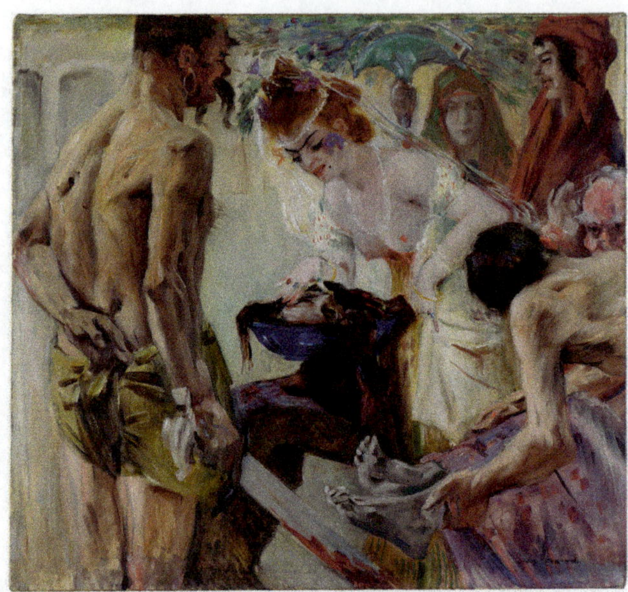

**Figure 5.4** Lovis Corinth, *Salomé*, 1899. Oil on canvas; 76.2 x 83.5 (30 x 32⅞ ins.). Harvard Art Museums/Busch-Reisinger Museum, Gift of Hans H.A. Meyn, BR53.60. Photo: Imaging Department © President and Fellows of Harvard College.

charger. She seems brutal and unfeeling. Adorned with flowers of evil (Baudelaire published *Fleurs du mal* in 1857), Salomé here not only takes possession of John's severed head, but she also subjugates it by penetrating it, forcing open his dead eyes. In Wilde's play, Salomé addresses the head,

> Why did you not look at me, Jokanaan? … You rejected me. You spoke evil words against me. … Well, I still live, but you are dead, and your head belongs to me. … I was a virgin but you took my virginity away from me. I was chaste, and you filled my veins with fire … If you had looked at me you would have loved me … and the mystery of love is greater than the mystery of death.[12]

Corinth's Salomé makes sure John's dead eyes look upon her. She offers him not her own eyes, which seem to wonder off past the charger, but rather her breasts, her sexuality. Salomé defies as she defiles him. Her red mouth alludes perhaps to the post-decapitation kiss – maybe imminent here – and its bitter, bloody after-taste. Perhaps, as in Wilde's opinion of Strauss's opera, Corinth too thinks that 'it's the shudder that counts'.[13] While kissing John's decapitating head may have been nauseating, forcing open his dead eyes is certainly shuddering.[14]

Picasso, however, chose to depict Salomé in the midst of itinerant acrobats, musicians and clowns, or *saltimbanques*. Between the autumn of 1904 and the spring of 1905, he found inspiration for his work in the world of travelling circus performers. Picasso's *Suite de saltimbanques* was first shown in 1905 as a collection of prints, though he created these works in etching and drypoint.[15] The two Picasso works in focus here are *Salomé Dancing before Herod* (Figure 5.5) and *The Barbaric Dance* (Figure 5.6). The first etching depicts Salomé dancing in front of Herod; her complete nakedness is exposed to him, her left leg kicking the air, while behind her the decapitated head of John the Baptist rests in the arms of a seated female servant, on a platter. The second etching focuses on a dance performed by *saltimbanques* for the entertainment of the ruling family, the performers naked and facing Herod and Salomé and also the viewer. Picasso's choice to

**Figure 5.5** Pablo Picasso, *Salome Dancing before Herod* from *La Suite des saltimbanques*, 1905. Drypoint. 400 x 348 mm. The Israel Museum, Jerusalem, Bl.14, F: DS. Gift of Max Palevsky, Los Angeles, to American Friends of Israel Museum, B99.0832(M). Photo © The Israel Museum, Jerusalem by Avshalom Avital.

**Figure 5.6** Pablo Picasso, *The Barbaric Dance (La danse barbare)* Plate XIV from *La suite des saltimabanques*, 1905. Drypoint. Private Collection. Photo © Christie's Images/ Bridgeman Images.

depict Salomé among the *saltimbanques* is an intriguing one, for it appears somewhat out of sync with the Salomé tradition contemporary to Picasso. Associations between Salomé's dance and acrobatic performances akin to those belonging at the circus were prevalent in mediaeval traditions,[16] the quality of her dance acrobatic rather than overtly seductive. However, by the end of the nineteenth and beginning of the twentieth century – and thus the immediate context of Picasso's *Saltimbanques* series – the emerging Salomé is very different, as we have seen above. For many of Picasso's contemporaries the primary quality of Salomé's dance, and indeed her character, is not agility but rather deadly seduction. The daughter of Herodias had become 'the symbolic incarnation of undying Lust, the Goddess of immortal Hysteria, the accursed Beauty exalted above all other beauties'.[17] This makes Picasso's choice to depict his Salomé among *saltimbanques* even more interesting.

The circus and the circus performer were themes that had a long tradition in French literature and art through the latter part of the nineteenth century to the middle of the twentieth century. Among the artists inspired by the circus we find Edgar Degas, Georges Seurat and Henri de Toulouse-Lautrec, the last of whom was one of the most prolific advocates for what became a genre, namely the circus poster.[18] Picasso's immediate inspiration for his *Suite de saltimbanques* came from performances of the Cirque Médrano (formerly Cirque Fernando, prominently featured in the circus posters of the time), which was located near his home and studio in Montmartre and which Picasso attended frequently. His partner at the time, Fernande Olivier, recounts that Picasso 'admired them [the circus performers] and felt a real sympathy for them'.[19] Despite their being part of the entertainment *de rigueur* in those days, circus performers were essentially other, social outsiders, on the outskirts of genteel society. Common in romantic and symbolist art and verse (from Daumier and Seurat to Baudelaire and Rimbaud), the *saltimbanques* were commonly portrayed as existing in a perpetual state of melancholy as well as social alienation. Picasso's *Suite de saltimbanques* belong to his Rose or Harlequin or Circus Period – called that because of the chalky red nuances that Picasso uses and because of his choice of subjects. Picasso's characters are no longer wooden, sculptural, immobile, as in his preceding Blue Period.[20] In his Rose Period, Picasso's characters become lively, some slender, even elegant. Nodding in the direction of Mannerism, Picasso begins to include in his work elements associated with classical themes of allegory, particularly *Vanitas* and *Impudicitia*, the unjustifiable human pride belied by the transient nature of all human experience, and the frivolous, shameless abandon to base compulsions, often as a direct response to human mortality.

Picasso's etchings based on the Salomé narrative harbour many such elements. In his *Salomé Dancing before Herod* (Figure 5.5), the composition is very elegant in its simplicity. Picasso chooses to focus on the protagonists of the biblical story: Salomé, Herod, Herodias and John the Baptist, or rather what is left of him, his head, which is carried by a servant or slave on a platter. The viewer can absorb the entire *tableau* in one glance: Salomé is dancing in front of Herod and Herodias; behind her the remains of the prophet. Salomé is naked, and so are the other characters ... mostly. Herod keeps his hat on, as well as his loin cloth, the knot of which falls rather limply between his legs. In his clothing Herod is mirrored by the slave, whose head covering and cloth skirt are also present. The direct line between Herod and the slave is further emphasized by the fact that they both gaze at Salomé; Herod looking down lustfully from the front – the left corner of his mouth turned up in a lascivious grin – and the slave looking up admiringly – almost in a motherly way – from the back, while with her right hand she is absent-mindedly caressing John's hair, which here may stand in for Salomé's.

Herodias stands at Herod's side, averting her eyes from the young, attractive woman's dance. Still beautiful and quite graceful herself, Herodias appears somewhat put out by the spectacle, and one almost expects a whistle of denial to escape her pretty pursed lips while her left hand is wistfully playing with her hair in a girly, flirtatious way – a vain attempt perhaps to distract herself, even Herod, from Salomé's display and to hang on to a very quickly fleeting illusion of youthful allure. She may wish to be the only woman to matter here, yet her full breasts and loose stomach, indeed the very presence of a grown-up Salomé, undermine that desire and betray both her age and her status as 'mother' and thus Other within the sexualized *tableau*. Herodias's somewhat disconnected presence and her averted eyes are balanced by, indeed linked through Salomé's open legs to, John's decapitated head. Cradled by the slave woman, the head is turned towards the audience and thus away from Salomé's dance; John's dead, empty eyes are averted from her nakedness, indeed her genitalia, which would have been in the prophet's direct line of sight.

These stylistic pairings between characters are not unique to Picasso. Wilde too connects John with Herodias and Salomé with Herod in his work, linguistically and aesthetically. In his rejection of Salomé, 'Back! Daughter of Babylon. Daughter of Sodom! By woman came evil into the world. Speak not to me. … I will listen but to the voice of the Lord God',[21] Jokanaan/John is paired with Herodias and her prosaic outlook. While Salomé and Herod realize the metaphorical dimensions of life – they both understand the moon and its many moods and portents – for Herodias, 'the moon is just the moon'.[22] Herod even echoes Salomé's aesthetic and her own painterly visions of Jokanaan/John when he barters for his head; having herself objectified Jokanaan, Salomé is offered objects as worthy replacements: 'an emerald, a great emerald … larger than Caesar's … the largest emerald in the whole world'; 'white peacocks; beautiful white peacocks … smeared with gold … their feet stained with purple'[23] and so on. Wilde wraps his dark, disturbing Salomé in beautiful language. By contrast, Picasso's Salomé is beautiful in form; dancing naked, with no need of embellishment. Her exposed body fits quite easily within the freedom of the composition, for Picasso does not restrict the biblical woman by prescribing an immediate context, an interior, even a frame. Picasso's Salomé is more akin to Auguste Rodin's *Iris, Messenger of the Gods* (Figure 5.7), modelled c. 1890 and cast in bronze c. 1895; and we will return to Rodin later. What is striking is that both Salomé and Iris are depicted as touching their raised feet with their hands (Salomé her left, Iris her right) while fully exposing their genitalia to their intended audience. Perhaps both Picasso and Rodin afford such freedom to their subjects because they pertain to the allegorical; Salomé and Iris are not 'real' women; they are, as Picasso would say, 'from a different kingdom'.[24] To exemplify artists' attitude to women in those days, Charles Baudelaire expands on the life of 'the painter of modern life' by stating,

> Woman is for the artist in general … far more than just the female of man. Rather she is divinity, a star … She is an idol, stupid perhaps, but dazzling and bewitching ….[25]

*Salomé* may be Picasso's first erotic work outside the world of brothels. He manages to liberate Salomé seemingly, by taking her out of the private, domestic world of a dining hall (a space usually perceived as quintessentially feminine) and bringing her out into the public, open spaces of artists (generally perceived as a masculine sphere), even if belonging merely to *saltimbanques* on the fringe. With the same stroke, however, Picasso sutures Salomé to her identity position as 'object', her role and beauty betraying her as 'a glittering conglomeration of all the graces

**Figure 5.7** Rodin, *Iris: Messenger of the Gods*, 1891. Bronze, modeled. Courtesy of Sourced Collection/Alamy Stock Photo.

of nature … dazzling and bewitching', but an object to be contemplated, nevertheless. Furthermore, she is yet again not only objectified but also renegaded to the margins of polite society, just like the *saltimbanques*.

Perhaps aware of such signification tensions, Picasso produces something very different in his *Barbarous* or *Barbaric Dance* (Figure 5.6). His lines are again clean and his hand firm, and there are no perceptible corrections here. Everything is how Picasso wanted it to be; and we seem to have a work of two halves: the upper, a caricature; the lower a classical *tableau*. Here is a group of *saltimbanques* performing in front of Herod and the young woman next to him, who is named by Picasso as Salomé. Herod is immediately identifiable here, for he is the same portly model as in the previous etching, yet Salomé is not immediately so, for she is somewhat different from the dancing girl. Salomé here is reclining on a sofa of some kind – perhaps a triclinium – her body nestled between Herod's large legs, her right arm resting on his large body; however, with her left hand Salomé is beckoning to a young attractive male, who stands proudly at the foot of her sofa with his back to the performing *saltimbanques*. Salomé's head is also turned towards the young man, and the two seem locked in a reciprocated gaze. Also looking at Salomé is a servant or slave (possibly male), who is kneeling in front of the royal couple, offering fruit on a platter. Herod seems to be unaware of Salomé's actions, instead paying attention to the strange performance in front of him.

While Picasso depicts Salomé's body somewhat reverentially in both etchings (inasmuch as she is beautiful in a conventional sense), the bodies of the three performers, the *saltimbanques,* are portrayed as grotesque. They are caricatures, lacking any grace or elegance. The body of the would-be-musician on the left has the look and proportions of a satyr, his large stomach overhanging small genitalia, and his bulbous head balanced by his equally exaggerated lips and phallic nose. His musical gesture – running a stick as a bow over the buttocks of a child who is stretched over his right arm like a violin – is not quite humorous; instead it is disturbing and rather tragic. The two dancers form a pair of sorts. Their gestures are probably meant to be synchronized (it has been suggested that their raised arms indicate that they are together performing a popular Andalusian dance[26]), and they do seem to be attempting to mirror each other: the woman's right hand is up and her left is down, her left hand raised slightly in what is meant to be perhaps a graceful gesture; the man's left arm is raised, while his right is down, hand raised. So far, so good. Yet the fact that their legs want to do the same thing – the woman's left leg is raised and so is the man's (well, slightly; he is not as nimble) – breaks that symmetry and the mirroring effect, and the result is disharmony. This disharmony is also achieved by their appearance: the woman is thin, and the man fat; her nose protrudes, while his has vanished; she is rather hairy, but he is not. The effect that the caricature has on the viewer is a mixture of amusement, puzzlement and repulsion. Tim Hilton states, 'This puzzling and unpleasant drawing seems to recede from the classic to the Oriental to the bestial. It is sour and negative. If its iconography has a meaning, it can only be, surely, in the bitter assertion that the bestial is closer to splendour that we think.'[27] It is certainly true that the identity markers of the performing *saltimbanques* are those of excess, and their nudity repels rather than attracts.

The indecorous quality of the performance is exactly what Picasso wanted. But why? Who is the dancing crone? Is she perhaps Herodias trying to demonstrate that she's still got 'it', when in fact she is far too old for the cancan, for stockings, kitten boots and no drawers? What of Herod? He doesn't sit too well within his designated, classical *milieu*. Herod may be enjoying the illusion of prowess: after all, the *saltimbanques* are performing for him; his royal head gear and sceptre are clearly exhibited; yet he too is a ridiculous and grotesque figure, a caricature, a fat jester with no clothes but a hat and a disproportionally small dick-on-a-stick. One is reminded that Herod had long enjoyed the dramatic reputation of a tragi-comic character, the ranting tyrant who is little more than a bragging buffoon, the ultimate victim of Vanitas. As far back as the beginning of the seventeenth century Shakespeare's Hamlet criticizes some players' inclination to overact, to out-Herod Herod, by hinting at the character's common depictions.[28] Perhaps the large male dancer is Herod's *alter ego*, devoid of royal garb and royal reservations – the entire performance a *memento mori* for him, another glance into the cycle of life. It may explain why Herod is the only one watching the spectacle.

While other artists were complicit in cementing her reputation as a lethal beauty, for Picasso Salomé was beautiful and graceful, perhaps a little misunderstood, perhaps a little stupid, not necessarily a *femme fatale*. As fleetingly as he engaged with stylistic influences, Picasso played with Salomé for a short while, for she was somewhat *de rigueur* and promising – possibly even delivering – a momentary *frisson*. However, it seems that Picasso soon wanted to sober himself up by producing an antidote to Salomé's transient allure, and so he created *The Dance*. In his *Salomé* and *The Barbaric Dance* etchings, Picasso oscillates between the divine and the ridiculous. It has been said that 'in high art, as opposed to popular art, ideal beauty and caricature have an intimate relationship, not as poles of an ideal style but as linked concerns … Caricature occasionally has a purgative role in the early stages of modernism as an antidote to cliché, a progressively weakened and confectioned repetition.'[29] Picasso does return to caricature throughout his career, even as he moves towards cubism, perhaps as a means of keeping himself in check. He does not, however, revisit the biblical narrative of Herodias's daughter, or indeed any other biblical narrative. Perhaps after Salomé he considered the Bible a little too sentimental, too cliché.

Wilde became fascinated with Salomé during his days in Oxford. Walter Pater, whom Wilde respected immensely, lent him in 1877 Gustave Flaubert's *Trois contes* (*Three Stories*), which contained the story 'Hérodias'. Wilde had great admiration for Flaubert, and he used a lot of his material unreservedly, although Flaubert did not consider this a compliment.[30] Flaubert may have wanted to expand on the biblical story in a sensitive way. He was more interested in exploring the political networks within the story. As a result, his Salomé is a spoilt princess, with a childish demeanour and a lisp, easily manipulated by her mother.[31] Although Wilde has been accused of deriving from Flaubert – and from Maeterlinck, for that matter, particularly his play 1889 *La princesse Maleine* – the same 'childish prattle' for his characters in *Salomé* (an accusation based possibly on the many repetitions in the character's speech), Wilde's princess has very little in common with Flaubert's or indeed Maeterlinck's imaginings. Wilde allows Salomé to become her own person, monstrous as that may be. In his play, she enunciates clearly, 'It is not my mother's voice that I heed. It is for mine own pleasure that I ask for the head of Jokanaan in a silver charger.'[32] No childish prattle there.

Wilde prefers an older, more self-aware and more passionate Salomé, it seems (in fact, he wrote the part for Sarah Bernhardt, the famous actress and socialite of the time, who was about 50 years old when Wilde wrote the play). However, Wilde may not have been the first to develop the lustful aspect of her character. The most nauseating element of the play, Salomé's kissing the severed head of the Baptist on the mouth, may not have originated with Wilde. In his 1841 poem 'Atta Troll' Heinrich Heine imagined a wild hunt with goblins and spirits on St John's Eve, in which the spirits of three dead women occupy centre stage. They are Diana of Greek mythology, Abunda of the Celts and Herodias of the Bible. Heine writes them as *femmes fatales*, sexual and violent; Herodias, an angel–demon hybrid princess with 'Oriental magic', acts as a result of spurned love when demanding the Baptist's head, which she kisses 'with fervour'.

Yes, she was indeed a princess,
Was the sovereign of Judea,
Was the beauteous wife of Herod,
Who the Baptist's head demanded.
…

In her hands she holds forever
That sad charger with the head of
John the Baptist, which she kisses –
Yes, the head with fervour kisses.

For, time was, she loved the Baptist –
'Tis not in the Bible written,
But there yet exists the legend
Of Herodias's bloody passion.

Else there were no explanation
Of that lady's curious longing:
Would a woman want the head of
Any man she did not love?

Was perhaps a little peevish
With her swain, had him beheaded;
But when she upon the charger
Saw the head so well beloved,

Straight she wept and mad became,
And she died of love's distraction –
Love's distraction! Pleonasmus!
Why, love is itself distraction![33]

Herodias kissing the head also appears in the work of an American poet, J. C. Heywood, whose dramatic poem 'Salomé' was published in Cambridge, Massachusetts, in 1862 and then in London during the 1880s. Wilde was familiar with Heywood's poem, for he reviewed it in 1888, three years before completing his play.[34] Still, for both Heine and Heywood the protagonist is Herodias, not Salomé. Perhaps Alice Bach is right when suggesting that the evacuation of the mother by concentrating on the daughter is, after all, 'in the interest of a patriarchal cultural system'.[35] Further, the kiss in Heine's poem occurs after her death, not as an act longingly desired by the woman but rather as punishment for her getting the prophet killed. Heine was, however, the inspiration behind Jules Laforgue's work, meant as a parody of Flaubert's 'Hérodias'. Laforgue wrote a piece caricaturing Salomé in one of the *Moralités légendaires* (published in *La vogue* of June–July 1886, then revised in the *Revue indépendente*, 1887). In it,

> No sooner was [John's head] the object delivered, than Salomé, in the spirit of scientific enquiry, tried those famous post-decapitation experiments which are so often discussed; she waited, but the electric currents drew nothing but grimaces from the face. …
>
> [She] kissed that mouth mercifully and hermetically, sealed it immediately with her corrosive stamp …[36]

Salomé's sadism developed by Laforgue occurs also in an 1894 performed drama by Antoine Sabatier called quite explicitly *Le baiser de Jean* (*The Kiss of John*). Sabatier draws her as a hysterical woman with a macabre fascination for the Baptist – an image similar, therefore, to Wilde's own portrayal of Salomé, perhaps yet another element that Wilde 'borrowed'.[37]

**Figure 5.8** Gustave Moreau, *Salomé Dancing before Herod*, 1876. Oil on canvas. 156½ x 41¹⁄₁₆ ins. (143.5 x 104.3 cm). The Armand Hammer Collection, Gift of the Armand Hammer Collection. Hammer Museum, Los Angeles.

The greatest literary influence on Wilde, however, and as mentioned earlier, appears to have been the Dutch novelist Joris-Karl Huysmans. Huysmans wrote in French, a choice he shared with Wilde, and his 1884 novel *A rebours* (translated in English as *Against Nature*) attracted Wilde's attention. The protagonist, the Duc des Esseintes, had acquired Gustave Moreau's 1876 painting *Salomé Dancing before Herod* (Figure 5.8), which he considered the very embodiment of Decadent spirit. Des Esseintes describes at length the painting,[38] and in doing so, his Salomé becomes a stylized icon. When it comes to style, even the biblical text allows for it, for Herodias's daughter adds her own request to her mother's instructions; it is Salomé who desires the silver platter. Strangely, it is this taste for precious metals and gems that penetrates, indeed dominates, the style of the Decadent movement and its imaginings of the Orient. While obviously taken by Moreau's Salomé, it was his watercolour *L'apparition* (Figure 5.9),[39] a precursor to his 1876 oil version of the same (now at the Louvre) that truly seduced des Esseintes. He writes,

**Figure 5.9** Gustave Moreau, *The Apparition*, 1876. Watercolour. 1.06 x 0.72 m. Paris: Musée d'Orsay. Photo by Christophel Fine Art/UIG via Getty Images.

> Here [Salomé] was a true harlot, obedient to her passionate and cruel female temperament; here she came to life, more refined yet more savage, more hateful yet more exquisite than before; here she roused the sleeping senses of the male more powerfully, subjugated his will more surely with her charms – the charms of a great venereal flower, grown in a bed of sacrilege, reared in a hot-house of impiety.[40]

In Alice Bach's interpretation of the same painting, Salomé 'points towards her work with pride. The Baptist is enclosed within the fire of cosmos. He is as complete as Salomé, an unearthly spectre to balance the very earthly woman … the figure with a body who has subsumed his.'[41]

**Figure 5.10** Aubrey Beardsley, *The Climax*, 1905. Photo courtesy of Culture Club/Getty Images.

Visually inspired, Wilde finished the play in January 1892, though its first production would not take place until 1896. Unsurprisingly, *Salomé* is a painterly work, a 'treasury of images – precious objects, jewels, garments, tropical fruits and exotic creatures', in the words of a critic.[42] The very choice of writing in French is for Wilde an aesthetic one (not a particularly popular choice at the time); he wished to write in the same language in which Moreau painted, for to write in French was to 'enlist the aid of language against nature … where words become precious images'.[43] Perhaps that is why Wilde was so possessive of the text, and when Lord Alfred Douglas (the infamous 'Bosie', his lover) translated the play into English, Wilde was very critical of his version and edited and re-edited the text before allowing its publication in English. He was equally critical of Aubrey Beardsley's drawings, which accompanied the John Lane, English edition of 1894 (Figure 5.10). Wilde described them as getting 'on one's nerves and … cruel.[44] However, it is for Beardsley's drawings that the John Lane edition of *Salomé* is considered the epitome of English Decadence.[45]

Wilde may have been uncomfortable with Beardsley's drawings, but most of its first English critics were as uncomfortable with Wilde's text, which they perceived, as *The Times* of London had it, 'an arrangement in blood and ferocity, morbid, bizarre, and very offensive in its adaptation of scriptural phraseology to situations the reverse of sacred' (23 February 1893).[46] Perhaps the intended beauty of Wilde's writing was only as obvious as Beardsley's rococo flourishes, overwhelmed by the macabre, brutal, ugly substratum, which finds true representations in Beardsley's cruel, grotesque, figures.

Salomé herself is in Wilde's play both beautiful and perverse, adorned and naked, painting and painter. In her three advances to Jokanaan, she describes him in landscapes. His torso is 'white like the lilies of a field that the mower has never mowed … white like the snow that lie on the mountains of Judea, whiter than the roses of the Queen of Arabia, whiter than the breast of the moon when she lies on the breast of the sea'. His hair is like 'the clusters of black grapes that hang from the vine-trees of Edom … like the great cedars of Lebanon that give their shade to the lions, darker than the long black nights when the moon hides her face; darker even than the silence that dwells in the forest'. Then his mouth is 'like a band of scarlet on a tower of ivory … a pomegranate cut in twain with a knife of ivory … the pomegranates that blossom in the gardens of Tyre and are redder than roses, redder than the red blasts of trumpets that herald the approach of kings, redder than the feet of the doves who inhabit the temples; it is like a branch of coral that fishers have found in the twilight of the sea, which they keep for the kings; it is like the vermillion that the Moabites find in the mines of Moab'.[47] (If the style of these descriptions sounds familiar, Wilde also acknowledges borrowing from the Song of Songs.[48])

It is clear that Wilde's Salomé is thoroughly enamoured with the prophet. Yet, how did John the Baptist become the poster boy of biblical masculinity? Certainly the figure of the Baptist emerging from Auguste Rodin's bronze statue 'Saint John the Baptist' (1880) (Figure 5.11) exudes virility: John is naked, tall, purposeful, with clearly defined muscles, proud genitalia and legs apart. Rodin is not alone in producing favourable depictions of the Baptist. In fact, he follows an already established artistic tradition. Two notable examples are Carlo Crivelli's *Saint John the Baptist* dated 1476 (Figure 5.12) and a painting produced by the circle of Annibale Carracci, *Saint John the Baptist Seated in the Wilderness*, dated late sixteenth, early seventeenth century (Figure 5.13).

Crivelli's Baptist is part of The Demidoff Altarpiece,[49] a polyptych originally designed for the high altar of La Chiesa di San Domenico in Ascoli Piceno, Italy. Of Venetian descent, Crivelli was schooled in Padua by Squarcione but returned to live and work in Venice until 1457, when he had to leave the region as a result of his being found guilty of adultery. Crivelli spent most of his creative life in the Marches (eastern central Italy), where his fine technique and vibrant and attentive colouring were appreciated – indeed he was considered a very successful altarpiece painter. His *Saint John the Baptist* is the far left principal panel, one of nine panels forming the Demidoff Altarpiece. The prophet's companions list the *Virgin and Child* (centre) and a number of other saints (Peter, Catherine of Alexandria and Dominic as same size panels; and Francis, Andrew, Stephen and Thomas Aquinas

**Figure 5.11** Rodin, *Saint John the Baptist*, 1902. Bronze modeled 1878–79. Copenhagen: Carlsberg Glyptotek. Photo courtesy of PRISMA ARCHIVO/Alamy Stock Photo.**

as smaller, top panels). John the Baptist is painted in a modest, prayerful position, standing but looking down, as if to avoid the direct attention of the viewer, and pointing with his right finger to a banner that he holds in his left hand that reads, 'ECCE AGNUS DEI QVI TOLLIT PECCATUM MUNDI'.[50] The pointing finger is an attribute that becomes associated with John the Baptist, as is the reed cross that John also holds in his left hand. In both the biblical and the artistic traditions, John the Baptist is the pointer, the precursor, the forerunner and announcer of Christ, the Lamb of God. Crivelli's Baptist is a beautiful man, with proportionate features, long, neat curly hair, and well-defined (though not bulging) muscles. He

**Figure 5.12** Carlo Crivelli, *Saint John the Baptist* from *The Demidoff Altarpiece*, 1476. The National Gallery, London, NG788.2. Bought 1868. Tempera on poplar, 138.5 x 40 cm. © The National Gallery, London.

is semi-naked, his right arm, upper torso and both lower legs exposed (the only figure to show this much skin in the altarpiece), wearing only a piece of camel skin against his body and a cloth wrap on top. On his feet he wears sandals, and it is telling that John is the only figure Crivelli shows in the midst of nature, on a river-bank (most likely Jordan), his toes almost touching the water.

The *Saint John the Baptist Seated in the Wilderness* created by the circle of Carracci is also beautiful, though in a more Classical fashion. Formerly attributed to Annibale Carracci, this painting is now thought to have been created by one of his pupils. Together with other artist members of his family (particularly his brother Agostino and his cousin Ludovico), Carracci founded an Academy in Bologna,

**Figure 5.13** Circle of Annibale Carracci, *Saint John the Baptist Seated in the Wilderness*, c. late sixteenth century. The National Gallery, London, NG25. Bought 1824. Oil on canvas, 133.7 x 96.6 cm. © The National Gallery, London.

training such great painters as Guido Reni and Domenichino. Working in Rome in later years, Carracci wished to influence the return of Italian art to pre-Mannerist and thus pre-Realist aspirations. By the seventeenth century, art had been firmly identified as belonging with the divine. Leonardo da Vinci had claimed that 'the knowledge of the painter transforms his mind into the likeness of the divine mind', and, like God, he creates in his own image; every painter paints himself [*ogni dipintore dipinge se*], but better.[51] And of course, clear differences were being drawn between 'good' and merely 'mediocre' art. Giovambattista Armenini made the distinction clear in his 1587 *De' veri precetti della pittura*, 'Even an artist of mediocre talent [*mediocre ingegno*] can master [portraiture] as long as he is experienced in colours'.[52] Armenini further implies that a truly good artist, a virtuoso, moves beyond the act of copying nature, the 'ritrare', for he cannot 'endure' the 'awkwardness and weakness' of natural faces. Therefore, a true virtuoso should invent and *perfect* a face, a process enunciated also by Vincenzo Danti: 'By the term *ritrare* I mean to make something exactly as another thing is seen to be; and by the terms *imitare* I similarly understand that it is to make a thing not only as another has seen the thing to be [when that thing is imperfect], but to make it as it would have to be in order to be of complete perfection.'[53] The idealized perfection, or *le arie del bel viso*, of creative invention came to represent the beauty of the art of painting itself.[54] When painting his John the Baptist, the pupil of Carracci creates idealized perfection. Naked but for a red cloak covering his groin and right leg, John is captured turning towards a brook, extending his right hand and gathering water in a dish. In his left hand, he holds a reed cross, with an inscribed scroll wrapped around it. The Baptist's body is strong, beautiful and arrests the gaze in its central position. There is nothing to mark John as suffering from rough living in the desert. In fact, the lush European landscape in which he is presented has less to do with a 'desert' and more to do with 'wilderness' as an idealized, uninhabited space.

The association between John the Baptist and the wilderness we owe primarily to the Synoptic Evangelists, who record that John 'grew and became strong in spirit, and he was in the wilderness until the day he appeared publicly to Israel' (Lk 1:80), 'proclaiming, "Repent, for the kingdom of heaven has come near"' (Matt 3:1–2); for 'John the Baptizer appeared in the wilderness, proclaiming a baptism of repentance for the forgiveness of sins' (Mk 1:4). Clothed in camel's hair and surviving on locusts and wild honey (Matt 3:4), John could be seen as the epitome of the 'wild prophet'. Living outside of the confines of societal formations seems to be a *sine qua non* condition for communication with the divine in the Hebrew Bible (consider for example Moses and Elijah, the latter of whom is mentioned to Zechariah by the visiting angel in direct connection to John's birth and mission in Lk 1:17), and it was also a known practice among the Qumran community of Essenes, Jewish monks contemporaneous to John. In the artistic tradition in focus here, however, it appears that the association with asceticism does not only guarantee John's sainthood but also his virility. He is not wild but wise; not emaciated but enticing; not dirty but daring. It seems that John's masculinity is predicated on his being defined by two main factors: wilderness and speech; animal skins and uncompromising 'virtue'. His rejection of 'civilised' – read 'corrupt' – society in favour of the wilderness acts as a choice for the pure and thus godly and a rejection of human sin; a voiced rejection of human sin, no less. As he declares himself, John is 'the voice of one crying out in the wilderness, "Make straight the way of the Lord," as the prophet Isaiah said' (John 1:23). By speaking in the wilderness, John occupies the space, or the 'crack' as Derrida would have it,[55] between sin and innocence; scorched land and the river; the desert and the garden – for in Eden God speaks; on Sinai he writes. 'The garden is speech, the desert writing.'[56] Both Crivelli and the pupil of Carracci show John as a healthy, beautiful man close to water and nature; an Adam of sorts and in somewhat Adamic surroundings. By denouncing sin and pointing to the Lamb of God, John signals the arrival of the one universally to restore the innocence of the garden.

If neither Crivelli nor the pupil of Carracci presented the Baptist fully naked – his modesty is preserved by animal skins or loose cloth respectively – Auguste Rodin had no such reservations. Rodin wanted to 'obey Nature in everything'.[57]

Declaring himself a 'seeker after truth and student of life',[58] Rodin saw the body as a vehicle for the spirit within and thus a body's movement as expressions of the spirit. Rodin detested formal poses and instead was captivated by free movement: women squatting; women dancing; having intercourse (the Sapphic way in particular); men walking. In his early years of training, Rodin was fascinated by Greek antiques and thus classical sculpture; he declared his masters to be Donatello and Michelangelo, particularly due to their realistic poses, which he saw as evidence of the expressive force of *non finito*. Even Rodin's fascination with dance was defined by his captivation with a soul's expression through movement. Unlike Degas and other artists who preferred classical ballet, Rodin admired experimental dance that moved away from convention and artifice, as performed by Isadora Duncan, Loie Fuller, Kijinsky and the Ballets Russes, indeed Japanese and Cambodian dancers touring or visiting France. As with his *Iris,* Rodin desired to express the veracity of nature through his work. Talking about an antique statue of Aphrodite, he is quoted to have said, 'It is truly flesh! … You almost expect, when you touch this body, to find it warm.'[59]

Certainly when one looks at Rodin's Baptist one expects him to continue walking, pointing, sowing, warm and alive. Building on Leonardo's principle of automimesis, Giorgio Vasari and other sixteenth-century writers frequently associate an artist's character and life force, indeed his soul, with the demeanour of his painted characters. Since the value of the soul at the time was linked closely to the Aristotelian understanding of the 'originative source' that possessed the 'principle of soul', namely the male *sperma*, it was expected that there would be a certain familial resemblance between the artist father and his creations.[60] Rodin acknowledges that he included in his creation his own self; a reproduction of the spirit of the subject as he saw it: 'The cast is less true than my sculpture! … The cast only reproduces the exterior; I reproduce, besides that, the spirit which is certainly also part of nature. I see all the truth, and not only that of the outside.'[61] Rodin modelled his John the Baptist on an Italian peasant from the Abruzzi called Pignatelli, though his work reflected his own interpretation of the *tableau vivant* in front of him. The artist's recollection demonstrates yet again the symbiotic relationship between biblical text, its interpretation and its representation:

> As soon as I saw him, I was filled with admiration; this rough, hairy man expressed violence in his bearing… yet also the mystical character of his race. I immediately thought of a Saint John the Baptist, in other words, a man of nature, a visionary, a believer, a precursor who came to announce one greater than himself. The peasant undressed, climbed onto the revolving stand as if he had never posed before; he planted himself firmly on his feet, head up, torso straight, at the same time putting his weight on both legs, open like a compass. The movement was so right, so straightforward and so true that I cried: 'But it's a man walking!' I immediately resolved to model what I had seen.[62]

Rodin thought of his model as 'a Saint John the Baptist' because he was 'hairy' and somewhat forthright and mystical; all attributes of the prophet as established both rhetorically and artistically by that time. While Rodin also exclaimed, 'But it's a man walking!' one can't help thinking of the retort, 'A dead man walking'. When Jokanaan rejects her in Wilde's play, Salomé destroys her painterly creations, with the tempest of a child who is not appreciated. 'Your body is hideous', she retorts. 'It is the body of a leper … like the plastered wall where vipers have crawled … where scorpions have made their nest … like the white sepulchre full of loathsome things. … Your hair is horrible. It is covered with mire and dust. It is like a knot of serpents coiled around your neck.'[63] She cannot bring herself to destroy the painting of the mouth, however. Instead she vows repeatedly, 'I will kiss your mouth, Jokanaan'. This is echoed at the end of the play with her famous, 'I have kissed your mouth (*J'ai baisé ta bouche*), Jokanaan',[64] Salomé's last words. Having made an image of herself through dance, she is ready to make an image of Jokanaan through murder; her possessing him worth her self-objectification. Perhaps that is the reason behind her own death at the end in the play; like her victim, she must be destroyed in order to be preserved, granted yet again the immortality of the image.[65]

In the biblical narrative, the daughter of Herodias is a little girl, *korasion*, or little *kore*, a little maiden. Yet, thanks in part to Wilde and Strauss, Salomé survives as the 'symbolic incarnation of undying Lust, the Goddess of immortal Hysteria, the accursed Beauty … the monstrous Beast, indifferent, irresponsible, insensible, poisoning …'[66] The connection that Alice Bach makes between Salomé and the secondary meaning of *kore*, namely that of 'pupil of the eye' – and here Salomé as the apple of Herod's eye, abducted like mythic Kore into the underworld of Herod's mind, indeed the reader's mind[67] – is certainly apt. As image, Salomé enjoys immortality. Not as Herodias's daughter, the rather innocent girl of the Bible manipulated into requesting the Baptist's head, but as Salomé who fell for the Baptist. After all, 'Would a woman want the head of any man she did not love?'[68] In other words, having buried the little girl of the Bible, *fin-de-siècle* European artistic traditions create and indeed suture Salomé's identity as a fallen and deadly woman; a fallen *femme fatale*. John the Baptist, forerunner of Christ, enjoys a tradition in which he appears to reflect the beauty and virility of an Adamic archetype, somewhat wild, unsophisticated, and thus godly. Occupying the gap between the garden and the desert, between innocence and the Law, he is a part of nature, full of creative *sperma* and as such compelling; the poster boy for biblical masculinity. Indeed, according to artists he is irresistible to Salomé. And yet, John the Baptist's established reputation is not that of *l'homme fatal*. Why not?

## Notes

1 Both Matthew and Mark describe Salomé as *korasion* (*talitha* in Aramaic, as used in Mk 5:41), which is the same term they use for Jairus's daughter (Matt 9; Mk 5), who is twelve years old (Mk 5:42).

2 It is Josephus who gives us her name. Even though he does not not mention Salomé in connection with the death of John the Baptist, he records, 'Herodias … was married to Herod, the son of Herod the Great, who was born of Mariamne, the daughter of Simon the Great Priest who had a daughter, Salomé; after whose birth Herodias took

upon her to confound the laws of our country, and divorced herself from her husband while he was alive, and was married to Herod, her husband's brother by the father's side, he was tetrarch of Galilee; but her daughter Salomé was married to Philip the son of Herod, and tetrarch of Trachonitis and as he died childless, Aristobulus the son of Herod the brother of Agrippa married her; they had three sons, Herod, Agrippa, and Aristobulus' (*Jewish Antiquities*, Book XVIII, Chapters 5, 4).

3 J.-K. Huysmans, *Against Nature* (Harmondsworth: Penguin, 1959), 65–66.

4 Richard Ellmann, *Oscar Wilde* (London: Hamish Hamilton, 1987), 323.

5 Huysmans, *Against Nature*, 65–66.

6 Gary Schmidgall, *Literature as Opera* (Oxford: Oxford University Press, 1977), 272.

7 Peter Conrad, 'Opera, Dance and Painting', in *Romantic Opera and Literary Form* (London: University of California Press, 1977), 144–78 (146).

8 My opinion is that this is a Judith, not a Salomé painting. Gustav Klimt's Judith paintings have been the subject of much confusion. Klimt's *Judith I* (1901) was first catalogued as *Salomé*, while Klimt was still alive and despite its being exhibited in the original golden frame embossed with the clear words 'Judith and Holofernes' (*Judith I* is currently at Österreichische Galerie Belvedere, Vienna). Klimt's second Judith painting, *Judith II/Salomé* (1909), is even now catalogued under both titles (currently at Galleria Internazionale d'Arte Moderna Ca' Pesaro, Venice).

9 Richard Strauss, quoted in Schmidgall, *Literature as Opera*, p. 286.

10 Rana Kabbani, *Europe's Myths of the Orient* (London: Pandora Press, 1988), 68–69.

11 Horst Uhr, *Lovis Corinth* (Berkeley: University of California Press, 1990), 166.

12 Oscar Wilde, *Salomé: A Tragedy in One Act* (Boston: Branden Publishing, 1996), 34–36.

13 Quoted in Schmidgall, *Literature as Opera*, 274.

14 Uhr, *Lovis Corinth*, 167.

15 The prints were exhibited at the Galerie Serrurier, and the exhibition featured prints from a small edition printed by Delâtre in 1905. In 1913, Ambroise Vollard purchased the plates from Delâtre, and had Louis Fort steel-face them (to harden their surfaces), and produced 250 sets of 15 prints. Most known prints are from the Vollard edition. Picasso worked in etching and drypoint for the prints in the *Suite*, and these techniques are generally known for capturing the original spontaneity of the artist's design. See Juan Carrete Parrondo, 'Picasso, la Suite Vollard y las técnicas del grabador', in *Picasso. Suite Vollard* (Madrid: Turner, 1991), 69.

16 For a brilliant analysis, see Diane Apostolos-Cappadona, 'Imagining Salomé, or How *la sauterelle* Became *la femme fatale*', in *From the Margins 2: Women of the New Testament and their Afterlives*, ed. Christine E. Joynes and Christopher E. Rowland (The Bible in the Modern World, 27; Sheffield: Sheffield Phoenix Press, 2009), 190–210.

17 Huysmans, *Against Nature*, 65–66.

18 Phillip Dennis Cate, 'The Cult of the Circus', in *The Pleasures of Paris from Daumier to Picasso*, ed. Barbara Stern Shapiro (Boston: Museum of Fine Arts, 1991), 38. For examples of circus lithograph posters in fin-de-siècle Paris, see the work of Jules Chéret, Adolphe Léon Willette, Henry Gray, Henri-Gabriel Ibels, Richard Ranft, Emmanuel Joseph-Raphael Orazi, Charles Paul Renouard and Edgar Chahine.

19 Fernande Olivier, *Picasso y sus amigos* (Madrid: Tarus, 1964), 106.

20 A few examples from his somewhat Symbolist Blue Period are *The Old Blind Guitarist* resembling Job; *The Soup*, with echoes an Annunciation, maybe even Eucharist; *The Two Sisters,* in which the two characters are a nun and a prostitute but recalling Mary

and an older Elisabeth; *The Tragedy*, reminiscent of an exile to Egypt; and *Evocation (The Burial of Casagemas)*, derived from El Greco and condensing a burial and an ascension; and the most revered and revealing of his blue works, *La vie*, which, when coupled with *The Evocation*, allows for speculation as to the true reason behind Picasso's depression, his blue mood. In *La vie* (not Picasso's title) one can identify the male in the foreground as Picasso's friend and fellow artist, another young Spaniard and Picasso's first Paris companion, Carlos Casagemas. Deeply in love and unable to come to terms with the fact that he was sexually impotent, Casagemas killed himself in 1901. His death seems to have had a great impact on Picasso. He was always rather reluctant to discuss *La vie*, though he seemed pleased with the attention it generated; Picasso is recorded to have said, 'It wasn't I who gave the painting that title … I certainly didn't intend to paint symbols; I simply painted images that rose in front of my eyes: it's for others to find a hidden meaning in them' (quoted in Hilton, *Picasso*, 32). Whether one looks for deeper meanings or not, *La vie* can be categorized as a Symbolist cycle-of-life work, the type of which was rather popular in *fin-de-siècle* Europe. Like possibly the best-known exemplar of its kind, namely Gauguin's *Whence come we? What are we? Where are we going?* cycle-of-life works (often murals) dramatize the brevity of life and condense within them key human experiences such as birth, childhood, adolescence, maturity, old age, death, sometimes rebirth. Set in an artist's studio, *La vie* depicts Casagemas standing semi-naked and communicating with an older woman, who is heavily covered in a draping garment and cradling a baby in her arms. The artist points to the child with his left hand, while his right is hidden behind the naked body of a young woman who clings vigorously to him, her left leg firmly positioned between his own, for stability. Resting between the naked couple and the older woman with the child are two canvases. In the top one a couple cling to each other, one looking out towards the viewer while cradling the other, who is in a foetal position. In the bottom canvas the artist has depicted one androgynous individual, in the same foetal position as in the top canvas. Perhaps Picasso not only laments the loss of his friend as a human being (his life is cut short and with it the prospects of procreation and thus continuity of life) but also the loss of Casagemas as the artist (his life is cut short and with it the prospect of artistic output and immortality).

21 Oscar Wilde, *Salomé: A Tragedy in One Act* (Boston: Branden Publishing, 1996), 11–12.

22 Wilde, *Salomé*, 15.

23 Wilde, *Salomé*, 30–33.

24 Françoise Gilot and Carlton Lake, *Life with Picasso* (London: Nelson, 1965), 116.

25 Charles Baudelaire, 'The Painter of Modern Life', in *The Painter of Modern Life and Other Essays,* trans. and ed. Jonathan Mayne (Oxford: Phaidon Press, 1964), 30.

26 Fernando Martin Martin, 'From the Blue of Hell to the Rose of Bateau-Lavoire: The Suite de saltimbanques', in *Picasso and the Circus: Fin-de-Siecle Paris and the* Suite de Saltimbanque, ed. Phillip Earenfight (Seattle: University of Washington Press, 2011), 60.

27 Hilton, *Picasso*, 52.

28 'O, it offends me to the soul to hear a robustious periwig-pated fellow tear a passion to totters, to very rags, to spleet the ears of the groundlings, who for the most part are capable of nothing but inexplicable dumb shows and noise. I would have such fellow whipt for o'erdoing Termagant, it out-Herods Herod, pray you avoid it' (*Hamlet*, III.ii).

29 Hilton, *Picasso*, 51–52.

30 Wilde is quoted as saying, 'But tell me now, is Flaubert still read? I regret to say we no longer speak; he, most foolishly, objects to the use of those few details I borrowed from him in my *Salomé* …' See John Espey, 'Resources for Wilde Studies at the Clark Library', in John Espey and Richard Ellmann, *Oscar Wilde: Two Approaches* (Los Angeles: William Andrews Clark Memorial Library, University of California Press, 1977), 21.

31 Gustave Flaubert, 'Hérodias', in *Three Tales,* trans. Robert Baldick (Harmondsworth: Penguin, 1961), 122.

32 Oscar Wilde, *Salomé: A Tragedy in One Act* (Boston: Branden Publishing, 1996), 29.

33 Heinrich Heine, *Atta Troll and Other Poems,* trans. T. S. Egan (London: Chapman & Hall, 1876).

34 Richard Ellmann, 'Overtures to Wilde's 'Salomé', in *Richard Strauss: Salomé,* ed. Derrick Puffett (Cambridge Opera Handbooks; Cambridge: Cambridge University Press, 1989), 21–35 (22).

35 Still, Richard Ellmann insists that 'to read other writers about Salomé is to come to a greater admiration for Wilde's ingenuity'. On the other hand, Mario Praz muses, 'as generally happens with specious second-hand works, it was precisely Wilde's *Salomé* which became popular'. See Alice Bach, *Women, Seduction and Betrayal in Biblical Narrative* (Cambridge: Cambridge University Press, 1997), 217.

36 Jules Laforgue, 'Salomé', in F. Ruchon, *Jules Laforgue* (Geneva: Editions Albert Ciana, 1924), 110.

37 Mario Praz, 'Salomé in Literary Tradition', in *Richard Strauss: Salomé,* ed. Derrick Puffett (Cambridge: Cambridge University Press, 1989), 11–20 (19).

38 'The painting showed a throne like the high altar of a cathedral standing beneath a vaulted ceiling – a ceiling crossed by countless arches springing from thick-set, almost Romanesque columns, encased in polychromic brickwork, encrusted with mosaics, set with lapis lazuli and sardonyx – in a palace which resembled a basilica built in both the Muslim and the Byzantine styles. In the centre of the tabernacle set on the altar, which was approached by a flight of recessed steps in the shape of a semi-circle, the Tetrarch Herod was seated, with a tiara on his head, his legs close together and his hands on his knees … Round about this immobile, statuesque figure, frozen like some Hindu god in a hieratic pose, incense was burning, sending up clouds of vapour through which the fiery gems set in the sides of the throne gleamed like the phosphorescent eyes of wild animals. The clouds rose higher and higher, swirling under the arches of the roof, where the blue smoke mingled with the gold dust of the great beams of sunlight slanting down from the domes. Amid the heady odour of these perfumes, in the overheated atmosphere of the basilica, Salomé slowly glides forward on the points of her toes, her left arm stretched out in a commanding gesture, her right bent back and holding a great lotus-blossom beside her face, while a woman squatting on the floor strums the strings of a guitar. … With a withdrawn, solemn, almost august expression on her face, she begins the lascivious dance, which is to rouse the aged Herod's dormant senses; her breasts rise and fall, the nipples hardening at the touch of her whirling necklaces; the strings of diamonds glitter against her moist flesh; her bracelets, her belts, her rings all spit out fiery sparks; and across her triumphal robe … the jewelled cuirass, of which every chain is a precious stone, seems to be ablaze with little snakes of fire, swarming over the mat flesh, over the tea-rose skin, like gorgeous insects with dazzling shards …' (Huysmans, *Against Nature*, 12).

39 Apparently Moreau found inspiration for the spectral head in a Japanese stamp, which he copied at the Parisian Palace of Industry in 1869.

40 Huysmans, *Against Nature*, 68.
41 Bach, *Women, Seduction, and Betrayal in Biblical Narrative*, 222.
42 Conrad, *Romantic Opera*, 160.
43 Conrad, *Romantic Opera*, 145.
44 Oscar Wilde, quoted in Gary Schmidgall, *Literature as Opera* (Oxford: Oxford University Press, 1977), 263.
45 Schmidgall, *Literature as Opera*, 263.
46 To illustrate the atmosphere of the day, in his 1895 burlesque play *Earl Lavander*, John Davidson has one of the characters remark in derision, 'It's *fang-de-seeaycle* that does it, my dear, and education, and reading French'; while another character retorts, 'I knew a woman who read French, and she ran away from her husband, and died of consumption. For it's the language. My husband says it's rotten and corrupt, and he ought to know, being a chemist by examination.' See John Davidson, *A Full and True Account of the Wonderful Mission of Earl Lavender: Which Lasted One Night and One Day* (London: Ward and Downey, 1895), 68, 73.
47 Wilde, *Salomé*, 11–12.
48 For an elegant analysis of the relationship between Wilde's text and the Song of Songs, see Bach, *Women, Seduction and Betrayal in Biblical Narrative*, 235–39.
49 Named after Prince Anatole Demidoff, who in the nineteenth century had the altarpiece framed as one, while in his collection.
50 Latin, 'Behold the Lamb of God who takes away the sin of the world' (John 1:29).
51 Jean Paul Richter, *The Literary Works of Leonardo da Vinci* (London: OUP, 1939); Martin Kemp, 'From Mimesis to "Fantasia": The Quattrocento Vocabulary of Creation, Inspiration, and Genius in the Visual Arts', *Viator* 8 (1977), 347–98.
52 Quoted in Fredrika H. Jacobs, *Defining the Renaissance* Virtuosa: *Women Artists and the Language of Art History and Criticism* (Cambridge: Cambridge University Press, 1997), 44.
53 Vincenzo Danti, *Il primo libro del trattato delle perfette proporzioni*, in Paola Barocchi (ed.), *Scritti d'arte del cinquecento*, 3 vols. (Milan, 1971–76), vol.1 (1960), 241.
54 Jacobs, *Defining the Renaissance* Virtuosa, 46.
55 Jacques Derrida, *Glas*, trans. J. P. Leavey, Jr and R. Rand (Lincoln, NE: University of Nebraska Press, 1986), 207.
56 Jacques Derrida, 'Edmond Jabès and the Question of the Book', in *Writing and Difference* (London: Routledge, 1990), 64–78 (65).
57 Auguste Rodin, Paul Gsell, *Rodin on Art and Artists: Conversations with Paul Gsell* (Courier Dover Publications, 1983), 11.
58 Gsell, *Rodin on Art and Artists*, 11.
59 Gsell, *Rodin on Art and Artists*, 21.
60 Jacobs, *Defining the Renaissance* Virtuosa, 49.
61 Gsell, *Rodin on Art and Artists*, 11.
62 Henry Dujardin-Beaumetz, *Entretiens avec Rodin* (Paris: Dupont, 1913).
63 Wilde, *Salomé*, 11–12.
64 Wilde, *Salomé*, 12, 36: 'Ich habe deine Mund geküsst, Jochanaan!'.
65 See further Conrad, *Romantic Opera*, 164–65.
66 Huysmans, *Against Nature*, 65–66.
67 Bach, *Women, Seduction, and Betrayal in Biblical Narrative*, 228–29.
68 Heinrich Heine, *Atta Troll and Other Poems*, trans. T. S. Egan (London: Chapman & Hall, 1876).

# 6

# FRAMING A HEROINE: JUDITH'S COUNTERPARTS IN BIBLICAL VILLAINS

Andrea Sheaffer

In 1901, Viennese Symbolist painter Gustav Klimt (1862–1918) enters his new work in the tenth Vienna Secession art exhibit (Figure 6.1).[1] Klimt's painting presents a supremely powerful, erotic, triumphant and fatal woman. Surrounded in gold decadence, a dangerously sexual woman gazes upon the viewer with fingers clenching the hair of a man's disembodied head. With dreamy eyes barely open and lips parted, art historians have compared Judith's expression of rapture to Italian Baroque sculptor Gian Lorenzo Bernini's (1598–1680) *The Ecstasy of St Theresa*, but her sexual climax takes on an entirely sinister note because it appears to be achieved at the expense, or death, of her partner (Figure 6.2).[2]

Although Klimt's portrait frame quite clearly identifies the painting's characters as 'Judith with the Head of Holofernes', within a few years, journals, critics and exhibition catalogues reproduced the painting without the identifying frame and Judith was consistently mislabelled as or mistaken for Salome. Art historian Alessandra Comini comments on the misidentification:

> People simply could not or would not believe that Klimt had intended a portrayal of the pious Jewish widow and courageous heroine of the Apocrypha, who, as Renaissance depictions had always shown, never actually delighted in her dreadful, heaven-directed mission of decapitating the plundering commander of the Assyrian army.[3]

The biblical text is quite clear to point out that the widow Judith remains celibate throughout her mission to save Israel, never compromising her honour while gaining the enemy's trust and later assassinating Holofernes with his own sword.

Salome, on the other hand, is no saviour. Both Mark 6 and Matthew 14 have given Herod's step-daughter notoriety.[4] The influence of Herodias and her daughter Salome upon Herod resulted in the decapitation of John the Baptist, his head brought to Salome on a platter (Mk 6:25; Matt 14:8). The Gospels identify the girl only as the nameless 'daughter of Herodias', but Jewish historian Flavius Josephus

**Figure 6.1** Gustav Klimt, *Judith and the Head of Holofernes*, 1901. Oil on panel, Österreichische Galerie Belvedere, Vienna. Wikimedia Commons.

(c. 37–100 CE) gives her name as 'Salome'.[5] Despite the fact that Josephus does not associate Salome with John the Baptist's death, and the Gospels are clear that Herodias is the person responsible for John's demise, over centuries this young girl has developed into an epitome of the *femme fatale*.[6] Scholars have noted Salome's evolution in the visual arts from a young, innocent acrobatic dancer in the Middle Ages, a seductive beauty in the high Renaissance and Baroque, culminating in her representation as seductive dancer, the archetype of destructive sexuality in Symbolist painting at the turn of the twentieth century.[7] Through a long and complex process of reception and representation of the biblical figure, for many interpreters, Salome became 'the indirect agent of John the Baptist's decapitation and thus a morally negative figure'.[8]

Traditionally, the biblical Judith and Salome resemble one another in only one simple respect: each is responsible for the killing of a man by decapitation.[9] But throughout Klimt's lifetime and beyond, Klimt's *Judith* is listed as *Salome*. The artist's apparent lack of concern over this is underscored by one of his contemporaries who comments quite simply on the painting, 'Judith . . . would be better renamed Salome'.[10] Years ago while researching Judith images I conducted an internet search. Like many of Klimt's contemporaries, I first saw the painting without the identifying frame and thought I was viewing Salome. My curiosity began with this painting, and I soon found several others in which artists portray Judith in exact likeness with notorious biblical villains: Salome and Delilah.

**Figure 6.2** Gian Lorenzo Bernini, *Ecstasy of Saint Teresa,* 1647–52. White marble, Cornaro Chapel, Santa Maria della Vittoria, Rome. Wikimedia Commons.

We begin our study in northern Europe, moving through the Renaissance comparing German Reform painter Lucas Cranach's (1472–1553) sixteenth-century depictions of Salome and Judith, then venturing to the Baroque with Flemish painter Peter Paul Rubens's (1577–1640) seventeenth-century portrayals of Delilah and Judith, and finally come full-circle back to Klimt and his rendering of Judith. The evolution in Judith art at this time, particularly in northern Europe during the Reformation (c. 1517–1648) is especially relevant to the topic of Judith and biblical villains, as this period witnessed a dramatic shift in Judith imagery. Depictions of Judith underwent a transformation from the conventional medieval iconography portraying her as a paragon of chastity – at times even as the Virgin Mary – to a more dangerous, deadly or erotic Judith, aligning her with other biblical *femmes fatales.*[11] The Bibles of the Reformation and Counter-Reformation – Luther's Bible devoid of Apocrypha and the Catholic Vulgate, in which the Apocrypha is considered sacred scripture – was reflected in social and artistic expression. In the visual conflation of Judith with biblical villains Salome and Delilah – figures who use their sexuality to triumph over powerful men – the canvas becomes a window into the society and culture from which it was produced. I propose that the conflation of the heroine and villain blur the line between 'saint' and 'sinner', and reflect societies in which women were often viewed with distrust. Reading the paintings in light of the 'Power of Women' *topos*, a popular literary and artistic theme prevalent especially in early modern Europe, this theme often depicted heroic or wise men dominated by women. I suggest that the 'framing' of Judith as a biblical villain in art underscores Judith's negative traits found in the biblical text, but is even more reflective of the pervasive distrust of women in the artist's social milieus of their day.

German Renaissance painter Lucas Cranach's c. 1530 *Judith with the Head of Holofernes* (Figure 6.3) presents Judith in elaborate contemporary costume, characteristic of Cranach's style as a court painter. Judith is set against a black background, her body in three-quarter length, turned to the left. She is richly clothed

**Figure 6.3** Lucas Cranach, *Judith with the Head of Holofernes*. c. 1530. Oil on linden, 35¼ x 24⅜ ins. (89.5 x 61.9 cm). Rogers Fund, 1911. The Metropolitan Museum of Art, New York, 11.15.

**Figure 6.4** Lucas Cranach, *Salome with Head of St. John Baptist.* c. 1530. Oil on panel. Szepmuveszeti Muzeum, Budapest. Wikimedia Commons.

in a slashed green-sleeve dress with black and white striped bodice, lined with elegantly patterned gold, vegetal motifs. She wears an ornate gold collar with red and green gems, and below that hangs a chain across her chest. Judith's red hair is pulled up under a netted cap of gold thread and a red velvet plumed hat is perched on her head. She wears gloves with multiple gold rings. Her left hand rests on the top of Holofernes' severed head, while her right hand grasps the hilt of the sword. Judith's gaze meets ours, a faint smile plays on her lips. Her fox-like eyes stare at us boldly, taking responsibility for her bloody trophy.

Cranach's *Salome* (Figure 6.4), from around the same period, bears such a startling resemblance to his *Judith* from The Metropolitan Museum of Art that it is nearly impossible to distinguish the two. There are a few differences to note: out Salome's window is a crisp forest, punctuated by a fortress perched on mountainous crags, a scene typical of Saxon landscapes. Salome is afforded an additional gold chain and she is gloveless. Her hand is not touching the severed head of John the Baptist, but supports the platter on which it rests. The two women look so much alike that art historian Erwin Panofsky famously used the pair to discuss what he called, 'the history of types', a means for distinguishing figures – in this case Judith and Salome – expressed by objects, themes and concepts.[12] In the case of the Cranach paintings, Panofsky posits that although they are practically identical, we can distinguish Judith from Salome because although there is a history of Judith with a head on a platter, there is no history or 'type' of Salome with a sword.

Why did Cranach paint Judith and Salome as identical, leaving us only Judith's sword to distinguish their identities? What can be inferred from the artist's choice to depict Israel's saviour as one of the Bible's villains? It is here that I suggest that we read the canvas in light of the society and culture from which it was produced in order to uncover possible answers.

At the time Cranach was working, the *Weibermacht*, or so-called 'Power of Women' *topos*, was a group of themes in literature and the fine arts that focussed on women who used their sexuality to triumph over men.[13] Especially popular in northern Europe, the 'Power of Women' imagery was one of the most prevalent themes of the day, the motifs and recurring stories were popular in literature, and images could be found on tapestries, enamels and furniture and in choir stalls.[14] Stories often involved biblical or classical subjects but the thrust of each was that 'women overcame men who were prominent, accomplished, or heroic'.[15] Comedic subjects like that of the peasant woman fighting with her husband over a pair of pants (symbolizing control of the household) or perhaps the most popular story of Aristotle and Phyllis, were common examples. In a woodcut by the late fifteenth-century German artist Hans Burgkmair, the famed philosopher Aristotle (Figure 6.5), who was deceived into serving as a beast of burden for Phyllis, is shown abjectly down on all fours, after having lusted after Phyllis.[16] H. Diane Russell notes that during the Renaissance and Baroque periods, men 'were considered to have the capacity for the highest forms of reason. The humiliation of Aristotle, paradigmatic man of reason, clearly conveys the dangers of women.'[17]

In the early sixteenth century, many of these 'Power of Women' subjects were treated together as a series, showcasing both virtuous and villainous women. For example, Judith was included in Burgkmair's 'Eighteen Worthies Series,' woodcuts depicting Judith alongside the virtuous Esther and Jael (Figure 6.6). But the most striking detail about these 'Power of Women' series, is that virtuous heroines and villainous seductresses were also lumped together into the same category. For example, Frederick the Wise, a patron of Cranach himself, commissioned a suit of armour etched with several 'Power of Women' themes.[18] Although Frederick's armour does not survive, we know from records that the décor on the armour featured not only the so-called women worthies and their male counterparts like Judith with Holofernes, but also women of negative reputation, such as Phyllis with Aristotle, and Delilah with Samson. Art historian Andrew Weislogel notes that the inclusion of these women was not seen as a protective power for the armour-wearer, but 'indicates a desire to keep a reminder of women's cunning constantly before him, lest he fall prey to them and thus the governance of society be jeopardized'.[19]

The story of Phyllis and Aristotle was one of the most popular themes in the 'Power of Women' *topos* and many northern artists captured Phyllis's use of her sexuality to literally bring Aristotle to his knees. Only a few years before Cranach painted his *Judith* and *Salome*, German engraver Barthel Beham completed his interpretation of Judith and Holofernes (Figure 6.7). Beham's engraving depicts a

**Figure 6.5** Hans Burgkmair, *Aristotle and Phyllis*, c. 1500. Woodcut; first state of two (Hollstein), sheet: 4⅞ x 3 15/16 ins. (12.4 x 10 cm). Harris Brisbane Dick Fund, 1931. The Metropolitan Museum of Art, 31.58.8.

nude Judith who sits on top of Holofernes' body. His head is wrenched out of its natural location as his hair is yanked back, his mane used as a grotesque bridle. This depiction of Judith is drastically different from the biblical narrative; Beham's *Judith* is instead an amalgam of the popular Phyllis and Aristotle story depicted by so many artists of the time, and the powerful female figure of Judith. Portrayals by popular artists such as Hans Baldung Grien who depict a nude Phyllis riding Aristotle doubtless had influence over the way Beham portrayed Judith.[20] Beham's Judith has wild hair that unravels in untamed curls, and the sword now serves as her riding crop to prod her lifeless beast. Judith's un-textual nudity in the engraving makes clear that her sexuality played a role in her victim's demise. The message here is clear: Judith's triumph over Holofernes is a warning to male viewers that, no matter how wise or powerful they may be, female sexuality is a dangerous and even deadly trait, and women will come out 'on top'.

Perhaps one of the clearest manifestations of Judith as a cautionary symbol of women's sexuality is seen in a Dutch print after Lucas van Leyden titled *Prostitution*.[21] In this mid-sixteenth century print, the sinfulness of lust is depicted

**Figure 6.6** Hans Burgkmair, *Hesther, Judith, Jael* (from *The Eighteen Worthies* series), 1519. Woodcut, image: 19 x 13.1 cm (7½ x 5³⁄₁₆ ins.), sheet: 21 x 13.8 cm (8¼ x 5⁷⁄₁₆ ins.). Hollsein no. 250. Rosenwald Collection, 1944.8.51. Courtesy of the National Gallery of Art, Washington.

in the foreground, represented by a naked prostitute who is fondled by her patron at the foot of a large, canopied bed. Deftly stealing from her customer, the woman pays her pimp, while a court jester and Death look on from their respective sides of the room. Looming in the background on the bed's headboard stands a triumphant Judith, holding the head of Holofernes and sword – thereby linking Judith, the heroine, with the whore.[22]

Returning to Cranach's paintings and bearing in mind the prevalent 'Power of Women' *topos* of the day it becomes clear, writes art historian Elena Ciletti, that 'the dramatically different circumstances and motivations of these two biblical characters, not to mention the results of their actions, are erased in favour

**Figure 6.7** Barthel Beham, *Judith Seated on the Body of Holofernes*, 1525. Engraving, Paul 'Barthel', no. 3. Rosenwald Collection, 1943.3.886. Courtesy of the National Gallery of Art, Washington.

of a presumed deeper truth: that whenever women exert power over men, it is by definition sexual and lethal'.[23] But a key theme that Ciletti touches on is also important here – erasure – and Cranach's conflation highlights a textual point often overlooked or *erased* in favour of a more salacious story. Judith 13:16 is very clear in stating that Judith's *face* seduced her victim, but she had no physical sexual contact with him, remaining celibate. Like Judith, Salome had no sexual contact with Herod, the text indicating only that her mysterious (and now infamous) dance 'pleased' Herod and his guests, the word being the Greek *aresko.*

Cranach's identical figures recall parallels and the story of Salome 'inverts the moral of Judith: Salome brings the…wicked to a (momentary) victory', while Judith brings them to defeat.[24] The helpless severed heads serve as deadly reminders, making it impossible to forget the dangers of woman. And although cultural memory and popular themes have had influence on the canvas, 'reading' these paintings from our own position can also engage us better with the biblical text.

In the Baroque period, we are presented with another conflation of Judith with a biblical villain: Delilah from Judges 16. Flemish artist Peter Paul Rubens's 1610 *Samson and Delilah* (Figure 6.8) depicts the quiet but dramatic moment just before Samson's downfall at the hands of his lover, Delilah. Bribed by Philistine leaders to learn the source of Samson's enormous strength, Delilah takes advantage of Samson's love for her and betrays his secret – and eventually his life – for money.

With Samson sleeping soundly on her lap, Delilah oversees the shearing of his locks, an act that will render him impotent before his enemies. Delilah looks down upon Samson, her creamy, round flesh and blond curls illuminated more by the lamp behind her than her maid's candle. Her bare, jutting breasts suggest her sexual duplicity. Though not in the biblical text, the old crone is especially common in Netherlandish pictures in the sixteenth century and is commonly understood as a procuress for her mistress. Mary Garrard suggests that the maid's depiction as an old servant could be understood subliminally as that of a procuress, an agent of her mistresses' sexuality.[25] In her article on this painting, Madeline Kahr notes further that Rubens's *Samson and Delilah* is 'related to the brothel scenes favoured especially by northern printmakers in the sixteenth century and later followers of the great Italian Renaissance painter Caravaggio (1571–1610) in the seventeenth century'.[26] Proffering her body for money, Delilah is the embodiment of 'men's

**Figure 6.8** Peter Paul Rubens, *Samson and Delilah*. c. 1609–10. Oil on wood, 185 x 205 cm. Bought 1980. NG6461. Courtesy of The National Gallery, London.

deep-rooted fear of the danger threatened by erotic involvement with a woman'; she represents the essence of the 'Power of Women' *topos*.[27]

About twenty years after *Samson and Delilah*, Rubens completes one of the most powerful and dangerous depictions of Judith. Art historian Mary Garrard calls it 'the most unforgettable evil of Judith art' before the nineteenth century.[28] *Judith with the Head of Holofernes* (Figure 6.9) presents us with the kind of seductress the 'Power of Women' *topos* has warned about for centuries now. Through her gaze and militant gesture, Judith looks menacingly out at us. Her thick, masculine forearms recall the brute strength needed to accomplish her grisly deed. This Judith is the emasculating virago. Both Delilah and Judith are typical of Flemish seventeenth-century female types. They wear traditional dress and their blonde hair is pinned and curly. But unusual for a virtuous saint of the Bible is Judith's untextual nudity. Like Delilah, Judith's breasts are bare and thrust upward, a visual cue signalling the sexual entrapment of her victim.[29]

Little attention has been given to the striking similarities between not only Delilah and Judith, but also the old maidservant, who continues to light the scene with her trusty candle. Caravaggio's (c. 1598) *Judith Beheading Holofernes* (Figure 6.10) is one of the first paintings to depict the maid as not only old, but hag-like, a trend that developed around the turn of the seventeenth century.

**Figure 6.9** Peter Paul Rubens, *Judith with the Head of Holofernes*. c. 1630. Oil on panel. Herzog Anton Ulrich-Museum, Braunschweig. Wikimedia Commons.

**Figure 6.10** Michelangelo Merisi da Caravaggio, *Judith Beheading Holofernes.* c. 1597–98. Oil on canvas. Galleria nazionale d'arte antica, Rome. Wikimedia Commons.

Much like the two Rubens paintings, in Caravaggio's work the maid's aged and witch-like face is contrasted with Judith's youthful and innocent appearance. Apprehensively slicing the neck of the nude and brutish Holofernes, Judith's smooth, ivory skin and stark-white blouse radiate purity. Judith is portrayed as a virtuous young woman whose assassination of a lust-filled tyrant is justified; the maid is Judith's antithesis.

Both Garrard and Kahr suggest the old maid's presence signals that she is a procuress for her mistress. This theory holds true of depictions of Judith with her maid primarily from northern Europe, in which Protestant artists and patrons were far less concerned with Judith's saintliness than were their Catholic neighbours to the south. It is more probable that Italian representations of the maidservant represented her as protector rather than procuress, because of the almost saintly veneration of Judith by Catholics at this time.[30] Like Caravaggio's rendering, many paintings depict the aged maid alongside Judith in Holofernes's bedchamber; the maidservant is a safeguard of chastity for the immaculate Judith.

However, in Rubens's works, the presence of the old maid in Holofernes's dark, cavernous tent links Judith to Delilah further: like Delilah, Judith's sexuality is being proffered for mercenary motives. The similarities between canvases also illuminate textual comparisons: Delilah's undoing of Samson has close parallels to Judith and her destruction of Holofernes. Both women use their sexuality to seduce and deceive their foes, and the acts of 'cutting' bring about the men's mortal demise. Rubens paints the men as slumbering innocents, reminding us that they are the victims of duplicitous women.[31]

Over 400 years between the height of the 'Power of Women' *topos* and Klimt's time has passed but the theme of the fatally seductive woman remains. The image of Judith changed gradually over time from a paragon of chastity and courage to a sexual and dangerous *femme fatale*, a transformation that was well underway in the sixteenth, seventeenth and eighteenth centuries.[32] Unlike Judith, who inspired a virtually steady stream of works from the Renaissance through the modern period, it was not until the nineteenth century that artists revived Salome's story and developed it with unprecedented zeal. 'First through poetry and prose, and through drama, and finally through the visual arts, Salome became almost an obsession' during Klimt's time.[33]

Perhaps the most important contribution to the rejuvenated interest in Salome in the nineteenth century can be attributed to French novelist Gustave Flaubert (1821–80). Fascinated by the Orient and influenced heavily by his travels to Egypt, Flaubert's personal experiences merge with the biblical tradition in his 1877 short novel, *Herodias*.[34] The culmination of the story is the impassioned description of Salome's sensual dance before Herod's guests: 'With eyes half closed, she twisted her waist, made her belly ripple like the swell of the sea, made her breasts quiver, while her expression remained fixed, and her feet never stood still'.[35] The vivid account of Salome's lascivious dance and the resultant beheading of John the Baptist anticipates the subsequent literary and visual representations of Salome as the ultimate *femme fatale*.

The stories of Judith and Salome were taken up by playwrights and composers. Friedrich Hebbel's 1840 drama *Judith* and later Oscar Wilde's 1891 *Salomé* began exploring the motivations and personalities of the characters, each giving radically new interpretation to the biblical text: that decapitation results from a sexually related act of revenge by a woman.[36] In both plays the women decapitate the men, but contrary to the biblical texts, Judith seeks revenge on Holofernes after he rapes her, and Salomé orders John's execution after he rejects her sexual advances. Art historian Nadine Sine's declaration concerning depictions of both Judith and Salome during Klimt's time sounds remarkably similar to sentiments expressed during the height of the *Weibermacht topos*. She writes: 'As [these artistic works] proclaim, turn-of-the-century woman was perceived by the men who observed and painted her as a purely sensual being, and because [of this]… she was also dangerous'.[37] These interpretations were of course not limited only to Europe: an American writer in the early twentieth century remarks:

> The cool ferocity of some young women is awful. Judith, Jael, Delilah, and Athaliah were not mythical. Is there a man who has not wakened from his dreams to find that the woman he trusted has stolen his strength or is just about to hammer the great nail through his temples?[38]

Viewed in light of the socio-cultural attitudes of the periods in which they were produced, it is clear that Judith has been 'framed', thrust into the category of the *dangerous woman* alongside her notorious biblical villain compatriots. But in conflating Judith with Salome and Delilah, the canvases and the cultural memory etched onto them paint the heroine as a complex, multifaceted, and contradictory character, supported by the text: Judith is a powerful widow; a lying liberator; a seductive celibate. Judith is compared – quite fairly – to Salome and Delilah because she, too, is an archetype for destructive femininity; Judith *is* the 'powerful woman' we both fear and cheer.

## *Notes*

1 The exhibit was organized and sponsored by the Vienna Secession, also known as the Union of Austrian Artists. See Nadine Sine, 'Cases of Mistaken Identity: Salome and Judith at the Turn of the Century', *German Studies Review* 11 (1988): 9.
2 Alessandra Comini, *Gustav Klimt* (New York: G. Braziller, 1975), 22.
3 Comini, *Klimt*, 22.
4 The narrative appears in Matt 14:1–12; Mk 6:17–29.
5 Josephus, *Antiquities of the Jews* 18.5.4.
6 Both Matthew's (14:11) and Mark's (6:28) Gospels use the term *korasion*, 'girl'.
7 For further discussion on the evolution of Salome in the visual arts and corresponding societal attitudes, see Diane Apostolos-Cappadonna, 'Imagining Salome, or How *la sauterelle* became *la femme fatale*', in *From the Margins 2: Women of the New Testament and their Afterlives*, ed. Christine E. Joynes and Christopher C. Rowland (Sheffield: Sheffield Phoenix Press, 2009), 190–209.
8 Mary Garrard, *Artemisia Gentileschi: The Image of the Hero in Italian Baroque Art* (Princeton: Princeton University Press, 1989), 292.
9 Sine, 'Cases of Mistaken Identity', 9.
10 See quote in Comini, *Klimt*, 29.
11 For discussions on Judith images in both northern Europe and the Catholic south during the Reformation period, see Elena Ciletti, 'Patriarchal Ideology in the Renaissance Iconography of Judith', in *Refiguring Woman: Perspectives on Gender and the Italian Renaissance*, ed. Marilyn Migiel and Juliana Schiasari (Ithaca: Cornell University Press, 1991), 35–70; Elena Ciletti, 'Judith Imagery as Catholic Orthodoxy in Counter-Reformation Italy', in *The Sword of Judith: Judith Studies across the Disciplines*, ed. Kevin R. Brine, Elena Ciletti and Henrike Lähnemann (Cambridge: Open Book Publishers, 2010), 345–70.
12 Erwin Panofsky, *Studies in Iconology: Humanistic Themes in the Art of the Renaissance* (New York: Oxford Press, 1939), 12–13.
13 H. Diane Russell, *Eva/Ave: Women in Renaissance and Baroque Prints* (Washington, DC: National Gallery of Art, 1990), 147.
14 Ibid.
15 Ibid.
16 The story of Phyllis and Aristotle has its origins in the writings of the thirteenth-century scholar Jacques de Vitry. In the sixteenth century it became popular as an illustration of the triumph of female seduction over masculine intellect.
17 Russell, *Eva/Ave*, 17.
18 Discussed in Andrew C. Weislogel, *Lucas Cranach's Judith and Lucretia: Fashioning Women in the Northern Renaissance* (Ithaca, NY: Herbert F. Johnson Museum of Art, Cornell University, 2005), 24.

19 Ibid.
20 See Hans Baldung Grien, *Aristotle and Phyllis*, 1513. Woodcut. *The Illustrated Bartsch*, vol. 12. Germanisches Nationalmuseum, Nuremburg.
21 After Lucas van Leyden, *Prostitution*, c. mid-sixteenth century. Print. Courtesy the Warburg Institute.
22 Elena Ciletti has brilliantly pointed out the appearance of Judith in this print and the connection with prostitution implied in the work; see the discussion in 'Patriarchal Ideology in the Renaissance Iconography of Judith,' 50.
23 Ibid.
24 Marina Warner, *Monuments and Maidens: The Allegory of the Female Form* (Berkeley: University of California Press, 2000), 167.
25 Garrard, *Artemisia Gentileschi*, 298.
26 Madlyn Kahr, 'Delilah', *Art Bulletin*, 54:3 (Sept. 1972), 296.
27 Ibid.
28 Garrard, *Artemisia Gentileschi*, 297.
29 The Book of Judith is clear that Judith uses her beauty to seduce her foe: 12:15–16; 13:16.
30 Ciletti, 'Patriarchal Ideology', 42.
31 In Judith 9 the heroine prays that she can use deceit to defeat her enemy and Judith lies repeatedly to Holofernes. For a few examples of Judith's lies, see Jdt 10:13; 11:5–6.
32 See Garrard's fine study of Judith in art, literature and theology, *Artemisia Gentileschi*, 280–302.
33 Sine, 'Cases of Mistaken Identity', 11–12.
34 Flaubert's interactions with Arab women, as well as his relationship with Kutchuk Hanem, his female companion while in Cairo, were influential in his writing, particularly in the description of Salome's erotic dance. See Udo Kultermann, 'The "Dance of the Seven Veils". Salome and Erotic Culture around 1900', *Artibus et historiae: rivista internazionale di arti visive e cinema*, 27:53 (2006), 190.
35 Ibid., 190–91.
36 Friedrich Hebbel, '*Judith: Eine Tragödie in Fünf Akten*', quoted in Edna Purdie, *The Story of Judith in German and English Literature* (Paris: H. Champion, 1927), 94–104; Oscar Wilde, *Salome: A Tragedy in One Act*, trans. Lord Alfred Douglas (New York: Dover Publications, 1967).
37 Sine, 'Cases of Mistaken Identity', 16.
38 Quote from novelist Francis Marion Crawford in *Soprano* (London: Macmillan & Co., 1905), quoted in Herbert Pentin, *Judith. The Apocrypha in English Literature* (London: Samuel Bagster and Sons, 1908), 68.

7

# BIBLICAL ELEGY AND *QUATTROCENTO* MARIAN ENCOMIUM: MARCANTONIO SABELLICO'S *CARMINA DE BEATA VIRGINE MARIA*

John Nassichuk

As a newcomer to the Venetian Republic in the 1480s, the Humanist from Vicovaro, Marcantonio Sabellico (1436–1506), made a name for himself among scholars and patrons, as well as a lucrative career as official historiographer, teacher of rhetoric in the San Marco schools and, finally, head librarian at the *Biblioteca marciana*. His celebrated history of Venice, dedicated to the Doge and the Venetian Senate, was published in 1487 and marked the beginning of a successful series of prose works on 'Venice or subjects of interest to Venetian rulers', many of which were dedicated to important local patricians.[1] Aside from this masterwork that inspired Pietro Bembo's vernacular prose version and lengthy continuation, Sabellico published an important collection of moral *exempla* in ten books, entitled *Exemplorum libri decem*, which became an editorial success Europe-wide, as well as several essays on philological themes.[2] All of these works, including Sabellico's voluminuous correspondence and his poetry, appear in the monumental, four-volume 1560 Basel edition organized by Caelius Secundus Curio.[3] Yet, despite his impressive stature among contemporaries and his seminal contribution to the literary corpus of Venetian humanism, Sabellico has to date received only scant attention from academic historians and critics.[4] One work which has seldom attracted commentary thus far is the curious little collection of thirteen elegies, written as a cycle in honour of the Virgin, which appears in the Basel edition under the title *Elegiae tredecim de Beata Virgine Maria*. This chapter is intended to mark a modest beginning in the correction of this oversight, by offering, first, a general overview of the elegiac sequence by way of introduction and, second, a more detailed examination of the Humanist's treatment of the *genethliacon* theme celebrating Mary's birth. A third and final section shall then be devoted to a brief description and analysis of the collection's second elegy, wherein Sabellico tries his hand at biblical poetry *per se*, elaborating an encomium of the Virgin's familial genealogy based on historical narrative from the books of Kings and of Chronicles.

The choice of the elegiac genre as a medium of Marian praise, by a Humanist who is clearly familiar with that poetic form's celebrated erotic pre-Christian antecedents, is in itself a curious innovation, which aptly reflects Latin elegy's remarkable thematic expansion under the plume of *Quattrocento* poets such as Giovanni Pontano in Naples, Enea Silvio Piccolomini in Siena and Cristoforo Landino in Florence. Several passages in Sabellico's collection may be read as a conscious Christianizing accommodation of ancient elegiac sources. Indeed, the birthday celebration topic, which constitutes the object of the first elegy, may be said to include poems of Tibullus, Propertius and Ovid among its primary generic models. As for the Marian theme as a privileged object of the Humanist's praise, there is little in Sabellico's published oeuvre to suggest a predilection for devotional poetry, other than perhaps the numerous references to Mary and other biblical figures in the *Exemplorum libri decem.* Neither the 1560 Basel edition of the *Opera omnia*, nor the 1513 Paris edition published by Jean de Gourmont contains any detailed explanatory preface revealing the author's intention in constructing a sequence of thirteen rather richly woven elegiac hymns in honour of Jesus' mother. If Sabellico's publication tendencies during his lengthy tenure in Venice may be taken as a parallel, it would seem reasonable to believe that the collection was composed for the private devotions of a patrician dedicatee, although none is explicitly named within the poems themselves. Even though Mary was a frequent addressee of public ceremonial worship in Italy during the Late Middle Ages, Venice's Festival of the Twelve Marys was formally abolished in 1379, due in part, it would seem, to the inherent incompatibility of this solemn ritual and the Bacchic Carnival season during which it took place.[5] The continuation of a more modest version of this annual event does allow for the possibility of some connection between Sabellico's work and the existence of a local ritual tradition in adoration of the Virgin Mary.

Sabellico's collection of elegies may be examined as an important instance of Renaissance biblical reception in both the Venetian and the wider European contexts. Before the advent of Paolo Veronese's spectacular contribution to the collective oeuvre of painted biblical narrative series during the middle of the sixteenth century, most notably through the remarkable scenes still visible in Venice's San Sebastiano church, this technique of public representation accorded to biblical story and genealogy occupied a central place in the Venetian churchgoer's visual experience, as evidenced by the celebrated Genesis cycle in the atrium of the Basilica San Marco,[6] as well as the Life of the Virgin represented on the west bays of both the south and the west transepts.[7] Thus, indelibly (and visually) stamped on the citizen's historical consciousness, pictorial sequences recounting the procession of generations leading from Eve to Mary undoubtedly constitute a powerful conditioning element of biblical reception both in the Venetian republic and elsewhere. On the literary side, Venice's unique status during this period as Europe's capital for the burgeoning field of Greek humanism made it a veritable cauldron of intellectual activity and the receiving house of a great variety of texts – biblical, apocryphal and classical.[8] Nicolas Jenson's Venetian printing operation produced at least two editions of the Latin Bible in 1476 and 1479, as well as an early edition of Antonio Cornazzano's *Vita della Vergine* (1471) and at least two runs of the *Officium Beatae Virginis* (1474, 1475).[9] Although Sabellico's elegiac cycle is heavily indebted to apocryphal sources, it is nevertheless also, as we shall see in our analysis of the collection's second elegy, the site of a thoroughgoing attempt at biblical poetic paraphrase.

Here it is also worth mentioning that the elegy as a poetic form represents something of an exotic new arrival in Venetian humanism, if indeed Sabellico did, as seems likely, compose this *opus* during his considerable career as a well-paid servant of the Most Serene Republic. Whereas nearly every major Italian city-state can boast of an elegiac poet of some renown during the *Quattrocento*, including Basinio Basini at Parma and Tito Strozzi in Ferrara, only Pietro Contarini's little-known collection entitled *Ad Gelliam*, still available only in manuscript at the Marciana,[10] may serve (to our knowledge) as a Venetian contribution to the genre's fifteenth-century Italian renaissance. Whatever its genesis may have been, the *Carmina de Beata Virgine Maria* are most certainly the result of an effort at creative syncretism, as the learned poet displays both his technical facility in the confection of elegiac distichs, and the breadth of learning which permits him to meld together such diverse lexical resources as Old Testament narrative and ancient erotic elegy. Sabellico's accomplishment is of considerable historical moment, insofar as it represents a very early stage of what shall become, during the sixteenth and seventeenth centuries, a tradition of sacred verse destined to elaborate a rich (extant) corpus of Marian praise in Latin elegiacs. Indeed, early sixteenth-century authors of individual Marian encomia composed in Latin distichs, such as Quinziano Stoa, Guillaume Du Bellay and Martin Conrard, often seem to be following the lead of *Quattrocento* elegists such as Sabellico and his Milanese contemporary Giovanni Biffi.[11]

## *The* Carmina de Beata Virgine Maria*: An Overview*

Sabellico's thirteen elegies to the Virgin Mary first appeared in late *incunabula*, the most important of which is the one published at Deventer in 1498, accompanied by the poetry of Gregorius Tifernatus and a commentary by Hermannus Torrentinus.[12] Unlike Contarini's *Ad Gelliam*, the *Carmina* seem to have gained a certain notoriety outside of Venice and indeed outside of Italy, as the 1513 edition produced by Jean de Gourmont's Parisian presses well attests.[13] In each text, the thirteen poems appear in an identical linear order, beginning with five elegies in which the author refers constantly to Mary's nativity, a theme increasingly celebrated during the later Middle Ages when much theological speculation was exercised upon the theory of Mary's own Immaculate Conception.[14] The sequence's opening piece is a sumptuous seventy-six-verse *genethliacon* celebrating the day of the Virgin's birth, followed by a shorter poem praising her distinguished genealogical origins. Next is a detailed, sixty-verse description, in language reminiscent of the Augustan poets, of the proper ritual to be followed when offering a sacrifice before the altar of Mary. The fourth elegy then offers a long paean to the town of Bethlehem described as the Virgin's 'birthplace', in which Sabellico develops a parallel between the natural fertility of the region's soil and that of the Virgin herself. Finally, in the fifth poem, which concludes what may be described as the collection's first section, devoted to the theme of the time and place of Mary's birth, the poet exhorts other Humanists, such as Pontano and Filelfo, to devote their talents to composing sacred verse, especially in honour of the Saviour's Holy Mother. These five pieces, which clearly form a cohesive thematic unit, constitute a grand opening encomium. They also provide the textual object of the present study. As for the eight remaining elegies, they contain praise of Mary's virginity (elegy VI), a narration of her presentation in the Temple (elegy VII), an account of her preaching and reasoning in the Temple (elegy VIII), a seventy-six-verse description of her triumphal chariot (elegy IX), a sixty-eight-verse narration of the Triumph itself (elegy X), an account of the 'causes' of the Annunciation (elegy XI), a defence of the Catholic faith against the pagans (elegy XII) and a final hymn of praise addressed to the Virgin (XIII). Altogether, this sequence falls into a carefully organized linear ensemble, wherein each part addresses a particular aspect of Mary's persona which is complementary to the whole. For our present purposes, the first two elegies of the collection form a remarkable opening thematic juxtaposition, which merits more detailed scrutiny than what this summary overview has been able to provide. The following analysis shall attempt to describe in some informative detail, first, the apocryphal theme of Mary's birth centred around the collection's opening elegy; second, the more biblical theme of Mary's (and Christ's) genealogy, grounded upon the opening chapter of the book of Matthew, which Sabellico addresses in considerable detail – even amplifying it – in the second elegy by adducing elements of Old Testament narrative borrowed from Kings and Chronicles.

## *Mary's Day: Elegies I, IV and V*

The collection's first elegy is a sixty-two-verse poem in which the author celebrates the birth of Mary herself; singing in the hymnic mode, Sabellico addresses the entire poem to praise of the venerable day. Opening a sequence of poems wherein mention of the Virgin's nascence is a central motif, this first one begins appropriately with the joyous exclamation that her day is fast arriving. All of Creation, exclaims the poet in the elegy's first distich, praises the coming of an anniversary which resonates majestically throughout the lands, the seas and the heavens. The very day, he further explains, shows itself in Nature to be "conscious of the celestial birth" (*coelestis conscia partus*), and the young girl to whom Nature shows such deference fully deserves the glorious reception that the entire universe has reserved in her honour. This centrality of the nativity motif in a cycle of poems dedicated to the praise of Mary certainly reflects the important influence of apocryphal sources such as the *Protevangelium of James*[15] (or indeed Cornazzano's *Vita della vergine* in *terza rima*), but it also provides evidence for the topical status of Virgil's fourth eclogue in Venetian Humanist poetry, as L. B. T. Houghton has well remarked in a recent article.[16]

Whatever its immediate literary source, this birth has long been the object of poetic praise, suggests Sabellico, for at this momentous event even the sibyls raised their voices in celebration. In a fashion similar to that of Baptista Mantuanus, whose poems of Christian praise frequently display a richly detailed knowledge of Greco-Roman mythology, the author does not hesitate to evoke several figures from the rich and varied pre-Christian Pantheon of natural divinities. First, the arrival of Lucifer, the morning star traditionally associated with Venus, puts the pagan world on notice that the incoming day shall also usher in a new world order. The poet here declares that the diurnal phase's celestial harbinger shines brighter than usual at the birth of this strange and momentous day.[17] Even the darkened underworld senses the imminence of a great advent.[18] Then Phoebus himself, as he rises above the ocean, perceives a radiant glow of unusual brightness:

Cynthius oceano nitidum cum tolleret arcem
  Et matutinis surgeret actus equis,
Vidit ut insolito radiantem lumine mundum,
  Numine nonnullo sensit adesse diem:
Quid cunctamur ait, tantos ne morabimur ortus?
  Nascere iam fas est, nascere sancta dies.[19]

Such unwonted celestial brilliance indeed seems to portend an event of extraordinary rarity, for it manifests itself with a great flash as soon as it breaks through darkness in the far Orient (*extremis...Indis*, v. 23). On this day, no storm clouds appear on the horizon, and birds of spring do not entrust themselves to the hazards of the winds, preferring to stay perched at home and bring forth joyous songs. Throughout all of Creation, predatory animals such as lions and wolves leave the hunt and refrain from conflict of any sort. Aggressive sea-beasts (*phocae*) quit the waters and sun themselves peaceably upon the adjacent shores; indeed, things are so tranquil that perhaps even the Stygian ferry remains idle on this day (vv. 24–31). The enthusiastic poet exclaims that the underworld itself, 'pale Orcus' (*pallidus . . . Orcus*), would have preferred to close up shop, if this were possible, and to accept no new shadows at its gates (32–34).

All of Nature thus makes way for a great arrival, one that is to usher in a new beginning in this world created by God, which mankind has foolishly tainted with sin. Having set the scene for Mary's birth through his description of Nature's obedient and joyous celebration of the coming event, Sabellico then apostrophizes the Holy Virgin's mother, Anne, declaring that such indeed was the day upon which the woman destined to be Jesus' Mother came into the world:

Haec est illa tui sacri lux conscia partus
  Anna parens tantae virginis, Anna parens;
Foelix cui matri mater veneranda tonantis,
  Annuit aethereo suspicienda throno:
Illinc maternos vultus miratur, et ulnas,
  Et quae se totiens sustinuere manus.[20]

In these verses, Sabellico seems to hint at a spiritual, pre-natal complicity between Mary and her own mother, one that mirrors the complex relationship subsisting between the divine, eternal Jesus and his chosen but earthly *genitrix*. As he evokes this relationship of joyous sympathy that links the heavenly and terrestrial maternal figures, the Humanist Christian poet describes a kind of crystallizing moment, as if this mutual, feminine contemplation of the celestial and the fleshly mothers had manifested itself, in Nature, by the unmistakeable advent of a 'conscious day' (*lux conscia*), one which affirms itself sympathetic to the harmonious and sacred conjoining of divine love and human admiration.[21]

These verses mentioning the maternal figure of Anne constitute in effect the culminating point of the elegy's development, in which the Holy Virgin's birthday is recognized to be at once a cosmic event reflected in Nature, and a moment of spiritual significance worthy of ritual commemoration. In the wake of this image of spiritual harmony and sympathy between heaven and earth, realized in the mutual gaze of each realm's feminine inhabitants, the elegy's final six distichs formulate a conventional peroration reminiscent of the ancient hymnic tradition which extends itself, with some variation, from Homer to Marullus.[22] Sabellico adduces a famous Virgilian image, taken from the eighth *Eclogue*, when he issues the traditional poet's promise to repeat, every year henceforth, the ceremonial singing of praise of which these verses represent the inaugural instalment:

> Ipse ego pampineo servatis mensibus anno
>  Virginis ante aras mascula tura dabo:
> Solennemque diem traducam carmine et hymnis,
>  Suspendamque sacro munera nostra tholo:
> Immodicasque preces addam: da virgo quotannis
>  Ipsa tuo vati mystica sacra coli.[23]

As the poet promises to 'suspend [his] offering from the sacred vault', he also announces a yearly renewal of hymnic praise for the Virgin. The scene he evokes through the use of Virgilian echoes is one of ancient, bucolic veneration, here suggesting an attempt to situate the origins of this idealized Marian worship at a time of pristine beginnings and relative innocence. Hence the formula *mascula tura*, or 'male incense', which seems perhaps a curious offering at the shrine of a female virgin, is an expression borrowed from Virgil's eighth Eclogue,[24] here apparently serving as a rustic feature reminiscent of an ancient, pre-urban authenticity. Indeed, the mention of this incense appears in the same pentameter as the genitive *Virginis*, indicating a direct homage and even the submission of male worshippers to Mary under a pagan-like *integumentum* of female divinity. Such direct appeal to pagan themes of primitivism also subtly announces the genealogical research and paraphrase carried out in the second elegy, where Sabellico resorts to Old Testament sources in order both to explain Mary's origins and to illustrate her salutary virtue.

This poem's objective is clearly to establish the solemnity of the celebration attached to Mary's nativity, using encomiastic structures and formulae borrowed from traditional hymns of pre-Christian origin. As such, it serves to foreground the central theme of Sabellico's collection, namely, the singular glory of Mary as an object of devotional veneration. Several other poems make mention of the Virgin's birth, and indeed two are explicitly devoted to the topic. In elegy four, the poet sings the praise of Nazareth, which he identifies as the heavenly Matron's birthplace, thus borrowing another common thematic aspect of ancient encomium. Here again, the complicity of the praised object as it obediently fosters a sacred event is underscored by Sabellico's use of the adjective *conscius*. Whereas in the collection's opening piece this word characterized the temporal moment of Mary's day – *lux conscia* – it is now employed to describe the parcel of soil, the *conscia terra*, upon which her mortal existence began. The poet also suggests a parallel between the fecundity of the soil beneath Bethlehem, and the miraculous fertility of the Virgin herself:

> Clarior una tamen terraque beatior omni:
> Nascentis Dominae conscia terra meae.
> Tu Bethlem summi regis veneranda creatrix,
> Crederis hoc ipsum praeteriisse decus!
> Hanc primam immensi coeli fabricator, et orci
> Factus homo mixto numine pressit humum.
> Haec igitur regum regem tulit illa parentem,
> Utraque terra suo clara puerperio.[25]

These lines illustrate the earthly, even fleshly, vitality of the connection between Mary, her Son and the natural world that is the theatre of their humanity. Sabellico's use of the genitive also subtly points up the delicate and complex relationship of interdependence between Mother (*summi regis…creatrix*) and Son (*immensi coeli fabricator*). Such insistence upon the status of Bethlehem as the conjoining locus of Mary and Jesus and of heaven and earth, is supported in large part by the Humanist poet's recourse to the ancient theme of the praise of one's native region, a commonplace frequently met with in pre-Christian Latinity and often imitated by Renaissance authors.[26]

Finally, the fifth elegy in this collection is perhaps the most conspicuously 'metatextual' piece of the entire ensemble, for the author addresses its forty-eight verses to his fellow humanists, in particular the poets, whom he implores to follow his lead in commemorating the day and place of Mary's birth. His intention is clearly to induce profane, classically oriented poets such as Pontano and Filefo to drink at the fount of Christian inspiration and contribute verses of praise to the annual poetic encomium of the Virgin. This piece nicely foregrounds the formal and generic innovation that Sabellico is attempting in his modest collection of elegies dedicated to Mary, for he views the Mother of God as a figure worthy of the rhetorical riches set forth in the literary monuments of pagan antiquity. While his contemporaries such as Mantuanus and Sannazaro made serious efforts to praise the Virgin in epic strains, the Venetian employee-poet's initiative here is to propose a similar thematic accommodation in Latin elegiac distichs. Sabellico borrows several bucolic strains from Virgil's *Eclogues* in order to create a primitive, golden-age, mythical framework in which to insert the biblical genealogy of Mary that he develops with much inventive amplification in the collection's second poem.

## Genealogy and Redemption: Elegy II

Sabellico's reference to St Anne in the first elegy's final part raises the question of Mary's (and hence Jesus') genealogical lineage, traditionally represented through the male line through the allegorical image known as the Tree of Jesse.[27] Although Mary's matrilineal genealogy is not developed systematically in any of the thirteen elegies, the poet's mention of Anne does at least constitute an acknowledgment of that side of her history, perhaps in accordance with the late Middle Ages' tendency to venerate female saints and, most conspicuously, the frequent iconographical representations of Anne as a figure who symbolizes precisely the important human and multigenerational side of familial intimacy, as P. Sheingorn has well demonstrated in several articles.[28] Yet despite this recognition of the centrality of Mary's maternal heritage to the very essence of her character as she is perceived in the fifteenth century, Sabellico chooses to adhere closely to his biblical sources, and thus to an agnatic lineage, when he attempts to praise Mary's familial origins.

The cascade of genitives near the end of the collection's opening elegy contains an expression – *regum regem tulit illa parentem* ('she bore him, the King, father of Kings') – which explicitly ties Jesus and Mary to a long line of royal succession. It is precisely this regal fecundity of Mary's lineage that Sabellico sets out to explore in the second elegy, now examining it from the side of her biblical antecedents. Here again, the poet begins by confirming that the celebration of Mary's birth is the central object of his praise.[29] After the collection's first poem, in which the author adds bucolic mythical images to the scene for an exploration of Mary's genealogy, this second elegy constitutes a further attempt at 'framing' the moment of her birth in a narrative, historical context, proceeding not from the miraculous event of her virginal birth foreshadowing virginal motherhood, but from the ancient origins of her familial race. Despite the initial promise of a far-reaching summary tracing the successive generations from their distant origin, Sabellico in fact dedicates the essential part of his poem to a detailed account of one of the most turbulent sequences in Israel's history: from the death of Solomon and the accession of Rehoboam (1 Kings 14) until the beginnings of Jehoiakin's ill-fated reign over Jerusalem (2 Kings 24), culminating, of course, in the destruction of the Temple. These verses represent an ambitious effort to inscribe one of the darkest periods of Old Testament narrative under Mary's redeeming mantle. They also constitute an inventive, amplifying attempt – using biblical material – to illustrate her exceptional, transformational powers in concrete historical terms. Indeed, Sabellico's use of contrast here becomes a powerful means of foregrounding her decisive impact on the course of human history in her mediational status as refuge and beacon towards salvation.

After the poem's initial verses, wherein the author addresses the Virgin and requests her blessing as he declares his renewed intention of praising the day of her birth, he quickly acknowledges the immensity of the task he has before him. To exhaust the narrative of Mary's ancient and illustrious race, he explains, would be an enormous undertaking. Indeed, such an endeavour far exceeds his humble abilities, even should the queen of heaven grant him the inspiration he has requested of her. For this reason, he hopes only to make a small contribution to the collective praise of Mary's family line. Though she is indeed his cynosure, the heavenly guide who leads him faithfully through ocean, mountain and wood, he timidly proposes to sing only a fragment of her history:

> Tu cynosura mihi medio dux certa profundo
> Montibus et silvis tu mihi fida comes;
> Sed quid, regalem repetam ne ab origine gentem,
> Et qui te sancti progenuere patres?
> Prodit in exhaustum series immensa laborem,
> Pauca sequar: multum sic quoque gliscet opus.[30]

Here it appears that Sabellico borrows an ingredient from the elegiac convention of *recusatio*, modestly declaring that he has no intention of revealing the entirety of Mary's genealogy. Such a massive, foundational undertaking, he implies, is better suited to a talent more considerable than his own. Indeed, his role shall be that of the encomiastic poet who hopes only to render faithful service to his Lady by revealing at least some small part of her greatness. By insisting on the modest portion that he aims to glorify – *pauca sequar* – , the author discretely borrows another rhetorical turn often met with in the Latin elegists of antiquity, who took much of their own inspiration from the dense, jewelled style of the Alexandrians.

According to Sabellico's elegiac restitution of Mary's origins, the Christian destiny of humanity was early revealed to the prophets. Well conscious of the traditional, genealogical association between Jesus and David, the poet begins his sequence with the 'pious prophet' (*pius vates*) who led Israel's people in times of peace and of tribulation. As 'author of the divine song' (*divini carminis auctor*), David the poet shows himself to be acutely aware of a divine presence, a triune godhead sitting atop the celestial regions.[31] Here the Humanist author invokes with obvious veneration the Davidic Psalms, the cornerstone of sacred verse in the Judaeo-Christian tradition, often imitated and paraphrased by sacred poets writing in Latin. David, in whom Sabellico flatters himself to perceive a significant poetic forebear, figures prominently in the elegy, appearing at once as a venerable, Old Testament ancestor of Mary and as a prestigious model of Christian Humanist invention. The King of Israel's considerable lyrical inspiration, explains the poet, was that of a prophet announcing a far-off, divine event:

> Coelitus o quotiens captus super aethera sensit
> Unius et trini numen adesse Dei:
> Ter veneranda tribus quotiens lux una figuris
> Est quoque sidereo visa sedere throno.
> Virgineos partus et mystica fata nepotis,
> Credibile est etiam tum didicisse senem:
> Caetera fatidico meditatus carmina plectro,
> Creditur ante ipsam praecinuisse diem.[32]

In the same way that David's lineage contains the seed which shall foster the Virgin birth of Jesus through his faultless Mother, so too shall the Psalmist's inspiration animate the talent of poets who use their lyrical gifts to sing the praise of God and of Mary, the queen of heaven. David is thus here described as the conscious bearer of news, which manifests itself subtly in his verse, though clearly enough to those blessed with the gift of understanding. Such talents of clear vision and comprehension are naturally to be found in the poets, suggests Sabellico at the end of the fifth elegy, where he encourages his Humanist colleagues to turn their talents to Mary's praise, using a language very similar to that which describes the inspired eloquence of David.[33] In these elegies dedicated to the Virgin, the Old Testament poet is characterized as both a divinely inspired visionary and a forerunner of the Christian Saviour.

The immense figure of King David serves here as the foundational moment, not only of Mary's lineage and the devotional hymnic tradition, but also, more specifically, as the starting point of Sabellico's enumeration of royal personages from the two Books of Kings. From this moment forward, the biblical figures are accounted for much more rapidly, at a rate of approximately one for each distich, as is well illustrated by the marginal indications that appear in the 1513 Paris edition. Next in line, of course, is Solomon, whose mention marks the beginning of the Humanist's rapid, generally chronological account of a tragic sequence in the history of Jerusalem. Ten verses evoke the period spanning from the accession of Solomon to the violent death of Jezabel (2 Kings 9: 33):

> Huius idumeae post fatum conditor arae,
>   Rege satus Solomon regia sceptra tulit.
> Nunc sequitur Roboam, Roboam trieteris Abiae,
>   Qui subit Aethiopem, contudit Asa ducem:
> Inde Philisateis ditissima regna tributis,
>   Ille tenet, cuius nomina pavit Arabs.
> Mox videre Joram non mitia sidera regem,
>   Sidus Ochozias tristius inde tulit.
> Difficiles audax populi molitur habenas,
>   Quae ruit ante sacras sanguinolenta fores.[34]

Here Solomon receives all of one distich and, unlike his father, is remembered not for any moral quality, but rather, more neutrally, as the builder of the 'altar' in Palestine (*idumeae…conditor arae*). He quickly disappears and is followed in the next distich by no fewer than three sovereign kings, each one mentioned by name. The first to appear is Solomon's son, Rehoboam, who became king of Israel in his father's stead (1 Kings 11: 43) – and whose turbulent reign marked the definitive separation of Israel and Juda (1 Kings 12: 19). He is followed by his own son, Abijam, a wicked king who reigned over Juda for only three years (1 Kings 15: 1–8) and then by his grandson, Asa, whose reign over Judah and Jerusalem lasted for forty years and is characterized by the biblical narrator as just in the eyes of God (1 Kings 15: 9–23). Asa's decisive military victory over Zerah the Cushite

(2 Chronicles 14: 8–14) is here cryptically evoked through *antonomasia* as his defeat of the 'Ethiopian leader'. His son Jehoshaphat, who reigned for twenty-five years, receives an entire distich in which he is described, again through *antonomasia*, as the warrior-king who, made rich by bountiful tributes paid by the Philistines,[35] instilled fear in the 'Arab' enemy, a reference to Jehoshaphat's military campaigns against the Syrians, the Moabites and the Ammonites. Rival kings of Judah and Israel, Joram and Ahaziah (Ochozias), are next mentioned, followed by a distich recounting the violent demise of Jezebel. All of these details are rapidly recounted as the poet follows the chronological line of the seed of David, listing the royal ancestors of Mary.

This precise enumeration of the links composing the familial line through the royal succession in Judah, beginning from the reign of Rehoboam, continues in the verses which follow these. Sabellico is now at great pains to follow this line until its historical conclusion with the reign of Jehoiachin (Joachim), the sack of Jerusalem and the destruction of the Temple, the event which marks the natural conclusion of the books of Kings and of Chronicles. Finally, after having duly recorded the reigns of Amon and Josiah within the space of a single distich, the poet asks rhetorically why he should endeavour to tell about King Jehoiachin and the other men who came after the fall of Jerusalem. Why repeat the songs and the sacred teachings of the prophets and the fathers? His real objective is to praise the redemptive and kindly figure of Mary, the Son of whom was to incarnate not only the messianic resurrection of a royal bloodline, but indeed the very Salvation of humanity. Here he is content to declare that Mary is the true glory of all her ancestors:

Quid Joachim reliquisque canam, post tristia regni
  Excidia illustris, qui subiere viri ?
Fatidicos ne senes, num carmina sacra revolvam,
  Coelicolumque patrum sancta ministeria ?
Tu mihi virgo satis summa ad praeconia, sive
  Epica plectra magis, seu magis ista placent:
Tu splendor, tu gentis honor, tu summa tuorum
  Gloria, et antiqui fama suprema laris.
Denique tu quicquid poterit succurrere vati,
  Ara tibi erecta est, ad tua sacra veni.[36]

Perhaps most remarkable in these verses, indeed in the entire elegy, is the poet's insistence upon Mary's venerated status within her own bloodline and the great dignity of her 'ancient house' (*antiqui…laris*). Such a perspective on praise even of the Virgin herself is nevertheless unsurprising in the context of Venetian humanism, which famously views marriage as an institution whose function is to guarantee the unsullied perpetuity of a purely aristocratic lineage.[37] To describe Mary of Nazareth as the summit of her ancient race, in the context of civic and class-oriented pride characteristic of many *Quattrocento* city-states, is in fact to pay her considerable homage within the context specific to *Quattrocento* Venice. Indeed, this elegy frames Jesus' Mother, not only as the zenith of her own familial history, but also as the woman whose surpassing splendour allowed her to become the very resurrection of a royal lineage which, when Jerusalem was sacked and the Temple overthrown, had fallen into great depths of misery and humiliation. This also likely explains Sabellico's insistence upon the (apocryphal) stories of Mary's presentation and ministry at the Temple in elegies eight and nine of this same collection, before the sequence of poems on her Triumph and Annunciation.

The exhortation to praise Mary's birth and familial origins, delivered by Sabellico even to his fellow Humanist poets in the collection's fifth elegy, largely constitutes the thematic material of the first five poems. Although the nativity and family themes hardly disappear in the remaining eight compositions, there is nevertheless a shift in focus, leading up to a joyous proclamation of Mary's triumphal procession and Assumption in elegies nine and ten. This shift is announced explicitly by the author at the beginning of the sixth elegy, where he proclaims that after having sung the praise of Mary's 'noble lineage', he now devotes his efforts to lauding the inimitable virtue of the Virgin herself. Sabellico's account of Mary's origins follows a chronological order borrowed directly from the biblical narration of the final decadence of Israel and the realm of Judah, culminating in the destruction of the Temple at Jerusalem and the captivity of all Hebraic survivors of this event under the hard yoke of Nebuchadnezzar.

By following the linear narrative development found in the concluding chapters of the books of Kings and Chronicles, the author presents only the agnatic, patrilineal side of Mary's family history. His reference to St Anne in the final part of the first elegy nevertheless constitutes evidence of an awareness of Mary's matrilineal side, perhaps as a reflection of this female saint's growing presence in fifteenth-century iconographical representations of the Holy Family. Yet even in the context of a lineage based here almost exclusively upon references to male antecedents, Mary is represented as a kind of Saviour figure in whom the fallen House of David finds both redemption and promise. Indeed, the poetic paraphrase of narrative material borrowed from Kings and Chronicles formulates a linear perspective in which Mary emerges, in historical terms, as something of a salvational figure in her own right, for the powerful contrast with the sad tale in intergenerational decline and failure of Judah's kings aptly highlights her unique virtue. In Sabellico's collection, the use of a 'minor' verse form allows for the free juxtaposition of parallel aspects of Mary's splendour in such a way that any linear ordering hardly suggests a moral hierarchy of qualities. As such, the poet's deployment of pagan elegiac motifs in commemorating the Virgin's birth is well supported by his rigorous use of scripture in the collection's second elegy. Hence the initial use of classical, bucolic, mythical images to underscore the theme of origins in the first poem is used to frame the precise use of biblical paraphrase in the second. Such inventive use of literary syncretism subtly underscores the inherently poetic nature of the Mother of Jesus, who, though present only episodically in biblical testimony, nonetheless occupies a central position in the long tradition of Christian praise, devotion and inquiry.

## *Notes*

1 On Sabellico's career, see M. L. King, *Venetian Humanism in an Age of Patrician Dominance* (Princeton, NJ: Princeton UP, 1986), pp. 73–74, 425–27; F. Tateo, 'Coccio, Marcantonio, detto Marcantonio Sabellico', *Dizionario biografico degli Italiani* 26 (1982), 510–15.
2 See F. Tateo, 'Marcantonio Sabellico e la svolta del classicismo quattrocentesco', in *Florence and Venice: Comparisons and Relations*. I. *Quattrocento* (Florence: La Nuova Italia Editrice, 1979), 41–63.
3 G. Cozzi, 'Intorno all'edizione dell'opera di Marcantonio Sabellico, curata da Celio Secondo Curione e dedicata a Sigismondo Augusto re di Polonia', in *Venezia e la Polonia nei secoli dal XVII al XIX*, ed. L. Cini (Venice: Istituto per la Collaborazione Culturale, 1965), 165–77.
4 See nevertheless, R. Chavasse, 'The *studia humanitatis* and the Making of a Humanist Career: Marcantonio Sabellico's Exploitation of Humanist Literary Genres', in *Renaissance Studies* 17 (2003), 27–38.
5 E. Muir, *Civic Ritual in Renaissance Venice* (Princeton, NJ: Princeton UP, 1981), 152.
6 M. Büchsel, H. L. Kessler and R. Müller, *Das Atrium von San Marco in Venedig: Die Genese der Genesismosaiken und ihre mittelalterliche Wirklichkeit* (Berlin: Gebr. Mann Verlag, 2014).
7 For an iconographical description of these mosaics representing the life of the Virgin, see O. Demus, *The Mosaics of San Marco in Venice*, vol. 1, pt. 1 (Chicago and London: University of Chicago Press), 127–47.
8 See on this topic the valuable contributions of D. J. Geanakaplos, *Greek Scholars in Venice. Studies in the Dissemination of Greek Learning from Byzantium to Western Europe* (Cambridge, MA: Harvard University Press, 1962); N. G. Wilson, *From Byzantium to Italy. Greek Studies in the Italian Renaissance* (London: Duckworth, 1992), 23–25, 124–56.
9 M. Lowry, *Nicholas Jenson and the Rise of Venetian Publishing in Renaissance Europe* (Oxford: Basil Blackwell, 1991), 239–54.
10 *Ad Gelliam elegiarum libri tres*, Marc. Lat. XII, 234 (4219), ff. 1–42.
11 *Ad beatam Mariam virginem gratiae et preces, vita S. Martini, vita Sanctae Caeciliae, vita S. Clementis, et alia quaedam I. Biffi carmina* (Milan: Leonhard Pachel, 1489); *Elegiae I. Biffi in quibus Virgo Dei genitrix commendatur* (Milan: s.e. 1512); *Carmina I. Biffi de annuntiatione beatae Mariae virginis* (Milan: A. Zarotum, 1493).
12 *Marci Antonii Sabellici Carmina elegantissima de beata virgine Maria cum commentario Hermanni Torrentini* (Daventer: J. de Brech, 1498).
13 *Sanctissime elegie de intemerata virgine Maria cum heroico carmine eiusdem in naufragatam Divi Petri Cymbam quibus nuper subjectam est Epigramma Petri de Ponte ceci bregen. ad honestos juvenes de casta incestaque poesi* (Paris: Jean de Gourmont, 1513).
14 J. Pelikan, *Mary through the Centuries. Her Place in the History of Culture* (New Haven and London: Yale UP, 1996), 189ff.
15 S. J. Boss, 'The Doctrine of Mary's Immaculate Conception', in *Mary. The Complete Resource* (Oxford: Oxford University Press, 2007), 208.
16 L. B. T. Houghton, 'Maritime Maro: Virgil's Fourth Eclogue in Renaissance Venice', in *Latin Literature and its Transmission. Papers in Honour of Michael Reeve*, ed. R. Hunter and S. P. Oakley (Cambridge: Cambridge University Press, 2016), 171–93.

17 1, 9–10: 'Iret et aurato conjunx Titonia curru, / Candidior cygnis, candidiorque nive.'
18 1, 15–16: 'Illius adventum manes sensere profundi, / Cerberus et stygiam quin regit arte ratem.'
19 1, 17–22: 'As Cynthian Apollo raised his radiant arch above the sea, / And arose, led on by the morning steeds, / Upon seeing how the world glistened with unwonted radiance, / He felt that the day was ushered in by a powerful deity: / "Why hesitate", he asked, "and risk delaying such a birth? / For it is well that it be born, this holy day!" '
20 1, 45–50: 'Here is the day complicit in your sacred birthing, / Anne, mother of such a Virgin, mother Anne; / Happy is that mother to whom the venerable Mother of God / Nodded, visible from atop her celestial throne: / Thence She admires the maternal visage, and the arms / And the hands which so often raised themselves to her.'
21 On this theme of a feminine solidarity which symbolizes the loving, nurturing relationship of *sympatheia* linking divine will and human adoration, J. Pelikan's *Eternal Feminines: Three Theological Allegories in Dante's Paradiso* (New Brunswick, NJ: Rutgers University Press, 1992) examines the seminal case of Dante's *Divina commedia*.
22 On the basic structure of the Homeric hymn, see of course R. Janko's seminal article, 'The Structure of the Homeric Hymns: A Study in Genre', *Hermes* 109:1 (1981), 9–24.
23 1, 59–64: 'As for myself, at the designated months of the growing season / Before the altars of the Virgin I shall offer male incense, / I shall spend the solemn day in song and hymns, / And I shall hang my offerings from the temple's arch. / Ardent prayers shall I add: every year, O Virgin / Let your poet adore your sacred mysteries.'
24 *Ec.* VIII, 66.
25 'Brighter one is, though, and more joyous, than every other land, / The land complicit in the birth of my Lady. / Yet you, O Bethlehem, venerable creator of the highest King, / Would have believed that this glory itself had passed you over! / On this place, first of all, the Creator of great Heaven and of Hell, / Once rendered human in His hybrid essence trod. / It was she therefore who brought forth the King father of kings, / Both places are glorious in her childbearing.'
26 See on this theme Madeleine Bonjour's classic study *Terre natale: études sur une composante affective du patriotisme romain* (Paris: Les Belles Lettres, 1975) and, for the Renaissance period, S. Laigneau-Fontaine's more recent edited volume: '*Petite patrie*'. *L'image de la région natale chez les écrivains de la Renaissance* (Geneva: Droz, 2013).
27 T. G. Gallino, *L'albero di Jesse: l'immaginario collettivo medievale e la sessualità dissimulata* (Turin: Bollatti Boringhieri, 1996); A. Watson, *The Early Iconography of the Tree of Jesse* (Oxford: Oxford University Press, 1934).
28 P. Sheingorn, 'Appropriating the Holy Kinship. Gender and Family History', in K. Ashley and P. Sheingorn, *Interpreting Cultural Symbols. Saint Anne in Late Medieval Society* (Athens and London: The University of Georgia Press, 1990), 178.
29 II, 3–4: 'Natales regina tuos en tollere cantu / Aggredior, coeptis intemerata fave.'
30 II, 7–12: 'For me you are the Cynosure, a sure guide amidst the deep, / Through mountains and forests you are my faithful companion; / But what then? shall I seek your royal race from its very origin, / And discern which saintly forebears gave you birth? / There stretches forth an immense succession in such labour, / Only a little of it shall I follow, for even thus the work of praise shall grow by much.'
31 II, 13–18.
32 II, 19–26: 'O how often did that captive from Heaven sense above the ether / The divine presence of a sole and yet triple God: / O how often did that unique, thrice venerable light, bearing three figures / Also appear seated on the celestial throne. /

Virgin births and the mystical destinies of his descendant, / It is conceivable that even then the old man learned of them, / For it is believed that he meditated other songs on his fated lyre / Sans these things in anticipation of their day.'

33 V, 41–48: 'Omnia virgineo resonent mihi carmine et hymnis, / Non nisi per laudes lux genialis eat; / Ipsa sui interea patris miranda creatrix, / Aetherea gratos spectet ab arce choros; / Illustresque viros nunc primum forte revulsos, / Fontibus Aoniis ad sua sacra vocet; / Et sibi facundo meditari carmina plectro, / Gaudeat aethereo conspicienda throno.'

34 II, 27–36: 'After his death the builder of the Palestinian altar, / Solomon born of royal seed, held the royal sceptre. / Thereupon followed Roboam, after Roboam then for three years Abijam, / Whose successor, Asa, crushed the Ethiopian king. / Thereafter, he whose very name made the Arab tremble / Held power, enriched by the tributes of the Philistines. / Unfriendly stars then looked down upon King Joram / Before Ochozias, sadder still, bore his own fateful star. / An audacious woman struggled to hold the people's difficult reins, / Then was thrust down, bloodied, before the sacred portals.'

35 2 Chronicles 17: 9–11: '(9) Docebantque in Juda habentes librum legis Domini, et circuibant cunctas urbes Juda atque erudiebant populum. (10) Itaque factus est pavor Domini super omnia regna terrarum quae erant per gyrum Juda. (11) Sed et Philisthei Josaphat munera deferebant et vectigal argenti. Arabes quoque adducebant pecora arietum septem milia septingentos et hircos totidem.'

36 II, 57–66: 'Why then should I sing of Joakin and the other men who followed him, after the / Sad destruction of the glorious kingdom? / Shall I recall the truth-speaking elders, the sacred songs, / Or the holy ministries of our heaven-dwelling fathers? / You, Virgin, are sufficient inspiration to the highest praise, or / Rather to the epic lyre, if this should please you more. / You are the splendour and the honour of your people, you are the highest glory / Of your race, and the supreme renown of an ancient house. / Finally, you who are are all that may second the efforts of your poet: / An altar stands in your honour, please be present at your mysteries.'

37 See on this theme M. L. King's excellent analysis of the Venetian (patrician) humanist Francesco Barbaro's celebrated treatise *De re uxoria*, dedicated to Lorenzo di Medici.

# 8

# THEATRICAL RELIQUARIES: AFTERLIVES OF ST MARY MAGDALENE IN EARLY SEVENTEENTH-CENTURY FLORENCE

Kelley Harness

On 22 July 1627, the feast day of St Mary Magdalene, a diarist of the Medici court recorded the following account of the occasion:

> The day of Saint Mary Magdalene. The feast day was commemorated in the chapel of the Most Serene Archduchess, the Mass was sung with music as was vespers, and after vespers the pages of His Highness performed a play that was called Saint Mary Magdalene Triumphant in Paradise, a small thing but very beautiful, being interwoven in it musical intermedi, a composition of Signor Balì Ferdinando Saracinelli ... The Most Serene Archduchess did not sponsor a banquet as in years past, for the *dame* were not there.[1]

Although brief, the diary entry is informative, describing the nature of the festivities as well as establishing their location, participants, and, importantly, sponsor. This sponsor was Archduchess Maria Magdalena of Austria (1587–1631), grand duchess of Tuscany beginning in 1609 and, since her husband's death in February 1621, co-regent, along with her mother-in-law Christine of Lorraine, of the grand duchy of Tuscany. During the period of the regency, which ended on her son Grand Duke Ferdinando II's eighteenth birthday (14 July 1628), chaste and active female protagonists dominated the archduchess's theatrical patronage: figures such as St Ursula and Judith replaced the mythological gods and goddesses that had populated the earliest Florentine operas. These were the sorts of operas presented to visiting dignitaries between 1621 and 1626, in performances that reiterated biblical, hagiographical and literary precedents for women's good governance, as I have discussed elsewhere.[2]

Archduchess Maria Magdalena also sponsored regular commemorations of her name saint's feast day (22 July) of the sort described in 1627, occasions comprising varied combinations of religious service, theatrical performance, music and banqueting. These annual events also served the conspicuously devout archduchess's political ends, providing illustrations of a particularly female spiritual authority with which she wished to identify, performed in an architectural space she controlled.[3] The works' focus on Mary Magdalene's speech – in most cases sung speech – rehabilitated the saint's singing voice through its use towards positive didactic ends.[4] At the same time the saint's voice served as the ventriloquizing medium by which Archduchess Maria Magdalena reminded courtiers and family members alike of her name saint's efficacy as devotional object and preaching subject.

The physical location of the St Mary Magdalene festivities played a key role in communicating these messages about the saint's contributions to Christianity. Between 1620 and at least 1629 the performances took place in the chapel adjacent to the archduchess's apartment in the Palazzo Pitti, known since the later eighteenth century as the Chapel of Relics (Figure 8.1). Maria Magdalena took possession

**Figure 8.1** *Chapel of Relics*. Florence, Palazzo Pitti. © 2017. Art Resource/SCALA Photo Scala, Florence, courtesy of the Ministero Beni e Att. Culturali e del Turismo.

**Figure 8.2** Workshop of Bernardino Poccetti, *Preaching of Saint Mary Magdalene in Provence,* c. 1612. Florence, Palazzo Pitti, Chapel of Relics. Soprintendenza per i Beni Artistici e Storici, Gabinetto Fotografico no. 250650.

of the chapel upon the death of her father-in-law, Grand Duke Ferdinando I, in 1609, and almost immediately embarked on extensive renovations, overseen by architect Giulio Parigi. Beneath overhead vault frescoes celebrating the Blessed Virgin Mary, Bernardino Poccetti and his workshop encircled the drum with a cycle of seven frescoed panels depicting scenes from Mary Magdalene's life: 1) Martha leads St Mary Magdalene to Christ; 2) St Mary Magdalene at Jesus' feet at the Last Supper; 3) Resurrection of Lazarus; 4) St Mary Magdalene preaches at Marseilles (Figure 8.2); 5) Baptism of the prince of Marseilles and the destruction of idols; 6) St Mary Magdalene transported by angels; and 7) Final communion of St Mary Magdalene.[5] Wall niches housed the archduchess's ever-expanding collection of relics, hidden behind locked doors adorned by eight canvases depicting religious figures of importance to Florence, the Medici, and Maria Magdalena herself, including the saints Cosmas and Damian, painted by Giovanni Bilivert, and Matteo Rosselli's *Assumption of Saint Mary Magdalene.*[6]

Archduchess Maria Magdalena's chapel was thus a locus where two of her most significant passions in terms of collecting intersected: relics and anything connected to St Mary Magdalene. Both interests were well known: beginning in 1610 the archduchess began requesting – and receiving – relics from around Italy,[7] while gifts of Mary Magdalene works of all sorts preceded her arrival in Florence and continued throughout her life there, beginning with Riccardo Riccardi's *Conversione di Santa Maria Maddalena ridotta in tragedia* (1609), which, according to an extant manuscript copy, was originally to have been sung as part of the festivities celebrating her marriage to Cosimo II in 1608.[8] She received the coveted relic of St Mary Magdalene's hair from Cardinal Del Monte in 1621.[9] On 27 August 1622 she thanked Abbot Belmonte Cagnoli of Rimini for sending her his 'Lagrime di Santa Maria Madalena', a poem, in her words, 'io entrai in desiderio di vedere' (I began to desire to see).[10] She was the dedicatee of Giovan Domenico Peri's five-act, unpublished play entitled *Madalena convertita.*[11] Her villa Poggio Imperiale, renovated with an emphasis on visual representations of heroic female *virtù*, became particularly well stocked as a repository of Mary Magdalene art: a 1625 inventory of the villa reveals that the archduchess surrounded herself with at least twenty-six Magdalene paintings, sculptures and *pietre dure* – the largest number of artworks devoted to a single subject in the villa and representing over a century's worth of artistic interaction with the saint's legend.[12] Paintings from the late fifteenth century, such as Perugino's *Saint Mary Magdalene*, were relocated to the villa,[13] as were more recent works by Alessandro Allori, Rutilio Manetti and Francesco Rustici, alongside several unattributed paintings of the saint 'nel diserto'.

Maria Magdalena exhibited these same interests in her Palazzo Pitti chapel. As a location for theatrical performances, allowing for the space necessary for performers, scenery and limited machinery, the octagonal chapel's small size – around ten *braccia* (approximately 5.836 metres) in diameter, according to Richa's estimate – would have accommodated only a handful of guests.[14] Access beyond the immediate family was therefore limited, granted by the archduchess as a means of demonstrating favour and reifying exclusivity.[15] She then took care both to amaze and to instruct these invited guests, presenting works designed to appeal to their senses and their intellects.

The Saracinelli play of 1627 noted above marks just such an integrated celebration, combining liturgical observance and theatrical event, both delivered musically. The earliest known description of a Mary Magdalene feast-day commemoration, which dates from 1619, that is, after the completion of the most extensive of the renovations, was much less elaborate, consisting of just a banquet with music.[16] In 1620, after Mass Christine of Lorraine sponsored the performance of a pastoral play with music by Francesca Caccini, followed by a *ballo*, after which the grand duke and his daughters stayed to hear the performance his wife (Maria Magdalena) had arranged in honour of her name saint.[17] This account by Cesare Tinghi, court diarist until his death in 1626, provides no additional information as to the nature of the Mary Magdalene work of 1620, but his precise accounting of time, which confirms that the pastoral and *ballo* began two hours before sunset (22 *ore*), that the *ballo* alone lasted half an hour and that the grand duke retired to his rooms but then returned for a meal at sunset, suggests that whatever it was that Maria Magdalena sponsored, it may have lasted only twenty to thirty minutes. In subsequent years, Maria Magdalena's feast-day celebrations regularly included a theatrical performance, usually with music, establishing a tradition that she maintained at least until 1629.

Tinghi's first unambiguous mention of a St Mary Magdalene play occurred on 21 July 1621, the vigil of St Mary Magdalene, when, after the vespers service held in the archduchess's chapel, four pages performed a dialogue with interlocutors St Cosimo, Amore Divino (Divine Love), Angelo Custode (Guardian Angel) and Amore Terreno (Earthly Love), who praised St Mary Magdalene and also the soul of the recently deceased Grand Duke Cosimo II, while a celestial choir pronounced words of protection on behalf of the Medici family.[18] The presence of Amore Divino, Angelo Custode and Amore Terreno suggests that the pages performed an adaptation of a play entitled *Disprezzo dell'amore e beltà terrena*, which the Florentine playwright Giovan Maria Cecchi had written c. 1580–87 for the

Florentine confraternity of the Arcangelo Raffaello and in which these personages appear.[19] Pages presented a similar adaptation the following year, when the archduchess, her children and her brother-in-law Cardinal Carlo de' Medici first heard vespers 'con la musica' then stayed to hear 'un dialagho della vita contemplativa et della vita ativa da Santa Maria Madalena et da Santa Marta et poi venuto la Pace li messe dacordo' (a dialogue by St Mary Magdalene and St Martha on the Contemplative Life and Active Life, after which Peace arrived to reconcile them).[20] Tinghi credits Jacopo Cicognini as this work's author and lists the performers – three of the grand duke's pages plus the brother of 'La Cecchina' (Francesca Caccini) – before praising the variety and embellishment of the costumes. As the only non-noble performer, Scipione Caccini's role was undoubtedly a musical one, possibly the only singing role in the work. He would return to sing the role of an archangel in the Magdalene play performed in the archduchess's chapel in 1624, and that same year he participated in the Andrea Salvadori/Marco da Gagliano opera *La regina Sant'Orsola*, a work that was repeated on 28 January 1625. For that second performance Francesca Caccini asserted her prerogative to compose the music her brother would sing, suggesting that she might well have composed all or some of the music for the 1622 Mary Magdalene play.[21]

The exact nature of the 1622 dialogue, as well as any music sung in it, can be established only tentatively. A manuscript version of a work corresponding, in part, to the description of 1622 survives in the Biblioteca Riccardiana of Florence, attributing the play to Cicognini but with a different title, *Il disprezzo nel mondo*.[22] According to information provided on the manuscript's title page, the Florentine confraternity of the Archangel Raphael had performed this play on 22 July 1624, a performance date borne out by the confraternity's own records.[23] Following a prologue in which Conversion (Conversione) addresses the confraternity brothers, interlocutors representing the active and contemplative lives debate the relative merits of their chosen paths. The Riccardiana manuscript appears to be incomplete, however, ending after the work's first dramatic climax – alternating one-line ripostes between the two title characters. The personage of Peace never appears, despite being mentioned on the work's title page, nor do a host of other interlocutors listed there, including Pride (Superbia), Vainglory (Vanagloria), Obstinacy (Ostinatione), Widowed State (Stato Vedovile), Married State (Stato Maritale), Virginity (Verginità), a chorus of angels and St Mary Magdalene herself. This list actually allows a clearer understanding of the play to emerge, for these personages are identical to those who interact in Cecchi's *Duello della vita attiva e contemplativa*, as are the lines delivered by the three interlocutors in the version preserved in the Riccardiana, confirming that, despite the attribution to Cicognini on the title page of that manuscript, the dialogue performed in 1624 by the boys of the Compagnia dell'Arcangelo Raffaello was the one written by Cecchi.[24]

As had occurred the previous year, Archduchess Maria Magdalena and her guests apparently heard an abbreviated version of Cecchi's play, one with only four personages, according to Tinghi's account: Vita Attiva, Vita Contemplativa, Pace and St Mary Magdalene. Excerpting the lines delivered by just those four interlocutors from the Cecchi play likely approximates the literary content of the 1622 play and also sheds light on the nature of the musical contributions. The work proceeds in *versi sciolti* (i.e. seven- and eleven-syllable lines of unpredictable rhyme) except for the first and only utterance by St Mary Magdalene – three stanzas that conclude the play and in which the saint revisits her past sinfulness, asserts her present joy and recalls her acts of physical mortification, now gloriously transformed. Since the description of the 1624 confraternity performance praises the saint's beautiful song (fol. 116r), performed on that occasion by a 'Cinganelli', identified by Eisenbichler as Piermaria di Michelangelo Cinganelli,[25] it seems likely that the character of Mary Magdalene also delivered her stanzas musically in 1622, sung by Scipione Caccini:

Io, che nel mar di colpe un tempo giacqui,
Non pria disposi al pentimento il core,
Ch'al sempiterno amore
Per l'interno dolor cotanto piacque,
Che in lagrime conversi il fuoco mio,
Ancor vivendo mi congiunsi a Dio.
Di vera penitenza erto sentiero
Sembrò dolcezza alla mia stanca vita;
Or provo al Ciel salita
Quel ben, cui non capisce uman pensiero;
Ed obliando ogni passata noia,
Non ho cor, che mi basti a tanta gioia.
Miro in perle converso il pianto amaro,
I lacerati miei biondi capelli
In rai del sol più belli,
E'l già livido sen splendente e chiaro;
E per digiuno il trasformato viso
La bellezza acquistar del Paradiso.[26]

(I, who at one time lay in the sea of sins, my heart not disposed earlier to repentance, let alone to eternal love, for the internal pain pleased so much, that my fire changed into tears; still living I joined with God. The steep path of true penitence seemed sweetness to my weary life; now I experience, ascending to heaven, that goodness that human thought cannot comprehend; and forgetting every past trouble, my heart cannot contain such joy. I perceive bitter tears changed into pearls, my lacerated blond hair [changed] into the beautiful rays of the sun, and my earlier bruised breast [now] shining and bright; my face, transformed by fasting, acquires the beauty of paradise.)

Although only a sung Mass and vespers marked the 1623 feast day of St Mary Magdalene, theatrical performances resumed in 1624, when Scipione Caccini, this time portraying an angel and a celestial archangel, joined a Cavaliere Incontri, who played Fidelity (Fedeltà), and three pages, portraying Divine Fear (Timore

Divino), Divine Love (Amore Divino) and Wisdom (Sapienza) to perform Cicognini's *Amore divino et del timore divino*, a work that is now lost.[27] Two of the pages, Francesco [Barbolani di] Montauto and Giovanni Artimis, returned in 1625, joined by Filippo di Orliens [Orléans?] and Camillo [Bourbon] del Monte, plus a boy listed as 'un filliolo del Cinganella', to recite Cicognini's *Trionfo del disprezzo del mondo* after vespers, a work whose title is quite similar to the play preserved in the Riccardiana manuscript discussed above, as well as to the St Mary Magdalene play performed at the Arcangelo Raffaello in 1623.[28] The Cinganella boy – likely the same youth who sang the role of St Mary Magdalene in the 1624 confraternity performance – recited the role of the repentant Mary Magdalene, singing music composed by Filippo Vitali ('Santa Maria Madalena in penitenzia recitata da un filliolo del Cinganella. Cantanto conposta l'aria di Filippo Vitali'), while the pages performed the roles of Disdain of the World (Disprezzo del Mondo), the World (Mondo), Youth (Gioventù) and Sin (Peccato). Both the play and its music are lost. Also lost is the unnamed play from 1626, which pages performed in the archduchess's chapel after vespers and before a banquet Maria Magdalena sponsored for her children in the ground floor rooms 'wanting to uphold tradition' ('volendo mantenere il stile antico').[29]

This brings us to 1627 and Francesco Saracinelli's *Santa Maria Madalena trionfiante* [*sic*] *in paradiso*, the play whose performance is the final one recorded in the official court diary. The modest, 189-line work survives in a manuscript (C.V.37) in Florence's Seminario Maggiore, with a title page that confirms the play's identity as the one recited in the archduchess's chapel on 22 July 1627. Dramatically, the Saracinelli work inaugurates a new approach to the Magdalene dramas: whereas in the Cecchi/Cicognini dialogue of 1622 allegorical personages debate ideals and issues directly illustrative of the Magdalene legend in order to contextualize the eventual on-stage appearance of the saint (a pattern that may have continued in the now lost plays of 1623 and 1625, as suggested by Tinghi's descriptions), Saracinelli heightens the impact of Mary Magdalene's presence by means of a dramatic 'reveal', one that maximizes her contrast to worldly views on women as objects of desire. The play begins with Asmodeus, the demon of lust, who complains that while he has caused thousands of women to burn with the sin of concupiscence, Mary Magdalene has remained beyond his reach. An angel appears and chases away the demon, which becomes the verbal cue to reveal the triumphant saint, who delivers three five-line stanzas in alternation with stanzas sung by her two companion angels. This scene is the first of three places in the play that seem to call for musical performance, likely the interwoven musical *intermedi* praised by the court diarist. At the first and last of these moments Saracinelli substitutes stanzaic closed forms for the *versi sciolti* that dominate the rest of the play's poetic language, and Magdalene's second and third speeches both follow an angel's reference to the act of singing. These are joyful celebrations of the saint's final triumph: as she affirms in the second stanza of her final song, a smile has been born from her tears ('nasce il riso dal mio pianto'). Yet even in such a short work Saracinelli appears concerned to provide an overview of the saint's life, dramatically analogous to the chapel's fresco cycle directly overhead. Shortly after Mary Magdalene's first musical stanzas, an angel recalls two of her previous interactions with Christ in which tears played a crucial role: the foot-washing scene at the house of Simon the Pharisee and the embrace of her Lord's feet at the Crucifixion.[30]

The second instance in Saracinelli's libretto that may have called for music occurs roughly halfway through the work. An angel asks Mary Magdalene to sing, and she complies by delivering the most emotionally charged utterance in the play, an 8-line speech in which she reminds the audience that her self-inflicted punishments were insignificant by comparison to the tortures her Lord endured:

Poco piansi, poc' arsi,
A così bella face,
Et allo stratio indegno,
Che fe del mio Signor', la gente audace,
Fu poco il fiero sdegno,
Fu poco quel ch'io fei,
Contro i capelli miei, inculti, e sparsi,
Poco piansi, poc' arsi.

(I wept little, and burned little at such a beautiful flame, and [compared] to the unworthy torture that the reckless populace inflicted on my Lord, my fierce disdain was but a small thing; it was but a small thing, that which I inflicted against my hair, unkempt and loose – I wept little, and burned little.)

This speech features a tighter organization than the play's other *versi sciolti*, framed by the refrain 'Poco piansi, poc' arsi' and with an emotional crescendo that begins with the anaphora of lines five and six, builds through the vivid adjectives at the end of the seventh line, and reaches its climax at the second statement of the refrain. The disheveled, weeping Magdalene appeared frequently in sixteenth- and seventeenth-century visual representations of the penitent Magdalene; here the saint herself recalls those images to the audience.

Mary Magdalene sings for a third time at the play's conclusion, this time in five *ottonari* (eight-syllable lines) quatrains in which she rejoices in her anticipated reunion with her beloved. While several of the *canzonetta*'s lines recall secular love poetry, the final stanza refocuses attention on the saint and the chapel's frescoes depicting her life. As she reminisces on the past physical contact with her Lord – washing his feet – she imagines recommencing the practice in heaven. The play concludes with a chorus addressed to the audience, promising heavenly rewards to those who follow Mary Magdalene's example and affirming the event's didactic purpose:

Chi di celeste Telo,
Porta piagato il seno,
Qual' Maddalena in Cielo,
Contentissimo appieno,
Godrassi delle stelle il bel sereno.

(The one who bears a breast wounded by the celestial arrow, such as Magdalene in heaven, will enjoy, thoroughly content, the serene beauty of the stars.)

Several lines in Saracinelli's play suggest that the actor portraying St Mary Magdalene was stationed on a higher plane than the rest of the performers, possibly actually ascending during the performance and thus occupying an elevation approaching that of the chapel's Magdalene frescos. This was certainly the case in 1628: on 5 July of that year the court disbursed funds to Cosimo Castiglione in order that he might build the *nuvola* – a machine capable of raising and lowering actors – that Parigi had designed for the archduchess's chapel.[31] That year the archduchess sponsored a performance of *La spelonca di Marsilia* (The Cave of Marseilles), an anonymous eclogue first uncovered by John Walter Hill.[32] As the court diary is silent on this and all subsequent Magdalene performances, the surviving manuscript remains the sole source of information. Like the Saracinelli play of 1627, *La spelonca di Marsilia* begins with an extended introduction, in this case a mildly comical dialogue among four shepherds – Tirsi, Dorindo, Alfesibeo and Ergasto – whose 306 lines account for well over half the work's 491-line total. Tirsi and Dorindo debate the relative merits of Mars and Cupid, after which Alfesibeo, acting as judge, calls both of them nitwits (*sciocchi*), scoffs at their weak reasoning and offers his own champion, Bacchus, as the god healthier to men. As in Saracinelli's Magdalene play of the previous year, the work's earliest mention of women is within the context of carnal love. Ergasto arrives and chastises his three companions, asserting that Jesus is their god and informing them that Jesus' faithful handmaiden, whose words earlier converted him (Ergasto), occupies the very cave next to which they have been arguing. Despite the work's title, only Ergasto's speech establishes the play's geographical and temporal locations, confirming that the action takes place in Marseilles where, according to eleventh- and twelfth-century accretions to the saint's legend, Mary Magdalene and her siblings travelled after the Crucifixion and where Mary Magdalene converted the populace through her preaching.[33] While depicted infrequently in sixteenth- and seventeenth-century visual representations of the saint, preaching scenes appeared in two panels in the reliquary chapel's Magdalene cycle (see Figure 8.2). Ergasto informs his companions that angels often lift the holy woman, who continually punishes her beautiful body, to heaven, possibly a cue for audience members to lift their eyes to the analogous fresco overhead. In the scene that follows, the shepherds witness the miracle and hear the voices of the saint and her cherubic companions, events that in turn convert them and confirm Mary Magdalene's role as an example whose contemplation facilitates repentance.[34]

This act of viewing appears essential to conversion: Dorindo informs Ergasto that if they could but see this apparition with their own eyes, they might put away their unworthy thoughts and turn their attention to heaven ('Oh' s'ancor si mostrasse agl'occhi nostri / questa si cara a Dio, / ogni men degno affetto / noi porremmo in oblio, / e tutti acceso il cor di nuovo zelo / volgeremo i pensieri, e'l core al Cielo' [fols. 86v–87r]). Ergasto asks the saint's angelic companions to reveal the treasure hidden in the grotto, using phrases such as 'dimostrate il tesor' (show the treasure), 'scopra la bella penitente' (unveil the beautiful penitent) and 'un' arra date à noi del Paradiso' (give us a foretaste of paradise) [fol. 87r]. As with Saracinelli's play of 1627, the moment of revelation acts as the dramatic climax of the play, here distinguished poetically by a sudden shift to rhymed *quinari* (five-syllable lines), as well as musically, as the chorus announces 'Ecco la bella' in a six-line refrain, likely the first music of the play. This refrain frames speeches by two angels, the first of which exhorts the shepherds (and the audience) to gaze at Mary Magdalene and then explains the purgative effect of this action (fol. 87v):

Rimirate Pastori
La bella Peccatrice
Cui santa penitenza
Ora rende del Ciel trionfatrice
A' sì gioconda vista
Scacciando ogni viltà dal vostro core
Ardete ancora voi di puro amore.

(Gaze, shepherds, upon the beautiful penitent, whose saintly penitence now restores her, triumphant, to heaven. At such a cheerful sight, chasing all cowardice from your heart, burn now with pure love.)

The second angel describes what is being witnessed, focussing in particular on the saint's tears, which he mentions in each of the last three lines of his five-line speech.

But viewing goes only one way here: Mary Magdalene does not interact with the shepherds, nor is she aware of their presence. At the beginning of her lengthy, 100-line speech she specifically calls attention to her privacy, noting the grotto's efficacy in shielding her from human eyes ('a' gl'occhi de Mortali io qui mi celo') [fol. 88r]. Formally her speech resembles the early seventeenth-century recitative lament, exemplified by Claudio Monteverdi's *Lamento di Arianna* (1608), in which poetic refrains punctuate and give shape to the utterance. In the *Spelonca di Marsilia* lament, four such refrains traverse the topics addressed in the speech, establishing a physical location before turning to the central focus of the lament, the description of actual acts of penitence: first 'O' Grotta, ò Speco, ò Sasso' (O grotto, O cave, O stone), then 'Mio Creator, mio Dio', followed by 'Peccai, signor, peccai / Io cadavere vile, io verme immondo / Offesi te che sei Signor del Mondo' (I sinned, my Lord, I sinned; I, vile corpse, I, foul worm, offended you who are Lord of the world) and finally 'Mani oziose, e vane' (idle and vain hands) [fols. 88r–89v]. As if in reaction to the shepherds' earlier comments on the joys and dangers of women's beauty, Mary Magdalene singles out those physical attributes that once defined her beauty and typified her idleness and transforms each into a symbol of her penitence: her eyes weep, her hair becomes a veil and her hands inflict blows (fols. 89r–90r):

Occhi che foste scorte
Agl' impuri diletti
Divenite di pianto eterne porte
Onde l'anima lavi i suoi difetti …

Chiome, ch'or per mia pompa
Erraste al vento sciolte
Ed'or intreccie accolte
Feste di mille cor misere prede
Chiome mi [è] troppo belle
Ma troppo à Dio rubelle
Chiome crescete tanto
Che voi facciate di voi stesse un velo.
Al Corpo indegno, acciò nol veggia il Cielo.
Mani oziose, e vane
S' or di fiori, or di gemme
Già con vano lavor m'ornaste il crine
D'acutissime spine
Or ghirlanda contesta
Passate questo core e questa testa.
Mani oziose, e vane
S' or mi cingeste al Collo
Prezioso monile
Primo del mar tesoro
Or mi cingeste al seno
Ricco trapunto d[']oro
Con più giusto lavoro
Mani da Dio contrite, ora con q*u*esta
Aspea Selve funesta
Battete questo petto
Di vanità ricetto
Mai non cessate, e le mie colpe intanto
Quinci lavino il Sangue, e quindi il pianto.

(Eyes that were the escorts to impure delights, become eternal doors of tears, so that you wash the soul of its defects … Hair, that sometimes for my display wandered loose to the winds and other times was gathered into braids, you made miserable prey of a thousand hearts. My hair is too beautiful but too rebellious towards God. Hair, grow so much that you become a veil to this unworthy body, so that it might see heaven. Idle and vain hands that earlier, with flowers or gems, would with vain labour arrange my hair – now place a garland braided from the sharpest thorns on this heart and on this head. Idle and vain hands that sometimes encircled my neck with precious jewelry, prime treasure of the sea, or other times surrounded this breast with rich, golden embroidery – with a more just labour, hands contrite before God, now with this hard, fatal wood beat this breast, shelter of vanity. Never cease, and my blows meanwhile will first cleanse the blood, and then the tears.)

Mary Magdalene concludes her speech by reiterating the transience of earthy life, as symbolized by the mirror and skull, two attributes that commonly accompanied her in art and were likely used here as props. This move from descriptive to moralizing speech marks a shift in focus, and she momentarily becomes the preacher praised by Ergasto and depicted in the frescos overhead, admonishing mortals to mark the fleeting nature of physical beauty before she dissolves in the flood of tears that will be, she claims, her only nourishment.

At the conclusion of the penitent Magdalene's lament, the angels – liminal beings who interact with both saint and shepherds – console her, promising that her desire to join with her beloved will now be satisfied. A new *ottonari* refrain (the only time this verse type appears in the play) frames this final section of the drama, delivered, possibly in music, by each angel in turn, then by both angels, and finally by the chorus (fols. 91r–92v):

Penitente avventurosa
Ch' innamori il Re del Cielo
Se piangente, se dogliosa
Qui t'affanni in vivo Zelo
Alla Croce il guardo gira
E dal duolo omai respira.

(Fortunate penitent, who is in love with the king of heaven, if with weeping and sadness you torment yourself here in animated zeal, turn your gaze to the cross and from sadness now respire.)

The refrain directs the Magdalene to refocus her tearful gaze on the cross, and she complies, embracing and adoring the very wood on which her Lord was sacrificed ('Deh voglia il Ciel ch'io spiri / l'anima mia su questo istesso legno / che sostenere il mio signor fu degno' [fol. 91v]). Once again her speech interacts dramatically with the physical location of the performance, through subject matter shared with the final panel in the chapel's Magdalene cycle as well as its utterance in a room filled with hundreds of relics, including one of the archduchess's own acquired relics of the holy cross.[35]

The machinery and scenery from the 1628 festivities were apparently reused the following year for a performance of a work entitled *Festa di Santa Maria Maddalena*, a work whose existence Michele Barbi noted in his monograph on Francesco Bracciolini, although he expressed scepticism as to its authorship.[36] The manuscript play indicates that it was to be performed in the archduchess's chapel ('da rappresentarsi nella cappella della Serenissima l'anno 1629'), and the 193-line work may be the final Magdalene play to have been performed in the Palazzo Pitti chapel during the archduchess's lifetime. In both its subject matter and its structure it recalls the earlier works. As secretary to papal nephew Cardinal Antonio Barberini, Bracciolini lived in Rome and probably did not attend the Florentine performances; if he did indeed write this play, someone from within the archduchess's inner circle must have given him a general idea of what was required. Like the plays of 1627 and 1628, over half the play elaborates on the subject of female beauty. This time the interlocutors are female: recalling the judgment of Paris but in a tone reminiscent of Bracciolini's *Lo scherno degli dei* (1618), Discord leads

Venus, Juno and Pallas Athena to a cave on the Tyrrhenian Sea then instigates an argument among them as to who is the most beautiful, promising a flower, rather than a golden apple, to whichever goddess emerges victorious. When Cupid arrives to award the prize, however, he informs the goddesses that Jupiter has decreed that the flower should instead be given to a new semi-goddess, whom he identifies as Anna, born of Austrian blood. The goddesses agree, and each praises this new deity, who not only receives, but apparently becomes the sought-after flower: Juno addresses her as Flora, and both Juno and Pallas promise to love her despite her Trojan heritage. Pallas's speech concludes: 'Io ami Flora e le bell'acque d'Arno' (I will love Florence and the beautiful waters of the Arno) [p. 192], references that point to Princess Anna de' Medici, whose thirteenth birthday had occurred the previous day.

As in the two previous plays an angel arrives to expel forcibly the secular world in favour of the Magdalene, shifting the dramatic focus by drawing the audience's attention to the new fruits and true roses about which the angel will speak. Aside from two brief interjections from the angel, Mary Magdalene's words dominate the remainder of the play. Once again the audience sees and hears Mary Magdalene the preacher, and the individuals who must learn from her example are not other characters in the play, but rather, actual members of the audience, who may have imagined themselves into the 'Preaching of Mary Magdalene' panel located to the right of the altar (see Figure 8.2). Gone are voyeuristic descriptions of the penitent, but still beautiful Magdalene, who describes her self-inflicted injuries in technicolour detail. This Magdalene begins her speech by contemplating the wounds of Christ on the cross and then explicating the role they played in the universal health of the world. She closes her sermon with a rhetorical discourse on the inadequacy of her own tears, then concludes the play by singing a four-stanza *canzonetta* in which she joyfully describes heaven opening to receive her, with a reference in the final stanza to flying ('ecco, ch'io me ne volo al patrio lido' [197]) that suggests reuse of the *nuvola*. The framing refrain sung by the Magdalene's angelic companion, 'Non più, non più lamenti', confirms the play's celebratory tone.[37]

Mary Magdalene's closing *canzonetta*, as well as the angel's two refrains, may well have been the only sung lines in the work. As with the other plays discussed above, music plays a crucial role in distinguishing the saint and her angelic companion from the play's other interlocutors, for they are the only characters who sing. In three of the four plays (of 1622, 1628 and 1629) Mary Magdalene's arrival also occurs well past the midpoint in the drama, creating a sense of revelation heightened by both the extended anticipation and the new sonic environment, while in the plays of 1627–29 the introductory material illustrates traits directly opposed to those the saint personifies. In Saracinelli's play of 1627 the emergence of the triumphant Mary Magdalene coincides with the singing of her three-stanza *canzonetta* 'Dall' orride foreste'. The shepherd Ergasto implores the angels to disclose the beautiful penitent to his unbelieving companions in the anonymous 1628 play, and the chorus's musical refrain, 'Ecco la bella', signals the angels' compliance. Bracciolini's play features a chastising angel who dismisses bickering goddesses, whom he describes as infernal shades ('ombre d'inferno'), then orders the audience to look and listen to the newly revealed 'peccatrice pentita', whose final four-stanza *canzonetta*, 'O puri campi', is the only closed poetic form in the play.

None of the music from these plays has survived, unfortunately, at least in recognizable form. Luckily, two surviving Florentine musical representations of St Mary Magdalene from this period shed light on the nature of at least some of the music likely heard in the archduchess's chapel: Andrea Falconieri's 'Maddalena chiedendo a Dio pietate' for soprano and basso continuo (Figure 8.3), one of two spiritual works published in his *Libro quinto delle musiche a una, due, e tre voci* (Florence, 1619), and, roughly a decade later, Girolamo Frescobaldi's spiritual sonnet 'Maddalena alla Croce' (Figure 8.4), published in the first volume of his *Arie* (Florence, 1630).

Falconieri's work is a likely candidate for performance at the 1619 banquet sponsored by the archduchess on behalf of her namesake: the court diary confirms the performance of music at the event, and the Falconieri volume had appeared in print just a few months earlier. Falconieri lived sporadically in Florence between December 1615 and July 1621, enjoying close ties with members of the Medici family. Dinko Fabris has noted the dramatic and virtuosic nature of some of Falconieri's works of this Florentine period, singling out 'Maddalena chiedendo a Dio' as an example of this style.[38] Fabris's discussion ends there, but a closer look at the work reveals that it serves a purpose similar to that of the visual and theatrical representations the archduchess collected and commissioned: it describes episodes from the saint's life and then guides the audience's interpretation of those events. Lines 1–3 of the poem present an image of the weeping, penitent Magdalene, while the final two lines celebrate her final, triumphant ascent to heaven – in short, a preview in summary form of the dramatic action of the plays of 1627, 1628 and 1629. The image of tears acts as the causal link between the two episodes, figuring prominently in the highly visual description of the saint's penitence and launching the series of exclamations that makes up the middle section of the poem.

Falconieri uses an arsenal of expressive devices to portray Mary Magdalene's keen grief. The work begins reverently, with the simple setting of a single word, 'Maddalena'. As the narrator describes the penitent saint asking for pity (mm. 4–8), Falconieri creates the effect of direct speech, encouraging the listener to hear the saint's actual voice: she repeats her petition a third lower, and then, in what appears to be the musical approximation of a groan, elongates her request for pity through the first of six lengthy vocal flourishes. Dissonance between voice and bass in the second half of measure 6 heightens the poignancy of the repeated request. Falconieri heightens the poetry's single-minded obsession with the saint's tears through expressive musical devices typical of the era: harsh dissonance (mm. 6, 11–12), vocal chromaticism (mm. 11, 14–15, 21–22), unexpected rhythmic pauses (m. 10) and melodically disorganized, jagged melismas (mm. 22–23).

At 'O lacrime beate', the phrase that marks the work's second half (m. 25), Falconieri reverts to the simple, uninflected opening of the work's first measures. Aside from a brief contemplation of Mary Magdalene's sighs (mm. 31–35), the text encourages the listener to dwell not on the tears themselves but on the rewards of true penitence. Consequently, for his setting of the poem's final lines the composer

**Figure 8.3** Andrea Falconieri, *Maddalena chiedendo a Dio*, in *Libro quinto delle musiche a una, due, e tre voci*, Florence: Zanobi Pignoni, 1619, 16–17.

**Figure 8.3** *Continued*

**Figure 8.3** *Continued*

reins in the expressive devices so characteristic of the first three quarters of the setting. In a manner similar to the poem he sets, he directs the listener to make causal connections between Magdalene's tears and her ultimate triumph: the effusive setting of the word *sede* at the work's conclusion recalls the earlier melismas that enacted the Magdalene's weeping, but this time the melody is patterned and consonant, and it leads logically to a concluding cadence as the ecstatic Magdalene is transported to heaven, the musical equivalent of the Rosselli painting that may have served as its backdrop. Directions to repeat this second half of the work add weight to the song's celebratory message.

Falconieri's madrigal, coupled with the interests of Archduchess Maria Magdalena, may have inspired the Roman keyboard virtuoso Girolamo Frescobaldi – who arrived in Florence in late 1628 – to publish his own musical setting on the subject, the spiritual sonnet 'Maddalena alla Croce' (Figure 8.4), which appeared in his first collection of vocal music.[39] The Falconieri and Frescobaldi works are roughly equal in length and in the same musical mode, and each composer heightens the Magdalene's despair musically by means of expressive melodic and rhythmic devices. But Frescobaldi's emotionally overwrought Magdalene captures the saint in a scene missing from the contemporaneous theatrical representations – the weeping Mary Magdalene at the Crucifixion.

The sonnet's two quatrains set the stage for the action through a concentration on visual images that is to some degree matched by Frescobaldi's music. In the three sections of the opening verse, a gradual vocal ascent encourages the listener's eyes to climb an imaginary cross, beginning at the foot ('A piè') and travelling upward to the languishing Jesus, whose suffering is made audible by an unexpected, dissonant disruption of the scalar ascent, one that remains unresolved (m. 3). By contrast to this dramatic opening, in line 2 (m. 5) Frescobaldi's narrator moves to the rapid speech rhythms and repeated notes of the more conversational recitative style. By minimizing the expressive possibilities inherent in the text line that depicts Christ near death, Frescobaldi renders the initial description of the saint all the more dramatic. This true subject of both the sentence and the sonnet – 'la sua fedele addolorata amante' (his faithful, distressed beloved) – appears in line 3,

**Figure 8.4** Girolamo Frescobaldi, *Sonetto Spirituale. Maddalena alla Croce* in *Primo libro d'arie musicali per cantarsi nel gravicembalo, e tiorba. A una, a due, a tre voci,* Florence: Landini, 1630, 15–16.

**Figure 8.4** *Continued*

and Frescobaldi draws attention to her disheveled appearance ('scapigliata così') by his abrupt return to the high register (m. 7), separating his description of Mary Magdalene from the preceding prepositional phrases and returning to the pitch on which the narrator earlier delivered the word 'croce', reminding the listener of the grieving saint's position at the foot of the cross.

While the first quatrain establishes the geographical and temporal location, as well as the subject of the scene to follow, the second focusses on vivid description, calling attention to Mary Magdalene's beautiful, weeping eyes and her golden, wavy, loose hair (mm. 13–22). Frescobaldi adopts a more narrative, emotionally neutral musical style for these lines, allowing the music of the first of the sonnet's two tercets – a highly dramatic imagining of the Magdalene's final words to her beloved – to stand in high relief. He matches the first person immediacy of these lines with the most musically expressive measures of the work. As Mary Magdalene demands to know how her Lord could leave her, her own words move ever higher but fall short of their presumed melodic goal (mm. 23–25). Frescobaldi uses register to separate her words from the narrator's 'dicea', but the specific pitches used also recall another well-known lament to a dead beloved – Orpheus's 'Tu sei morta' as set by Claudio Monteverdi in his opera *L'Orfeo* of 1607. At the second of her rhetorical questions (mm. 29–31), Mary Magdalene's frantic fervour yields to despair. The rhythmic syncopation that marks each of the question's three sections, 'Come', 'morendo tu' and 'viver' poss' io', gives the effect of stammering, and the slowly descending chromatic vocal line sinks into the cadence (m. 31). Frescobaldi repeats the phrase, retaining the same initial pitch and basic rhythmic outline. But this time Magdalene is insistent, demanding an answer: her earlier chromatic descent is inverted, and the slight alteration of the rhythmic shape of 'morendo' gives an added sharpness to her question, which also reaches the melodic goal of d' that was earlier denied in measure 25.

The impassioned questioning of the first tercet gives way to a newly found resolve in the second, as Mary Magdalene vows to unite her soul with Jesus and thereby share in not only his life, but also his death. The sudden harmonic shift at measure 35 signals this change of mood, and her earlier expressive chromaticism gives way to more neutral declamation. In the repetition of her final line, she exhibits the control that comes with resolve, as her melodic line gradually ascends an octave before participating in an extended final cadence. As in the surviving Mary Magdalene plays performed in the archduchess's chapel, audience members would thus have had the opportunity to hear the saint speak – an audibility that differs from the communicative abilities of visual art and continues the tradition of Magdalene as preacher that was, by the seventeenth century, less prevalent in the visual tradition.

As patron of these works, Archduchess Maria Magdalena assumed indirectly a preaching role. But unlike the large-scale theatrical works she sponsored during the period of the regency, commissioned to mark state events, the 'congregation' for the Mary Magdalene plays and music consisted of a small circle of her intimates as well as, reflexively, the archduchess herself. These works were partly for her own devotional consumption, hidden from public view much as were the relics housed in the chapel in which they were performed. But she was seen to be consuming them; just as courtiers and her family knew that she possessed relics, they knew about the performances in that chapel, even if they themselves did not attend them. During the period of the regency, at least, the events were part of the official court record. The Mary Magdalene performances occupied an intermediate space between public and private events, representing a private act of piety whose existence was to be known by – although not necessarily witnessed by – a broader public, in a manner analogous to the saint in her grotto. Archduchess Maria

Magdalena consciously fostered identification with her namesake throughout her tenure as grand duchess, most notably by commissioning Justus Sustermans to depict her visually as the penitent Magdalene (Figure 8.5), but also through public acts, such as her establishment of a Holy Thursday tradition of publicly washing the feet of twelve women with her own hands.[40] Her Palazzo Pitti chapel and its associated artistic activities also seem to have been designed to encourage guests to connect the archduchess to both the penitence and eventual triumph of her namesake. Each year her small chapel was transformed into the Magdalene's grotto, an analogy made explicit, for example, in the 1629 play, in which characters situate the play geographically through references to both the Tyrrhenian Sea and

**Figure 8.5** Justus Sustermans, *Archduchess Maria Magdalena as Saint Mary Magdalene*, c. 1625–30. Florence, Palazzo Pitti, Galleria Palatina. Soprintendenza per i Beni Artistici e Storici, Gabinetto Fotografico no. 153327.

the Arno river. The message was clear: for an hour or so Florence had become the new home of Mary Magdalene, enclosed within a beautiful receptacle to which a living Magdalena granted access.

## Notes

1 Florence, Archivio di Stato [=I-Fas], Misc. Med., 11, fol. 201r: 'Giorno di Santa Maria Madalena. Si fece festa nella Cappella della Ser.ma Arc.a, si cantò la Messa con Musica et il Vespro, et doppo Vespro si fece dalli Paggini di S.A. una Rapp.ne che fù S. Maria Madalena trionfiante in Paradiso, cosa breve, ma belliss.a essendovi intromesso intermedi di Musica, composizione del S.re Bali Ferd.o Saracinelli . . . la Ser.a Arc.a non fece fare il Banchetto conforme alli anni passati per non ci esser Dame'.

2 Kelley Harness, *Echoes of Women's Voices: Music, Art, and Female Patrons in Early Modern Florence* (Chicago: University of Chicago Press, 2006).

3 On the archduchess's commissioning and collecting of sacred objects and non-theatrical experiences see Alice Elizabeth Sanger, 'Women of Power: Studies in the Patronage of Medici Grand Duchesses and Regentesses 1565–1650' (PhD thesis, University of Manchester, 2000), 132–88; Alice E. Sanger, *Art, Gender and Religious Devotion in Grand Ducal Tuscany* (Farnham, Surrey: Ashgate, 2014), esp. 71–111. Sanger also explores the archduchess's highly visible devotional acts in 'Maria Maddalena d'Austria's Pilgrimage to Loreto: Visuality, Liminality and Exchange', in *Medici Women as Cultural Mediators (1533–1743)/Le donne di casa Medici e il loro ruolo di mediatrici culturali fra le corti d'Europa*, ed. Christina Strunck (Milan: Silvana Editoriale, 2011), 253–65. In the same collection see also Ilaria Hoppe, 'Maria Maddalena d'Austria e il culto delle reliquie alla corte dei Medici: Scambi di modelli dinastici ed ecclesiastici', 227–51.

4 On the tradition of a singing Mary Magdalene, see H. Colin Slim, 'Mary Magdalene, Musician and Dancer', *Early Music* 8:4 (October 1980), 460–73.

5 I have here followed (but translated) the titles given in Lisa Goldenberg Stoppato, 'La cappella delle Reliquie di Palazzo Pitti', in *Fasto di corte: La decorazione murale nelle residenze dei Medici e dei Lorena*, ed. Mina Gregori, 3 vols. (Florence: Edifir, 2005–7), 1:139.

6 The chapel's present-day cupboards date from 1712, but the paintings that adorn them date to Maria Magdalena's commissions of 1618; see Alessandro Conti, 'The Reliquary Chapel', *Apollo* 106:1 (1977), 198–201; Marco Chiarini, 'La cappella delle Reliquie', in *Palazzo Pitti: L'arte e la storia*, ed. Marco Chiarini (Florence: Nardini, 2000), 54–56; Goldenberg Stoppato, 'La Cappella delle Reliquie', 137–43; and, most recently, Lisa Goldenberg Stoppato, 'La decorazione della Cappella delle Reliquie', in *Sacri splendori. Il tesoro della 'Cappella delle Reliquie' in Palazzo Pitti, catalogo della mostra (Firenze, Palazzo Pitti, Museo degli Argenti, 10 giugno–2 novembre 2014*, ed. Riccardo Gennaioli and Maria Sframeli (Livorno: Sillabe, 2014), 32–49, who thoroughly documents the history of the paintings along with the other renovations of that decade, including numerous colour plates. See also Sanger, *Art, Gender and Religious Devotion*, 84–90.

7 Sanger, 'Women of Power', 150–69; Sanger, *Art, Gender and Religious Devotion*, 71–91; Goldenberg Stoppato, 'La cappella delle Reliquie', 137.

8 Florence, Biblioteca Riccardiana (=I-Fr), Ricc. 2242, fols. 27r–55v, 195r–201v, 203r–206v. For more on this play see Kelley Ann Harness, '*Amazzoni di Dio*: Florentine

Musical Spectacle under Maria Maddalena d'Austria and Cristina di Lorena (1620–30)' (PhD diss., University of Illinois, 1996), 271–74.

9 Sanger, 'Women of Power', 152–53; Sanger, *Art, Gender and Religious Devotion*, 71–72.

10 I-Fas, Archivio Mediceo del Principato (MDP) 105, fol. 281r.

11 I-Fr, Ricc. 3093. She may also have been the intended recipient of Ottavio Rinuccini's unfinished dialogue between saints Mary Magdalene and Martha, which survives in a manuscript in Florence, Biblioteca Nazionale Centrale (=I-Fn), Magl. VII.902, fols. 105r–107r. Rinuccini's *Versi sacri* (Florence, 1619) had been sung in the archduchess's chapel on 2 April 1619. See Francesca Chiarelli, 'L'inedita "Santa Maria Maddalena" di Ottavio Rinuccini', *Studi italiani*, 6:1 (1994), 115–20; Harness, '*Amazzoni di Dio*', 271, 415.

12 I-Fas, Guardaroba Medicea, 479. See Harness, '*Amazzoni di Dio*', 256–70. The inventory has since been published: Paola Barocchi and Giovanna Gaeta Bertelà, eds., *Collezionismo Mediceo e storia artistica*, vol. 2, *Il Cardinale Carlo, Maria Maddalena, Don Lorenzo, Ferdinando II, Vittoria della Rovere 1621–1666* (Florence: Studio per Edizioni Scelti, 2005), 271–314. See also Ilaria Hoppe, *Die Räume der Regentin: Die Villa Poggio Imperiale in Florenz* (Berlin: Dietrich Reimer, 2011), esp. 58–76. Hoppe (61–62) briefly discusses Francesco Curradi's lunettes for Villa Poggia Imperiale, which date from 1632, shortly after the archduchess's death but possibly commissioned by her. On the Curradi cycle see also Marilena Mosco, 'La cappella della Maddalena nella villa di Poggio Imperiale a Firenze', in *La Maddalena tra sacro e profane*, ed. Marilena Mosco (Milan: Mondadori, 1986), 237–39, who dates the cycle roughly a decade earlier, following Silvana Cuzzocrea, 'Francesco Curradi ovvero la pittura di devozione', *Paradigma* 6 (1985), 107–30.

13 Mosco, 'Cappella della Maddalena', 237. According to the 1625 inventory (opening 6) the small panel painting, there misidentified as a work by Leonardo, was set into the small ebony altar in the archduchess's bedroom.

14 Giuseppe Richa, *Notizie istoriche delle chiese fiorentine*, 10 vols. (Florence: Pietro Gaetano Viviani, 1762; reprint, Rome: Multigrafica, 1989), 10:217. An eighteenth-century plan of the palace, one that includes a scale in *braccia*, appears to corroborate Richa's estimate; see Alessandra Contini and Orsola Gori, eds., *Dentro la reggia: Palazzo Pitti e Boboli nel Settecento* (Florence: Edifir, 2004), 162–63.

15 See Patricia Waddy, *Seventeenth-Century Roman Palaces: Use and the Art of the Plan* (Cambridge, MA: MIT Press, 1990), 7, on the perception of chapels as private territory. In my thinking about the political messages conveyed by the archduchess's chapel I have been especially influenced by Helen Hills, 'Theorizing the Relationships between Architecture and Gender in Early Modern Europe', in *Architecture and the Politics of Gender in Early Modern Europe*, ed. Helen Hills (Aldershot: Ashgate, 2003), 3–22.

16 I-Fn, Gino Capponi, 261, vol. 2, fol. 216r. A few months before that, on 14 November 1618, Maria Magdalena sponsored a musical performance in her chapel to celebrate the unveiling of the St Mary Magdalene painting (I-Fn, Gino Capponi, 261, vol. 2, fol. 173v, transcribed in Angelo Solerti, *Musica, ballo e drammatica alla corte Medicea dal 1600 al 1637* [Florence: Bemporad, 1905; reprint, New York: Benjamin Blom, 1968], 142). A digitial reproduction of this volume of the Tinghi diary, along with the others held at the Biblioteca Nazionale Centrale, is available at the library's website, specifically at http://teca.bncf.firenze.sbn.it/ImageViewer/servlet/ImageViewer?idr=BNCF0003469476#page/1/mode/2up.

17 I-Fn, Gino Capponi, 261, vol. 2, fol. 259r, partially transcribed in Solerti, *Musica, ballo e drammatica*, 155. Solerti's transcription ends just before the mention of the Mary Magdalene play. See also Suzanne G. Cusick, *Francesca Caccini at the Medici Court: Music and the Circulation of Power* (Chicago: University of Chicago Press, 2009), 283, 300.

18 I-Fn, Gino Capponi, 261, vol. 2, fol. 401r.

19 The play remained unpublished until the nineteenth century, when it appeared in Giovammaria Cecchi, *Commedie*, ed. Michele Dello Russo (Naples: Francesco Ferrante, 1869), 121–40. On this and other Mary Magdalene plays performed by the confraternity of the Arcangelo Raffaello, see Konrad Eisenbichler, *The Boys of the Archangel Raphael: A Youth Confraternity in Florence, 1411–1785* (Toronto: University of Toronto Press, 1998), 214–17. According to the confraternity's records, members performed a similarly titled play (*Il disprezzo d'amore, et bellezza terrena*) in 1623, although it is attributed to Jacopo Cicognini (I-Fas, Compagnie religiose soppresse [CRS], 162, no. 22, fols. 102v–103r).

20 I-Fn, Gino Capponi 261, vol. 2, fol. 523r, transcribed in Solerti, *Musica*, 163, here emended slightly to reflect the original. Near the end of that same year, the archduchess wrote to the Florentine ambassador in Rome, Francesco Niccolini, reminding him that she sought an indulgence for her Palazzo Pitti chapel that would cover all the solemn feasts of the year, 'especially for our feast of Santa Maria Maddalena' ('et di più per la n.ra Festa di S.ta Maria Madd.na), as she added near the end of the letter (I-Fas, MDP, 105, fol. 456v, draft dated 12 December 1622).

21 I-Fas, MDP 111, fols. 182r–v; transcribed and discussed in Harness, *Echoes of Women's Voices*, 79–109. See also Cusick, *Francesca Caccini at the Medici Court*, 87.

22 I-Fr, Ricc. 2782, fols. 343r–348v. This work was discovered by John Walter Hill, who kindly informed me of its existence.

23 I-Fas, CRS, 162, no. 22, fols. 115r–116v, transcribed and translated in Harness, '*Amazzoni di Dio*', 374–76.

24 Cecchi, *Commedie*, ed. Dello Russo, 97–120; Eisenbichler, *The Boys of the Archangel Raphael*, 397n30. In a private correspondence Prof. Konrad Eisenbichler, who is at present working on an English translation of this and other sacred plays by Cecchi, has reiterated to me his belief that the attribution to Cecchi is correct.

25 Eisenbichler, *The Boys of Archangel Raphael*, 216.

26 Cecchi, *Commedie*, ed. Della Russo, 119–20.

27 I-Fn, Gino Capponi, 261, vol. 2, fol. 605v (for 1623); I-Fas, Misc. Med., 11, fol. 60r (for 1624), the latter transcribed in Solerti, *Musica*, 173. A 1690 inventory of the company's belongings (I-Fas, CRS, 155, B, p. 20, lists numerous manuscript plays by Jacopo Cicognini, including 'opere varie sopra S. Maria Mad.na penitente' (various works on the penitent St Mary Magdalene).

28 I-Fas, Misc. Med. 11, fols. 133v–134r.

29 I-Fas, Misc. Med. 11, fol. 175r.

30 Archduchess Maria Magdalena and her guests would have understood St Mary Magdalene to be the woman who appears in several biblical passages, including the female sinner who anointed Christ's feet with her tears at the house of Simon the Pharisee (Lk 7:36–50) and the woman who stood beside the cross during his crucifixion (Jn 19:25), a tradition accepted in Western Catholicism beginning with Pope Gregory I. The literature addressing the cult and legend of St Mary Magdalene

is vast; see, for example, Victor Saxer, *Le culte de Marie Madeleine en Occident des origines à la fin du moyen âge*, 2 vols. (Paris: Librairie Clavreuil, 1959); Susan Haskins, *Mary Magdalen: Myth and Metaphor* (New York: Harcourt Brace, 1993); Katherine Ludwig Jansen, *The Making of the Magdalen: Preaching and Popular Devotion in the Later Middle Ages* (Princeton: Princeton University Press, 2000); Diane Apostolos-Cappadona, *In Search of Mary Magdalene: Images and Traditions* (New York: American Bible Society, 2002); Bruno Phalip, Céline Perol and Pascale Quincy-Lefebvre, eds., *Marthe et Marie-Madeleine: Deux modèles de dévotion et d'accueil chrétien* (Clermont-Ferrand: Presses Universitaires Blaise-Pascal, 2009); Michelle A. Erhardt and Amy M. Morris, eds., *Mary Magdalene: Iconographic Studies from the Middle Ages to the Baroque*, Studies in Religion and the Arts 7 (Leiden: Brill, 2012).

31 I-Fas, MDP, 1839, fol. 72r. On *nuvole* see Nicola Sabbatini, *Pratica di fabricar scene e machine ne' teatri*, ed. Elena Povoledo (Rome: Carlo Bestetti, 1955), 105–23; and *Enciclopedia dello spettacolo*, ed. Francesco Savio et al., 9 vols. (Rome: Casa Editrice le Maschere, 1954–62), s.v. 'Nuvole' (by Elena Povoledo).

32 I-Fn, Magl. VII.604, fols. 78r–92v. I would like to thank Prof. Hill for kindly sharing this discovery with me.

33 See, for example, the extraordinarily popular thirteenth-century *Legenda aurea* by Jacobus de Voragine, translated as *The Golden Legend: Readings on the Saints* by William Granger Ryan, 2 vols. (Princeton: Princeton University Press, 1993), 1:374–83.

34 The conversion of on-stage spectators as a result of witnessing Mary Magdalene's example is a dramatic trope apparently derived from earlier Florentine plays on the subject, appearing in *Rappresentazione di un miracolo di S. Maria Maddalena*, in Alessandro d'Ancona, ed., *Sacre rappresentazioni dei secoli XIV, XV e XVI*, 3 vols. (Florence: Successori Le Monnier, 1872), 1:391–425; Antonio Alamanni, *Commedia della conversione di Santa Maria Maddalena*, ed. Pierre Jodogne (Bologna: Commissione per i testi di lingua, 1977).

35 Sanger, *Art, Gender and Religious Devotion*, 81–82. See also Estella Galasso Calderara, *La Granduchessa Maria Maddalena d'Austria* (Genoa: Sagep, 1985), 88.

36 Michele Barbi, *Notizia della vita e delle opere di Francesco Bracciolini* (Florence: Sansoni, 1897), 164. Pietro Parducci subsequently published an edition of the work, which he believed to be by Bracciolini, based on the surviving manuscript (Arezzo, Biblioteca della Fraternità di Santa Maria, Ms. 103); see his *Spigolature letterarie* (Rome: Albrighi Segati & Co., 1904), 181–97. Subsequent references will be to this edition. See also Solerti, *Musica*, 195. Two biographical studies on the poet remain silent on the issue: *Dizionario biografico degli Italiani*, s.v. 'Bracciolini (Dell'Api), Francesco', http://www.treccani.it/enciclopedia/francesco-bracciolini_%28Dizionario-Biografico%29/ (accessed 18 October 2016); and Laura Benedetti, 'Francesco Bracciolini', in *Seventeenth-Century Italian Poets and Dramatists*, ed. Albert N. Mancini and Glenn Palen Pierce (Detroit: Gale, Cengage Learning, 2008), 55–64.

37 Parducci (*Spigolature letterarie*, 197) assigns the second occurrence of the refrain to St Mary Magdalene, but the text's reference to 'your tears' suggests that the angel sang it both times.

38 Dinko Fabris, *Andrea Falconieri napoletano: Un liutista-compositore del Seicento* (Rome: Edizioni Torre d'Orfeo, 1987), 84.

39 Frederick Hammond, 'Girolamo Frescobaldi: New Biographical Information', in *Frescobaldi Studies*, ed. Alexander Silbiger (Durham, NC: Duke University Press, 1987), 22. For a contextualized analysis that studies the work within webs of Mediterranean influence, see Susan McClary, 'Mediterranean Trade Routes and Music of the Early Seventeenth Century', *Inter-American Music Review* 17:1–2 (Summer 2007), 135–44. The work has been recorded by soprano Maria Cristina Kiehr with Concerto Soave, dir. Jean-Marc Aymes, on *Canta la Maddalena* (Harmonia Mundi, HMC 901698).

40 Galasso Calderara, *La Granduchessa Maria Maddalena*, 126.

# 9

# GUERCINO'S *CHRIST AND THE WOMAN OF SAMARIA* IN THE KIMBELL ART MUSEUM: THE EVOLUTION OF BIBLICAL NARRATIVE AND VISUAL MEANING

Heidi J. Hornik

The Italian seventeenth-century artist Guercino painted the *Christ and the Woman of Samaria at the Well* (Figure 9.1) in the collection of the Kimbell Art Museum, Fort Worth, Texas.[1] The painting, dated 1619–20, marks the culmination of Guercino's early (pre-Roman) artistic style and has been previously published only once.[2] Guercino's use of composition and gesture creates a rich visual depiction of John 4:1–26 that is critical to our understanding of the theme during the Baroque period of art history. The meaning of the Gospel story to the artist and to his contemporaries is further revealed in the context of biblical interpretation.

## *The Artist*

Giovanni Francesco Barbieri was christened on 8 February 1591 in the small town of Cento, twenty miles northeast of Bologna.[3] According to his friend and biographer of Emilian painters, Malvasia (1616–1693), he was the son of Andrea Barbieri and Elena Ghisellini.[4] Giovanni Battista Passeri (1610–1679), another contemporary biographer, writes that Guercino's father was a woodchopper.[5] Giovanni was given the nickname, 'the squinter' due to a childhood malady that left him 'wall eyed' or cross-eyed. Guercino was largely self-taught, but studied with Benedetto Gennari (1563–1658) in Cento in 1607.[6] In 1628, Guercino's sister Lucia married Benedetto's brother (and one of Guercino's assistants), Ercole Gennari (1597–1658).[7] Lucia and Ercole had two sons, both of whom joined Guercino's workshop. As Guercino never married or had children, he left his estate to his nephews when he died in Bologna on 22 December 1666.[8]

We do not know exactly when Guercino first came to Bologna but scholars agree that he was influenced by Ludovico Carracci (1555–1619) and his cousins, Annibale Carracci (1560–1609) and Agostino Carracci (1557–1602). The Carracci artists emphasized the importance of preparatory drawings, drawing from nature and other methods that clearly define what is today known as the Bolognese

**Figure 9.1** Guercino, *Christ and the Woman of Samaria at the Well,* 1619–20. 38¼ x 49⅛ ins. Oil on canvas. Kimbell Art Museum. Credit Line: Kimbell Art Museum, Fort Worth, Texas. Acquired in 2010 in memory of Edmund P. Pillsbury, director of the Kimbell Art Museum, 1980–98.

Academic style of painting that was shared by Guercino. Recent scholarship clarifies that whenever Guercino arrived the first time in Bologna, he probably knew only Ludovico personally.[9] Passeri tells a delightful tale of how Guercino met the Carracci brothers while delivering firewood with his father and was quite taken by their drawing. So, Annibale showed him how to use a pen. This is not possible as Annibale and Agostino left Bologna in 1595 and 1597 respectively, when Guercino, born in 1591, was a small child.[10]

Guercino did meet Bolognese cleric Canon Antonio Mirandola of San Salvatore in 1612. Mirandola was responsible for convincing Don Biagio Bagni to give Guercino his first important commission in 1613 for the church of S. Spirito in Cento. By 1616, Guercino had opened the first 'Accademia del nudo' in the house of Centese patron Bartolomeo Fabri. According to Malvasia, the school of life drawing, patterned after the Carracci academy in Bologna, was considerably successful, having twenty-three students in 1617.[11]

Alessandro Ludovisi, archbishop of Bologna (who will be elected Pope Gregory XV in 1621), calls Guercino to Bologna to paint four panels. Ludovico Carracci wrote to Don Ferrante Carlo, secretary to Cardinal Scipione Borghese, on 19 July 1617, reporting the arrival of Guercino in Bologna. A few months later, on 25

October 1617, Ludovico writes again to Carlo and praises Guercino by saying, 'There is a young man here born in Cento who paints with the happiest of inventiveness. He is a great draftsman and a felicitous colourist: he is a phenomenon of nature and a wonder capable of astounding all who see his work'.[12]

By 1618, Guercino's reputation is established and he makes a brief trip to Parma and Venice. While in Venice, Guercino meets Japopo Negretti (known as Palma il Giovane and a student of Titian) and encounters the works of Titian. Malvasia recounts the patronage of Cardinal Jacopo Serra, papal legate of Ferrara, as occupying Guercino's efforts in 1619. Three paintings, *The Return of the Prodigal Son* (Kunsthistorisches Museum, Vienna), *St Sebastian* (Pinacoteca Nazionale, Bologna) and *Samson Seized by the Philistines* (Metropolitan Museum of Art, New York), were executed for Cardinal Serra.[13] In Ferrara, Guercino encountered the paintings of Scarsellino (1550–1620) and Carlo Bononi (1569–1632). Guercino then goes to Mantua in 1620 to work for Duke Ferdinando Gonzaga and then was summoned to Rome by the new Pope Gregory XV (Alessandro Ludovisi) in 1621.[14]

Art historians recognize a change in style from the early works to the late works of Guercino but do not necessarily agree with why this happens. The works painted between 1615 and 1620 are quite different stylistically from those of the 1650s. Francesco Scannelli, Guercino's friend and biographer, commented on this stylistic change in the seventeenth century.[15] Denis Mahon attributed the change to the influence of Monsignor Agucchi's classicistic art theory encountered by Guercino during his time in Rome (1621–23).[16] David Stone revised this theory by dividing the works according to those produced before and after Rome, not based on theoretical influences, but on internal artistic reasons.[17] This stylistic (pre-Rome versus post-Rome) division will be applied in support of the dating of *The Christ and the Woman of Samaria at the Well* in the Kimbell.

## *The Painting*

The Kimbell *Christ and the Woman of Samaria at the Well* (Figure 9.1) should be dated stylistically alongside the *Samson Captured by the Philistines* in New York (Figure 9.2) and *The Return of the Prodigal Son* in Vienna (Figure 9.3) commissioned by Cardinal Archbishop Jacopo Serra of Ferrara in 1619–20.

Keith Christiansen, the John Pope-Hennessy Chairman of European Paintings at the Metropolitan Museum of Art in New York, comments that '*Christ and the Woman of Samaria* is, I believe, the finest painting by the artist to appear on the international market in years'. He noted that the work is among the handful of paintings, including the Metropolitan Museum's *Samson Captured by the Philistines* (Figure 9.2), 'that are generally considered to mark the culmination of his early phase, in which he achieves a quality of dramatic movement through the use of gesture, pose, and brilliant, theatrical lighting. But there is another side to this aspect of Guercino, as beautifully exemplified in the *Christ and the Woman of Samaria*, and that is an interest in psychological characterization; the story is told

**Figure 9.2** Guercino, *Samson Captured by the Philistines*, 1619. Oil on canvas. 75¼ x 93¼ ins. The Metropolitan Museum of Art. Credit Line: Gift of Mr and Mrs Charles Wrightsman, 1984. Image © The Metropolitan Museum of Art. http://www.metmuseum.org/.

not as an unfolding drama but as a moment of revelation, in which the viewer is less an observer than an eavesdropper of a private moment, and this confers on the work a particularly mesmerizing quality.'[18] This aspect of the psychological characterization will be examined below in light of the biblical narrative.

These three paintings, rightly considered Guercino's early mature works, are defined by a compelling vitality and a forceful brush. The fluidity and tactile quality of the garments and the dramatic *chiaroscuro*, as well as the compositional arrangement, are reminiscent of Caravaggio. The value of gesture is also apparent in the prominence and placement of hands in each of the three paintings. The report of the chief conservator at the Kimbell, Claire Barry, supports the authenticity of the painting as an original composition and the importance gesture plays in the work.[19] Two important *pentimenti* (under paintings) were discovered when the painting was x-rayed. The existence of major *pentimenti* is evidence of an original work of art rather than a copy because the artist has changed his mind while creating the composition. Guercino twice remodelled Christ's right hand, making his gesture more open and inclusive. Conservator Barry explains, 'And in so doing he helps connect the figure of Christ more closely to the viewer. The importance of this gesture is also seen in how Guercino rests the tip of Christ's finger right

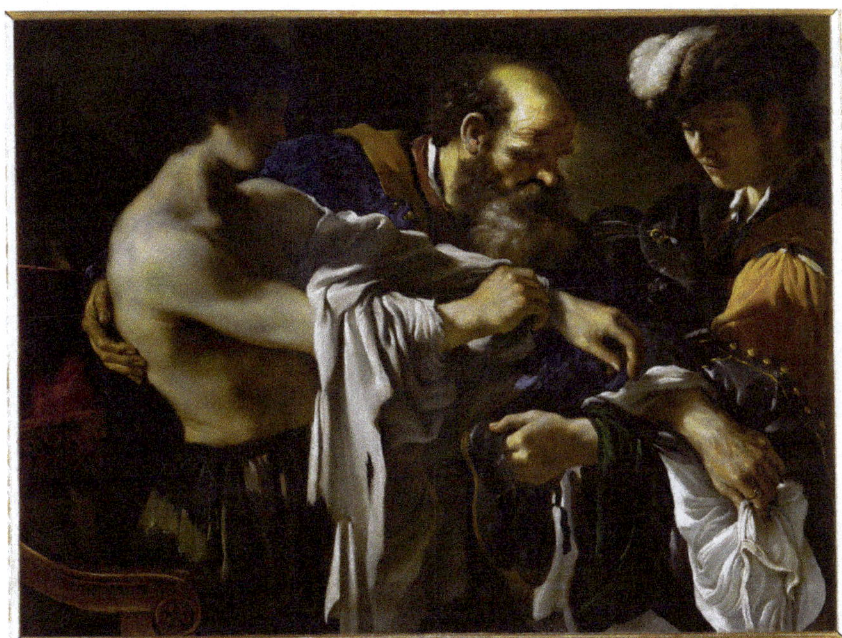

**Figure 9.3** Guercino, *Return of the Prodigal Son*, 1619, 47 x 63½ ins. Oil on canvas, Kunsthistorisches Museum, Vienna. Photo Credit: Erich Lessing/Art Resource, NY.

on the edge of the painting. He also changed the tilt of the head of the woman of Samaria. He tilted her head back just slightly as if to convey that she was very actively engaged in the act of listening – as if she were just beginning to absorb Christ's message.'[20]

The half-length figures are pushed to the foreground and gaze at each other with closed lips. The full-cheeked woman balances her bucket on the ledge of the well and steadies it with her right hand while the handle encircles her left forearm. Her hair is pulled away from her face and secured above the nape of her neck. There is a very small amount of space between her right sleeve and the blue cloak over the left arm of Christ. Christ's face is loving and attentive. The light accentuates the centre of Christ's face and both of their necks. The woman, whose face is in *chiaroscuro*, gazes at him. The lines of the composition have subtle diagonals from her right shoulder to Christ's left hand that holds his outer garment and then downwards to his dramatically foreshortened open right hand. The right hand is the only part of the composition that is tense, movemented and demonstrative during their conversation. That is the area that Guercino changed twice according to the *pentimenti* to get this final gesture.

A thematic study of other versions of the *Christ and the Woman of Samaria* paintings attributed to Guercino and to his workshop is useful as further evidence of attribution and dating. The theme is very popular and numerous copies were made during Guercino's career.[21] The paintings at the Detroit Institute of Art

**Figure 9.4** Studio of Guercino, *Christ and the Woman of Samaria at the Well,* 1620. 44.6 x 61 in. Oil on canvas. City of Detroit Purchase. Detroit Institute of Arts. Purchased 1926. Photo Credit: Detroit Institute of Arts, USA, City of Detroit Purchase/Bridgeman Images.

(Figure 9.4) and at the David Museum and Cultural Center at Wellesley College (Figure 9.5) are dated 1620 and are closely related to the original Kimbell painting that inspired them. Ward Bissell described the Detroit painting as an excellent replica, produced in the studio of Guercino, of a painting that the artist had conceived and executed about 1620.[22] The Wellesley College painting is a much-darkened version that scholars agree did not reach the level of quality of the Detroit picture.[23] Nonetheless, it is dated 1620 and belongs with this compositional grouping.

The basic principles of a composition from c. 1620 includes half- or three-quarter length figures seen close up, imposing their presences upon the picture plane and upon the viewer.[24] Mahon and Bissell found that the impelling force of Guercino's brush brought incomparable vitality to the works of his early maturity, wherein forms of convincing corporeality seem nonetheless caught in a universal flux missing from the Detroit painting.[25]

Bissell supported this conclusion by explaining specifically what is lacking: 'Christ's robes have the design but not the fluidity of garments painted by Guercino, by the uniformity of the shadows on the flesh areas, resulting in passages (as the head of the woman) of flattened forms, and by the lack of animation in the hair, foliage, and clouds'.[26] Mahon and Bissell both cited a lost painting (perhaps the original) known only in a black-and-white photograph published by Luigi Salerno.[27] Due to the minor *pentimenti* and variations in pigment application in

**Figure 9.5** Studio of Guercino, *Christ and the Woman of Samaria at the Well,* 1620. 37 x 50 ins. Oil on canvas. Davis Museum and Cultural Center, Wellesley College. Credit Line: Gift of Dr and Mrs Arthur K. Solomon.

the Detroit painting, Bissell concluded that this hand belonged to a member of the master's studio employing workshop methods rather than to a later copyist.[28] More importantly for our discussion, Bissell established that the issue is not whether the master himself produced replicas of his inventions, for especially in his later years he clearly did, and indeed qualitative differences between the prime versions and autograph replicas may sometimes be observed, but rather that there are stylistic differences that occur in compositions two decades later.

During those two decades, Guercino works in Rome 1621–23, returns to Cento in 1623 and moves to Bologna in 1642 until his death in 1666. Guercino goes to Rome after his former patron Alessandro Ludovisi, the Archbishop of Bologna, was elected Pope Gregory XV on 9 February 1621. The new pope also brings his nephew to Rome and, on 15 February 1621, nominated him Cardinal Ludovico Ludovisi. Ludovico commissions Guercino and Agostino Tassi to paint the *Aurora* (Figure 9.6) on the ceiling in the central room of the ground floor in the Casino Ludovisi and the work is documented as already in progress by 29 July 1621.[29] In the Villa Ludovisi, Guercino abandons the Baroque *chiaroscuro* for a lighter palette and adjusted his earlier asymmetrical compositions to a more classical style of symmetry and balance.

The paintings after Guercino's Roman period, as related to this theme, have pronounced idealization, pictorial refinement and a less intimate narration. Two paintings of the *Christ and the Woman of Samaria at the Well* that date two decades later are illustrated here (Figures 9.7 and 9.8) and exemplify the changes in palette, lighting and figural relationships. Three different versions of *Christ and the Samaritan Woman* are listed, in the *Libro dei conti* (accounts book) kept by the artist's brother Paolo Antonio until his death in 1649 and then continued by another member of the workshop.[30] Roberto Contain believes the picture in the Thyssen-Bornemisza Collection, Madrid (Figure 9.7) should be dated 1640. Giuseppe Baroni of Lucca documented the work as being first chronologically in the group of Christ and the Woman of Samaria thematic paintings.[31] The painting in the National Gallery of Ottawa (Figure 9.8) is the second painting listed in the ledger; it was for the patron Abbot Bentivoglio in 1641.[32] Both of these paintings indicate a post-Roman style of handling the subject that is closer to the style of Guido Reni (1575–1642) and is more typical of the Bolognese Academic style of painting. It lacks the dramatic lighting with chiaroscuro and the intimate relationship between the two figures. There is more physical and emotional separation between the Samaritan woman and Christ. In both paintings her right arm pulls the rope from the well, and as she draws the bucket she also draws herself away from Christ. The moment in the biblical narrative is also different than in the Kimbell, Detroit and Wellesley College paintings. This will be discussed below.

Similar compositional changes occur in pre-Rome and post-Rome Guercino paintings of another biblical narrative, the Return of the Prodigal Son. By

**Figure 9.6** Guercino and Agostino Tassi, *Aurora's (Dawn's) Chariot.* Detail from the ceiling fresco of the *Allegory of Dawn* or *Aurora*, 1621–23. Ceiling fresco. Villa Ludovisi, Rome. Photo Credit: Scala /Art Resource, NY.

**Figure 9.7** Guercino, *Christ and the Woman of Samaria at the Well*, 1640. 51.5 x 69.3 ins. Oil on canvas. © Thyssen-Bornemisza Collection Foundation, Madrid. Purchased 1976. Photo Credit: Museo Thyssen-Bornemisza/Scala /Art Resource, NY.

comparing *Return of the Prodigal Son*, dated 1619, in the Kunsthistorisches Museum, Vienna, and the third painting commissioned by Cardinal Jacopo Serra of Ferrara with the *Prodigal* in the Museo Diocesano, Wloclawek, Poland, and in the Timken, San Diego, the same compositional and stylistic changes occur.[33]

## *Interpretation of the Biblical Narrative: Lapide, Guercino and* Christ and the Woman of Samaria at the Well

Guercino lived during the Catholic Reformation in Italy. The Italian Baroque style of art is largely a product of the decrees made at the Council of Trent in the twenty-fifth and final session held on 3–4 December 1563. The decree 'On Invocation, Veneration, and Relics of Saints, and on Sacred Images' directed bishops to see to the proper preaching on these subjects. Trent dealt with the veneration of sacred images, a subject that first received solemn church ratification of the Second Council of Nicea (787), in reaction to the violent outburst of iconoclasm in the Eastern Empire.[34] Nicea had declared that sacred images were legitimate and helpful for instruction and devotion. Trent went further by saying they should be free of all 'sensual appeal' (*lascivia*), false doctrine and superstition.[35]

**Figure 9.8** Guercino, *Christ and the Woman of Samaria at the Well*, 1640–41 or 1647. 51.9 x 69.3 ins. Oil on canvas. National Gallery of Canada, Ottawa. Photo Credit: National Gallery of Canada. Purchased 1965.

The Council of Trent declared that sacred images must be instructive and decorous.[36] It is critical for this study to ask whose written works and commentaries would have been of importance to Guercino and to his patrons. The writings of contemporary seventeenth-century theological writer Cornelius à Lapide (1567–1637) were very popular and his presence in Rome proves invaluable in discussing the evolution of the biblical narrative in the Kimbell *Christ and the Woman of Samaria* painting.

Cornelius à Lapide was born in Bocholt, a German border city with the Netherlands. He studied humanities and philosophy at Jesuit colleges in Maastricht and Cologne. His theological studies began with six months at the University of Douai and continued with four more years at Louvain. He entered the Society of Jesus on 11 June 1592, and after two years' noviciate and another year of theology, was ordained a priest on 24 December 1595. A Lapide became Professor of Scripture at Louvain in 1596 and, a year later, was also named Professor of Hebrew. In 1616, he was called to Rome by his Jesuit superiors to assume the same positions there. A Lapide's *Great Commentary* incorporates the writings of the Patristic Church Father from the second to the fourth centuries. In particular, he commented on the works of Jerome, Origen, Tertullian, Irenaeus, Augustine, Ambrose and John Chrysostom.[37]

The relationship and meaning of the biblical verses in light of the painting combined with an application of à Lapide's commentary on the scripture and on earlier historical interpretations allows us to 'interpret' the painting as a type of visual exegesis. The context of the narrative of John 4 offers several questions that are relevant to our understanding of the painting.

> When Jesus therefore understood that the Pharisees had heard that Jesus maketh more disciples, and baptizeth more than John, (Though Jesus himself did not baptize, but his disciples,) He left Judea, and went again into Galilee. And he was of necessity to pass through Samaria. He cometh therefore to a city of Samaria, which is called Sichar, near the land which Jacob gave to his son Joseph. (John 4:1–5; Douay Rheims)

The circumstances of the travel of Jesus are essential to the context of the story and are explained thoroughly by our commentators. Why was he travelling? Jesus was travelling, according to Augustine, because John was now in prison. A Lapide explains: 'Jesus knew John was in prison and feared the envy and calumny of the Pharisees, who had already stirred up Herod against John, that they might not be the means of casting Himself also into prison through the instrumentality of Herod or Pilate, and put Him to death before the time predetermined by the Father, prudently retired out of Judea into Galilee'.[38] Where was he going? A Lapide quotes John Chrysostom that Jesus was retiring into Galilee so that he might mollify the envy of the Pharisees.[39] Previously, Jesus' activity was centred on the people and places of official Judea. Jesus was passing through Samaria, which lies between Judea and Galilee. According to à Lapide he told his disciples not to go into Samaria, nor to continually evangelize them, or else they would prejudice the Jews, who were their enemies.[40] Jesus stops at Jacob's Well or Be'er Ya'akov near the capital of the district of Samaria known as Sichem or Sychar.[41] He stopped because it was the noon (or sixth) hour and, insisting that he travel on foot, was thirsty. It would have been a fifty-two hour trip by foot. Lapide takes the opportunity to say that Jesus was weary and reminds his readers that Chrysostom says that this teaches us to live with labours and difficulties. Xavier and his followers recently used Jesus' travels and weariness as a model as they journeyed through India.

In addition to setting the context of the journey, it is also necessary to understanding the socio-political context between the Jews and the Samaritans. The Jews and Samaritans had a dispute about the correct location of the cultic place of worship. The Samaritans built and worshipped at a shrine on Mount Gerizim (Figure 9.9) that competed with the Temple of Jerusalem. The Jews destroyed the shrine in 128 BCE.[42] The Jews and Samaritans were bitter enemies.

> There cometh a woman of Samaria, to draw water. Jesus saith to her: Give me to drink. For his disciples were gone into the city to buy meats. Then that Samaritan woman saith to him: How dost thou, being a Jew, ask of me to drink, who am a Samaritan woman? For the Jews do not communicate with the Samaritans. (John 4:7–9; Douay Rheims)

**Figure 9.9** Roman Provincial Coin of Neapolis, Judaea. *Philip II,* 247–49 CE. Mt Gerizim on reverse. Neapolis, Judaea. Photo Credit: CNG auction 321 (26 February 2014), lot 429.

The second complication with this situation was regarding a man speaking to a woman. Not only was the woman a member of an enemy people, she was a female without her husband present. This would have been considered a scandalous conversation. A Lapide comments that Jesus took the imitative in conversing with her. He knew that the woman, being a Samaritan, would not give him a drink, but would dislike him for being a Jew. The woman recognized Jesus to be a Jew from his dress and speech; and because the Jews have no dealings with the Samaritans, there should be no contact with a heretic.[43] Yet, the conversation occurs and the significance of it can be understood through the à Lapide commentary and the Guercino painting at the Kimbell.

## *Conversation of Conversion*

The conversation between Jesus and the Samaritan woman leads to conversion that is achieved through a series of four successive steps. The first part of their conversation is about living water. This is symbolic for the 'doctrine' or message that Christ is offering to the woman. The woman desires to have the physical (earthly) water to quench thirst while Christ offers something more substantial, living water. This is the first step for the woman towards conversion.

> Jesus answered, and said to her: If thou didst know the gift of God, and who he is that saith to thee, Give me to drink; thou perhaps wouldst have asked of him, and he would have given thee living water. The woman saith to him: Sir, thou hast nothing wherein to draw, and the well is deep; from whence then hast thou living water? Art thou greater than our father Jacob, who gave us the well, and drank thereof himself, and his children, and his cattle? Jesus answered, and said to her: Whosoever drinketh of this water, shall thirst again; but he that shall

> drink of the water that I will give him, shall not thirst for ever: But the water that I will give him, shall become in him a fountain of water, springing up into life everlasting. The woman saith to him: Sir, give me this water, that I may not thirst, nor come hither to draw. (John 4:10–15: Douay Rheims)

A Lapide says: 'Christ leads her from earthly to spiritual water by analogy. Let religious and apostolical men do likewise. Note, as a stagnant lake, or pool, is termed "dead," because it moves not; so, on the contrary, flowing water is called *living water*, especially that which leaps forth, as it were, from fountains, as though animated by a living spirit.'[44] Quoting Ammonius, à Lapide clarifies that Christ's evangelical doctrine is called *living water* because it incorporates the Holy Spirit and grace. Christ infuses and breathes these into his followers by his teaching.[45] Water has the power to cleanse the soul from sin while grace is the supernatural elegance, beauty and adornment of the soul. A Lapide cautions that water, although it washes, likewise corrupts, weakens, destroys and consumes. He says, 'For we see that clothes which are washed, are cleansed indeed, but are worn away. But it is not thus with the Holy Ghost, for he cleanses and fortifies souls, and they gain more strength the more they are cleansed'.[46]

The setting for the scene, and for Guercino's painting, at a well or source of water is also quite valuable in further understanding the biblical narrative. A Lapide tells us that St Augustine says that living water is so-called because it flows in such a manner that is united with its fount or source, from which it bubbles up. Grace, therefore, is called living water, because it is never separated from its fount which is the Holy Ghost.[47] The setting of the Kimbell painting is not only at the well, but the well creates the ledge in the front of the picture plane that separates the viewer from the pair. It serves as the bottom frame in the Kimbell painting. This is more intimate than the Thyssen-Bornemisza painting (Figure 9.7) where the three sides surrounding the hole of the well are visible and come between the figures and the viewer.

Jesus explains to the woman that his living water is far better because it will quench all, even further thirst. At the conclusion of this first step, she desires the water on a purely physical level. Jesus is not limited by conventions and restraints. He speaks and teaches a member of a despised people who is also a woman. The grace of God is available to all peoples and not bound by social constraints.

The second step towards conversion is one of ethical reproof and theological dialogue that results in the woman having a deeper understanding of Jesus and moving her closer to conversion. Jesus questions her lifestyle and ethics.

> Jesus saith to her: Go, call thy husband, and come hither. The woman answered, and said: I have no husband. Jesus said to her: Thou hast said well, I have no husband: For thou hast had five husbands: and he whom thou now hast, is not thy husband. This thou hast said truly. The woman saith to him: Sir, I perceive that thou art a prophet. (John 4:16–19; Douay Rheims)

Chrysostom, along with other early commentators, interpreted that Christ was instructing the woman to get her husband because it was not proper to give such a great thing as the living water to a married woman without the knowledge of her husband.[48] A Lapide corrects that saying, 'But Christ really intended to open out to her hidden things of her life, and her secret fornication, that so he might draw her confession from her, and arouse her to repentance. At the same time he would show her that He was more than a mere man, that He was the Christ, from whom she might ask and expect remission of her sins and everlasting salvation.'[49]

The woman acknowledges that Jesus is a prophet and then questions religion beginning with a discussion of Mount Gerizim:

> Our fathers adored on this mountain, and you say, that at Jerusalem is the place where men must adore. Jesus saith to her: Woman, believe me, that the hour cometh, when you shall neither on this mountain, nor in Jerusalem, adore the Father. You adore that which you know not: we adore that which we know; for salvation is of the Jews. But the hour cometh, and now is, when the true adorers shall adore the Father in spirit and in truth. For the Father also seeketh such to adore him. God is a spirit; and they that adore him, must adore him in spirit and in truth. (John 4:20–24; Douay Rheims)

A Lapide explains: 'There was a famous and unending controversy between the Samaritans and the Jews concerning worshipping and sacrificing in this mountain … Here Christ gives a direct answer to the woman, and decides the Jews to be in the right in the controversy concerning the worship of God.'[50] The post-Roman paintings by Guercino illustrated here from the Thyssen-Bornemisza Collection (Figure 9.7) and the National Gallery of Canada (Figure 9.8) both depict this moment in the biblical narrative. Christ points in the distance to Mount Gerizim on his right. The well was probably located in the valley of Shechem with Mount Gerizim on one side and Mount Ebal on the other. Mount Gerizim was frequently depicted on Roman coins (Figure 9.9) with a ladder leading up to a temple.

Jesus takes the opportunity of the woman's questioning about worshipping on Mount Gerizim to tell her that true worshipers will believe in spirit and truth neither in the temple of Jerusalem nor on Mount Gerizim. Christ will die for the salvation of all at the determined time. A Lapide interprets Christ's words as, 'Now is the time of My evangelical law, in which the true worshippers, namely, Christians, whether the descendants of the Jews, or the Samaritans, or other nations, nor in Jerusalem only, by the carnal sacrifices of beasts, as the Jews and the Samaritans, but rather in all nations throughout the world in spirit and in truth.'[51]

*In spirit* and *in truth* indicates that Christians do not make sacrifices in body but worship God in spirit and instead of in shadows, falsehood and ignorance, adore God in truth, for God is an incorporeal Spirit, most true and most pure.[52] Spirit therefore signifies the spiritual worship of faith, hope, charity, religion, devotion, contrition and other virtues, by which God is most rightly worshipped by Christians.[53] For a more mystical reading, à Lapide quotes Theophylact: '"Mystically, by the spirit is intended action: by truth, contemplation" for all Christians serve God either by an active or a contemplative life.'[54]

In the third step towards her conversion, Jesus declares his identity and he is revealed to her.

> The woman saith to him: I know that the Messias cometh (who is called Christ); therefore, when he is come, he will tell us all things. Jesus saith to her: I am he, who am speaking with thee. (John 4:25–26; Douay Rheims)

A Lapide's meaning: I am the Messias, or the Christ. Have faith in Me: receive My doctrine and my law, that thou mayest be saved and blessed.[55] A Lapide comments, 'Christ spoke this with the outward voice, but still more with an inward voice, illuminating the woman's mind, and kindling her will, to love and reverence Him. Whereon the woman believed straightway, and moved her whole city to believe in Him.'[56]

This unstated acceptance by the woman is caused by her revelation of Jesus as the Messiah. Her reaction to evangelize is the fourth and final step in their conversation to conversion. She is inspired to spread the word to all in the city.

> And immediately his disciples came; and they wondered that he talked with the woman. Yet no man said: What seekest thou? or, why talkest thou with her? The woman therefore left her water pot, and went her way into the city, and saith to the men there: Come, and see a man who has told me all things whatsoever

**Figure 9.10** Annibale Carracci, *Christ and the Woman of Samaria at the Well,* 1593–94. Oil on canvas. Pinacoteca di Brera, Milan. Photo Credit: Scala/Ministero per i Beni e le Attività Culturali /Art Resource, NY.

I have done. Is not he the Christ? They went therefore out of the city, and came unto him. (John 4:27–30; Douay Rheims)

Annibale Carracci illustrates this final portion of the story in his version of *Christ and the Woman of Samaria at the Well* (Figure 9.10) in Milan. The disciples have returned on the left of the composition just as the woman, who no longer holds her water pot, is about to run off to tell everyone about the Messiah. St Augustine remarks, 'I am he, who am speaking with thee, and having received the Lord Christ into her heart, what could she do but leave her pitcher, and run to preach the gospel?' A Lapide continues: 'For she knew that Jesus was a prophet and a great man, because He had revealed to her the secrets of her heart. When therefore He declared that he was the Messias, she believed him, Knowing that He was a man worthy of credit, who could neither deceive, nor be deceived.'[57]

## Conclusion

Through the analysis of both form and content, a richer study of the stylistic elements and narrative details of *Christ and the Woman of Samaria at the Well* in the Kimbell is offered to the reader. The painting is placed stylistically in Guercino's pre-Roman period and can be dated 1619–20. Iconographically, the Kimbell work illustrates the first three steps in the conversation of conversion: doctrine, understanding and revelation. By examining the commentary of Cornelius à Lapide, a contemporary of Guercino, the evolution of the biblical narrative of John 4:1–30 is used to further comprehend the visual meaning in the artist's paintings of *Christ and the Woman of Samaria at the Well.*

## Notes

1 This paper was originally presented in a lecture series at the Kimbell on 12 November 2014. The painting was purchased in 2010 in memory of the eminent art historian and director of the Kimbell Art Museum, Edmund P. Pillsbury, 1980–98. I wish to thank Nancy E. Edwards, curator of European art, and Eric M. Lee, director of the Kimbell, for this opportunity.

2 See Nicholas Turner, 'Two Studies for Guercino's Early *Christ and the Samaritan Woman* at Fort Worth', in *Master Drawings* 53:4 (December 2015), 439–42.

3 Daniel M. Unger, *Guercino's Paintings and his Patrons' Politics in Early Modern Italy* (Farnham, Surrey and Burlington, VT: Ashgate, 2010), 17, 22 nn. 1, 2.

4 Carlo Cesare Malvasia, *Felsina Pittrice: Vite de' pittori bolognese*, 2 vols, ed. Giovanni Pietro Cavazzoni Zanotti, Luigi Crespi and Vicente Victoria (Bologna: Tipografia Giudi all' Ancora, 1841), 2:257.

5 Giovanni Battista Passeri, *Vite de' pittori, scultori ed architetti: che anno lavorato in Roma morti dal 1641 fino al 1673* (Rome: Gergorio Settari, 1772), 369.

6 Unger, *Guercino's Paintings*, 17.

7 Julian Brooks, *Guercino. Mind to Paper* (Los Angeles, CA: Getty Publications, 2006), 4.

8 David M. Stone, *Guercino. Catalogo completo dei dipinti* (Florence: Cantini, 1991), 7.
9 Unger, *Guercino's Paintings*, 18.
10 Unger, *Guercino's Paintings*, 17. Unger recounts this story and validates its historical impossibility.
11 Stone, *Guercino. Catalogo completo*, 7.
12 Andrea Emiliani, 'Guercino: From Natural Talent to the Romanticism of Reality', in Dennis Mahon, *Guercino. Master Painter of the Baroque* (Washington DC: National Gallery of Art, 1992), 14–15.
13 Dennis Mahon, 'Guercino and Cardinal Serra: A Newly Discovered Masterpiece', *Apollo* 114 (Sept. 1981), 172–73.
14 The later works, although not part of this study, benefit from the *Libro dei conti*, an account book begun by Guercino's brother Paolo Antonio Barbieri in 1629 and concluded by his nephew, Benedetto Gennari in 1666. See Barbara Ghelfi, ed., *Il libro dei conti del Guercino 1629–1666* (Bologna: Nuova Alfa, 1997).
15 Francesco Scannelli, *Il microcosmo della pittura* (Cesena, 1657); reprinted in 2 vols. (Bologna: Nuova Alfa Editoriale), 1989, as cited by Sybille Ebert-Schifferer, '"Ma c'hanno da fare i precetti dell' oratore con quelli della pittura?" Reflections on Guercino's Narrative Structure', in Mahon, *Guercino*, 75, 108 n. 1.
16 Ebert-Schifferer, ibid., 75.
17 Stone, *Guercino*, 5–15. Mahon's theory, as noted by Ebert-Schifferer, 75, was doubted earlier by Donald Posner, 'The Guercino Exhibition at Bologna', *Burlington Magazine* 110 (1968), 600.
18 'Guercino', *The Kimbell Art Museum*. Web accessed 1 April 2016 (https://www.kimbellart.org/collections/recent-acquisitions/guercino).
19 'Kimbell Art Museum Creates iPad App Featuring Permanent Collection', *Dallas Art News*. 7 October 2012. Web. accessed 1 April 2016 (http://www.dallasartnews.com/2012/10/kimbell-art-museum-creates-ipad-app-featuring-permanent-collection/).
20 Transcript of audio, 'How the Kimbell Decided that the *Christ and the Woman of Samaria at the Well* was Guercino's Original Work and Not a Copy' by Claire Barry, Conservator, Kimbell Art Museum in personal email correspondence from Regina Palm, Curatorial Assistant, Kimbell Art Museum to Heidi J. Hornik, 29 October 2014.
21 My intention here is not to evaluate the attributions made for each of the comparative works but only to discuss the similarities in the paintings in order to support a stylistic dating of 1619–20 for the Kimbell painting.
22 Ward Bissell, *Masters of Italian Baroque Painting*, Detroit Institute of Art (London: Giles, 2005), 112.
23 Ibid., 112.
24 Ibid.
25 Ibid., 112, n. 2.
26 Ibid.
27 Ibid. See Luigi Salerno, *I dipinti del Guercino* (Rome: Ugo Bozzi, 1988), 143, cat. no. 64. Although I have seen the Salerno catalogue black and white illustration, the size is unknown and a conclusion regarding the identification of the Kimbell work as the one illustrated by Salerno cannot be made at this time.
28 Bissell, *Masters*, 112.
29 Armando Schiavo, *Villa Ludovisi e Palazzo Margherita* (Rome: Amor, 1981), 122. See also Stone, *Guercino*, 99–101, cat. no. 78.
30 See note 3 above and Roberto Contini, *Seventeenth and Eighteenth Century Italian Painting. The Thyssen-Bornemisza Collection* (London: Philip Wilson, 2002), 48–53, cat. no. 10.

31 Ibid., 50–51. See also Stone, *Guercino*, 184, cat. no. 167; Salerno, *Dipinti*, 272, cat. no. 189.

32 Ibid., 50, Figure 9.1.

33 See chapter six on the *Prodigal Son* by Guercino (Luke 15:11–21) in Heidi J. Hornik and Mikeal C. Parsons, *Illuminating Luke: The Public Ministry of Christ in Italian Renaissance and Baroque Painting*, vol. 2 (London: T&T Clark International, 2005), 134–64.

34 John W. O'Malley, *Trent: What Happened at the Council* (Cambridge, MA: Belknap Press of Harvard University Press, 2013), 244.

35 Ibid.

36 For the 'Decree of the Council of Trent concerning Images', see Martin Chemnitz, *Examination of the Council of Trent*. Part IV (St Louis: Concordia, 1986), 53–54, and exact date cited by James Waterworth, ed., *The Council of Trent. Canons and Decrees* (Chicago: Christian Symbolic Publication, 1848).

37 For biographical information, see Charles A. Coulombe, 'Foreword', in *The Great Commentary of Cornelius à Lapide. The Holy Gospel according to Saint Matthew*, vol. 1. Translated by Thomas W. Mossman, revised and completed by Michael J. Miller (Fitzwilliam, NH: Loreto, 2008), vii–xv.

38 A Lapide, *The Great Commentary John*, 134–35.

39 Ibid., 135.

40 Ibid.

41 Ibid., 136–37.

42 Carol Ann Newsom and Sharon H. Ringe, eds., *Women's Bible Commentary* (Louisville, KY: Westminster John Knox Press, 1998), 295. For more on the Woman of Samari, see Janeth Norfleete Day, *The Woman at the Well. Interpretation of John 4:1–41 in Retrospect and Prospect* (Leiden: Brill, 2002).

43 A Lapide, *The Great Commentary. Saint John*, 139.

44 Ibid., 140.

45 Ibid.

46 Ibid.

47 Ibid., 142.

48 Ibid., 147. Theophylact (eleventh-century Greek archbishop and commentator) and Euthymius also held this perspective.

49 Ibid.

50 Ibid., 149–50.

51 Ibid., 151.

52 Ibid., 152.

53 Ibid.

54 Ibid., 153.

55 Ibid., 156.

56 Ibid.

57 Ibid., 157.

# 10

# PICTURING THE WOMAN CLOTHED WITH THE SUN (REVELATION 12): IMAGES OF APOCALYPTIC CONFLICT, PIETY AND STRENGTH

Natasha O'Hear

## *Introduction*

The Woman Clothed with the Sun of Revelation 12 is a figure that is often overlooked in contemporary surveys of the art inspired by Revelation. While perhaps lacking the immediate recognizability of the Four Horsemen, Revelation's satanic Trinity of Beasts, the Last Judgment or the New Jerusalem, the Woman Clothed with the Sun has a rich and complex visual afterlife. Indeed, in one of the examples discussed below, Diego Velázquez's *St John the Evangelist on the Island of Patmos* (1618), the Woman Clothed with the Sun narrative, essentially the battle of the chaste woman protecting her baby son against the satanic dragon, is presented as the defining episode of John's apocalyptic vision.

Velázquez's exegetical insight was in many ways spot on. While perhaps not *the* defining episode, Revelation 12 certainly has a key role to play both within the narrative of Revelation and in terms of the themes that it draws together and the issues that it raises. With regard to its narrative function, Revelation 12 can be seen as part of the hinge or turning point within the narrative. Following John's renewed prophetic commission in Revelation 10, and Revelation 11, which is concerned with the theme of prophetic witness *on earth*, we are abruptly transported to heaven at the beginning of Revelation 12, where we are introduced to our protagonist, the Woman Clothed with the Sun, who is fleeing her enemy, the Dragon, while in the midst of labour.[1] This vision ushers in a series of new visions focussing on the Beasts of the Apocalypse and their violent, coercive and deceptive methods (the Dragon, Sea and Earth Beasts of Revelation 13 and the Whore of Babylon of Revelation 17). Hitherto, following the introductory sections and the heavenly throne room scene of Revelation 4–5, the narrative of Revelation has been ordered around the first two sequences of seven woes (the seals and the trumpets).[2] Revelation 12's placement at the head of these new visions is noteworthy, particularly when contrasted with the closing vision in this sequence, that of the Whore of Babylon of Revelation 17, which presents a polar opposite vision of femininity to that of the virtuous Woman Clothed with the Sun (hereafter, the Woman).

As well as occupying a place of narrative significance, therefore, the fight between the Woman and the Dragon plays an important thematic role. For what are the Beasts, if not manifestations of Satan in all his many guises? Who or what does the Woman represent? Interpreters have ranged fairly widely in their answers to this question. As stated above, although initially thought, by the earliest interpreters, to be the Holy Spirit, Israel, Jerusalem or the Church, later interpreters have favoured a Marian interpretation.[3] At any rate, as Velázquez incisively depicts, in symbolic terms there is no more powerful way of encapsulating the great struggle between good and evil that runs throughout the narrative of Revelation for an audience than by presenting it as the battle between a 'great red' Dragon and an innocent woman in the midst of and shortly after labour. Additionally, in contrast to Revelation 13 which focusses entirely on the Beasts' activities on earth and Revelation 17 which centres on the earthly rise and fall of the Whore of Babylon, Revelation 12 is very much a two-level drama. The fight between good and evil rages first on earth, then in heaven and finally on earth again. This encompassing of the two realms, the heavenly and the earthly, and the acknowledgment of the close relationship between the two, makes this one of the most apocalyptic of apocalyptic visions.[4]

Importantly for this volume on Biblical Women, it is the characterization of the Woman of Revelation 12 as the epitome of goodness alluded to above that has both led to many stereotypical artistic depictions of the figure and troubled and indeed divided feminist commentators. While controversial nineteenth-century suffragist and author of *The Woman's Bible* Elizabeth Cady Stanton (1815–1902) praised Revelation 12 for its respectful portrayal of the Woman as the Church and Yarbro Collins sees the chapter as evidence of John having to acknowledge the 'feminine aspect of the divine', others such as Schüssler Fiorenza and Pippin see the sexism invoked in Revelation via the resolutely dualistic presentations of femininity as either whorish or pure and/or maternal as deeply problematic.[5] Pippin famously rejects Revelation from the Christian canon altogether on account of its thoroughgoing sexism.[6]

While I would not presume to advance this discussion from within the parameters of feminist debate, I would argue that the images selected of the Woman for this chapter combine to present a more rounded image of the figure than some argue is possible. In the interests of offering a representative sample, some of the images, due to their contexts, of course offer a rather two-dimensional view of the Woman as pure, virginal (in many cases, she *is* the Virgin Mary) and somewhat passive. It could be argued that this is a faithful rendering of the text in the sense that the characterization of the Woman is limited and the fact that she has to be rescued by heavenly forces not once but three times. But there are also images of strength here (sometimes from surprising sources), whose artists have clearly read between the lines of the struggle between the Woman and the Dragon and inferred and imagined a more spirited response from her and depicted this accordingly. The final images in this chapter, created by two contemporary female artists, attempt to reclaim the figure from her idealized pedestal and ground her in the reality of contemporary female life.

My desire to present a rounded survey of how the figure of the Woman of Revelation 12 has been visualized has in part informed my decision to present a selective but representative chronological survey of the figure. However, this is also a legitimate approach to the task of visual reception history and one that I use often.[7] Trends within visual histories of biblical texts can be approached and classified in many different ways. However, it is often useful to isolate trends within certain time periods and then select examples that typify those trends, which can then be compared and contrasted with typical (or in other instances atypical) examples from other time periods. This allows for a fuller and more robust appreciation of the trends that occur and are recapitulated in the visual reception of biblical narratives and figures. One is not constrained to a narrow time period but the fact that the examples chosen have been selected by virtue of their typicality means that there is a robustness to the analysis that would be lacking if examples from different time periods were chosen for comparison at random or just by virtue of their particular fascinating qualities. An obvious caveat to this methodology is that 'typicality' can be hard to define and that this task becomes more difficult the closer one moves to the modern and post-modern eras. However, the range of examples that follow *either* represent certain key trends within the visual history of the Woman of Revelation 12 *or* in the case of some of the later, more idiosyncratic examples, represent thought-provoking interpretations which help to open up new ways of approaching the figure that stand in clear contrast to previous trends and stereotypes. In both cases, the visual interpretations offered should be seen as a vital counterpart to the textual reception history of the Woman. Visual exegesis has a key role to play in both complementing and challenging textual exegesis and in many ways our predecessors have embraced this truth more readily than modern biblical scholarship. Until the Blackwell Commentary series, Biblical commentaries were rarely illustrated, and those that were often presented the images as an interesting addendum rather than as a part of the exegesis. This stands in contrast to the illuminated manuscripts of biblical books that were produced in the middle ages in which the biblical text, commentary passages and images were presented as a whole 'package', the one informing and illuminating the other.[8] Likewise many of the first printed bibles were fully illustrated, such as Luther's Bible of 1534, although ironically the Protestant emphasis on the primacy of the word led to a suspicion of illustrations and the eventual decline of anything that could be called visual exegesis.

In the case of the Woman of Revelation 12, I would argue that some of the visualizations explored below help to illuminate and challenge elements of the source-text (Rev 12) more incisively than textual interpretations have done.[9] The very nature of the image as a synchronic entity means that different and sometimes contrasting elements of the source text can be brought together in one visual plane, often helping us to reflect afresh on the source text. Similarly, the decisions that artists have had to make regarding what to prioritize and what to omit, generally as a result of economic constraints, can result in surprising and revealing exegetical choices. I would argue that the images by German Renaissance master Albrecht Dürer (1471–1528) and seventeenth-century Spanish painter Diego

Velázquez (1599–1660) discussed below both move into the category of visual exegesis by virtue of their intentional visual prioritization of Revelation 12, which in turn reveals a particular understanding of the text. Meanwhile the idiosyncratic English artist and poet and self-proclaimed visionary William Blake (1757–1827) and the contemporary Chicana artist Yolanda Lopez (b. 1942) offer fairly radical re-interpretations of Revelation 12 while remaining in close continuity with both the subject matter and the spirit of the chapter. In what follows, a brief overview of the source text (Rev 12), its distinctive features and its major interpretative strands will lead into an analysis of the carefully curated eight images (or collections of images) that I have selected of the Woman.

## *The Woman Clothed with the Sun in Revelation*

As with other passages in Revelation, Revelation 12 switches between the heavenly and earthly planes without explanation or warning and encompasses three main sections. In the first section (Rev 12:1–6), a woman who is described as 'clothed with the sun', standing on a moon and crowned with stars appears on earth in the process of giving birth. Suddenly she is confronted by a 'great red dragon with seven heads and ten horns' who has descended from heaven and seeks to kill her child 'as soon as it is born'. Before this can happen, the child, who is destined to 'rule all the nations with a rod of iron' (Rev 12:5), is snatched up to safety in heaven and the woman finds sanctuary in the wilderness. The second stage of the narrative then moves up to heaven where Michael and his angels fight against and defeat the Dragon and cast him and his angels down to earth (Rev 12:7–9). After a hymn of praise for the Lamb and his 'comrades' who have defeated the 'accuser' in heaven, and a warning that Satan now dwells on earth, the narrative enters its third stage with the Dragon pursuing the Woman on earth, with two distinct threats. First, he tries to persecute her and she is given eagle wings to escape from him (it is unclear by whom). Again, she finds sanctuary in the wilderness. Secondly, he tries to sweep her away with a flood and (Mother) earth (γή) swallows the water and protects her. Frustrated, the Dragon goes off to 'make war' on the Woman's children and their descendants.

Revelation 12 is exegetically noteworthy for several reasons. First, it is a discrete chapter with a self-enclosed narrative, which sets it apart from much of the rest of Revelation, which involves significant recapitulation of characters and themes. Although the great red Dragon appears again in Revelation 13 (handing over power to the Sea-Beast) and at the denouement of the vision in Chapters 16 and 20, the Woman and her child do not appear again, nor do Michael and his angels who fight against the Dragon and his angels (Rev 12:7–17). The Woman appears without warning and just as quickly departs from the wider narrative.

As stressed above, however, thematically many of the motifs and ideas that permeate the wider narrative of Revelation are recapitulated here. The Dragon is another manifestation of the evil forces that recur frequently in Revelation (the Four Horsemen, the Beasts, the Whore of Babylon, etc.) and the battle that he fights against the Woman and her descendants and Michael and his angels on the heavenly plane is a clear recapitulation of the on-going battle between good and evil that pervades the text. Thus, although a discrete chapter in terms of its specific characters, Revelation 12 is well synthesized into the overall narrative. In terms of visual interpretations of the entirety of Revelation, images of the Woman are given visual coherence via the figure of the Dragon himself and via visual links with the underlying themes of the text.

Secondly, more than any other chapter in Revelation, as well as drawing upon Old Testament sources (such as the story of Eve and the Serpent from Genesis 3), this chapter draws upon mythological, non-biblical sources and ideas. The Greek birth myth of Apollo is especially significant here. Apollo's mother Leto, pregnant with Zeus's twins Apollo and Artemis is pursued by the dragon Python and has to be rescued by Zeus and Poseidon. These connections with wider mythologies, which Boxall argues would have been familiar to John's first hearers in Asia Minor, give Revelation 12 a more mysterious, even mystical feeling, than the rest of Revelation's narrative.[10] These mystical qualities are often reflected in visualizations of the Woman Clothed with the Sun episode, particularly in the later representations.

### *Interpretative Trends*[11]

The textual reception history of Revelation 12 necessarily impacts upon the visual reception, particularly in the earlier manuscript images which were always presented alongside both the text of Revelation and commentary extracts. As Kovacs and Rowland stress, the interpretative history of Revelation 12 covers 'the whole gamut of interpretative methods and exegetical possibilities'.[12] However, in a general sense, the textual reception of the figure of the Woman herself has been dominated by the Marian interpretation since the fifth century when Bishop Quodvultdeus identified the Woman of Revelation 12 with Mary, an identification that was taken up more explicitly by Oecumenius in the sixth century.[13] Prior to this, the Woman had been interpreted variously as the Holy Spirit, as Israel or Jerusalem and also as the Church. Prior to the Marian interpretation when the Woman's child was identified with Christ, the child was also interpreted as a manifestation of the Church.[14] Tyconius, for example, saw the battle between the Woman and the Dragon in Revelation 12 as symbolic of the struggle between his own Donatist church and its enemies.[15] The fourth-century Methodius meanwhile saw the battle at the heart of Revelation 12 more in terms of the inner struggle that takes place within all Christians between good and evil. Interestingly for our purposes he also saw the Woman herself as 'an inspiration to virgins to lead a celibate life'.[16] These variant readings did continue in spite of the strength of the Marian interpretation and the growth of Marian devotion in the Late Mediaeval era. As late as the thirteenth century, commentaries still identified the Woman with the church, the twelve stars of her crown with the apostles and the sun which clothes her (rather than her child) with Christ.[17]

Following the authorization of the feast of the Immaculate Conception by those dioceses who wished to introduce it by Pope Sixtus IV in 1476, there was a renewed interest in Revelation 12 as it was one of the scriptural readings chosen for the corresponding feast.[18] This perhaps also accounts for the renewed visual interest in the figure from around this time, starting with Hans Memling's *St. John Altarpiece* of 1474–79 and Hieronymus Bosch's *St John on Patmos*, c. 1500, and also in two of the image collections discussed below (Albrecht Dürer's *Apocalypse Series* of 1498 and Diego Velázquez's pair of paintings from 1618).[19]

In terms of historical identifications or actualizations, the Dragon has been identified with figures as various as several Roman Emperors, including Nero, Pope Gregory IX (and XIII), Mohammed and George III (see William Blake). Spenser identified Elizabeth I as the Woman of Revelation 12 in the *Fairie Queen* and Hal Lindsey, author of *The Late Great Planet Earth*, identified her with US Airforce jets carrying Jews to safety.[20] Hildegard of Bingen describes the Woman entering her visions and the nineteenth-century self-styled prophet Joanna Southcott famously identified herself with the Woman of Revelation 12 and inspired an influential prophetic movement after her death (The Panacea Society).[21] Different aspects of many of these interpretations are reflected in the visualizations offered below.

## *Selected Images*

The first three examples that have been selected for discussion are representations of the Woman of Revelation 12 from the Bamberg, Trinity and Dürer Apocalypse Series of c. 1000, c. 1260 and c. 1498, respectively. While details of the interpretations offered of the Woman are actually very different in all three of these representations, they all exemplify an episodic, manuscript-based approach to the task of visualizing this figure. The *Trinity Apocalypse*, for example, devotes a full five images to Revelation 12, resulting in a very comprehensive, literal interpretation.

*The Bamberg Apocalypse* is the only extant Ottonian Apocalypse manuscript and was created for Holy Roman Emperor Otto III and completed for his successor Henry II around 1020 after Otto's death. The manuscript, from which these two images of the Woman are taken, contains the text of Revelation accompanied by fifty-seven illuminated images (Figures 10.1 and 10.2). This first image of the Woman is typical of the images throughout the series: uncluttered, sparse even, but simultaneously effective at conveying both the narrative and the essence of Revelation. The art historian van der Meer draws our attention to the 'shifty eyes' of the main protagonists which are never centrally focussed but dart to the left or right conveying silent horror.[22] The Woman is an imposing figure, almost as big as the Dragon, which hisses menacingly from the bottom right-hand corner. She has a sun-wheel around her head (with eleven points, the twelfth being concealed behind her back), stands on a crescent moon and holds a male child with enlarged genitals, which serves to underline his masculinity and possibly therefore his status as messianic king.[23] Apart from this implied reference to the Christ-child, there are no clear iconographic links between the Woman and Mary. If she had been meant to represent Mary, she might well have been smaller, less hieratic and certainly more human, more like other contemporary Marian images.

**Figure 10.1** *The Bamberg Apocalypse*, c. 1000. *The Woman Clothed with the Sun: Woman, Dragon, and Child*. Bamberg: Bamberg State Library. © Bridgeman Art Library.

It is far more likely that here she is intended as the Church, presiding over Salvation History. In the second Bamberg image, a representation of the flight of the Woman into the wilderness (Rev 12:6 or 13–17), despite her upturned eyes, which may imply the horror that Van der Meer senses, the Woman is again a huge and imposing figure, more a contending cosmic force against the Dragon that attempts to drown her from below than the historical figure of Mary. What is striking about these images (as with all the images in the *Bamberg* series) is their uncluttered quality. By removing all extraneous details, the *Bamberg* artists were able to focus the viewer's attention (in both images) on the conflict at the heart of the chapter, the struggle between the Woman and the Dragon. In this rendering, the determined calm of the Woman is powerfully contrasted with the coiled and spitting venom of the Dragon.

Our next example is drawn from *The Trinity Apocalypse* of 1260, a striking example of the trend for Apocalypse Manuscripts among the French and English aristocracy in the thirteenth and fourteenth centuries. *Trinity* for example was possibly created for Elenore of Provence, wife of King Henry III.[24] By 1260, there

**Figure 10.2** *The Bamberg Apocalypse*, c. 1000. *The Woman Clothed with the Sun: The Flight of the Woman*. Bamberg: Bamberg State Library. © Bridgeman Art Library.

was an established Anglo-Norman apocalyptic iconography, which *Trinity* follows in many respects, despite a unique artistic style. The defining feature of the genre is the sheer number of miniatures or images devoted to the task of visualizing Revelation. With seventy-one miniatures, *Trinity* is no exception. The representations of Revelation generated by these large numbers of images are detailed and episodic, with the detail of the text coming to the fore. This sequence of these five images of Revelation 12 is a typical example of the genre. The first folio depicts the first part of Revelation 12, the menacing of the Woman by the Dragon as she gives birth (Figure 10.3). The image on the upper register depicts the Woman reclining, as if she has just given birth. She wears a blue stole, which had come to be an integral part of Marian iconography by the thirteenth century. She hands the baby to the angel on the right while the muscular red Dragon flies in from the left, trailing a clutch of stars (Rev 12:4). The lower register of the first folio in the series depicts the Woman in the wilderness for the first time. The third image depicts the heavenly battle between St Michael and his angels and Satan and his angels (not depicted), while the second double-tiered image shows the

**Figure 10.3** The *Trinity Apocalypse*, c. 1260. *The Woman and the Dragon* (Rev 12:3–5). Cambridge, Trinity College. © The Master and Fellows of Trinity College, Cambridge.

second attack on the Woman by the Dragon and also the giving of the eagle wings, enabling her once again to fly to the wilderness (Figure 10.4). Here the wilderness is protected by an enclosed garden of rainbow-coloured plants, a natural *hortus conclusus* and in an interesting visual gloss she is nourished by the Eucharist by an angel descending from heaven.[25] The convent-like setting of this Woman, and the

**Figure 10.4** The *Trinity Apocalypse*, c. 1260. *The Woman Enters the Wilderness* (Rev 12:6–17). Cambridge, Trinity College. © The Master and Fellows of Trinity College, Cambridge.

way she is depicted with a gentle demeanour and cloak of blue and gold, would, in this case, certainly suggest an identification with the Virgin. And even when she is being threatened by the Dragon, her calmness and inner repose are very typical of contemporary representations of the Virgin Mary, intimating that in this case, at least, Marian devotion is being interwoven with apocalyptic struggle. In the bottom right-hand corner of the lower register we see the descendants of the Woman being attacked by the Dragon as described in Rev 12:17. This detail closes *Trinity's* characteristically faithful visualization of Revelation 12, which leaves no narrative detail unexplored.

Turning now to Albrecht Dürer's revolutionary Apocalypse woodcut series of 1498, we are greeted with a very different sort of visualization.[26] Gone are the detailed episodic visualizations and liberal use of gold leaf. In their stead are his iconic and much larger (they measure 38.8 x 29.1 cm) full-page black and white woodcut evocations of the essential strands of Revelation's narrative. In condensing Revelation into just fifteen images (largely for reasons of economic viability), Dürer had to make theological decisions about what was crucial to the narrative and what wasn't. It is therefore fascinating that he devoted two precious images to the Revelation 12 narrative, one to the Woman and one to the War in Heaven between Michael and his angels and the Dragon, testament to the contemporary importance (and also the visual currency) of this biblical passage. Dürer also infused the narrative with a Renaissance sensibility and a physical and psychological realism hitherto unseen in depictions of this text. Although Dürer's *Apocalypse* Series images were eventually to supersede the text (they were published as a standalone picture book in the early sixteenth century), it is also worth noting that at its inception the images and the text were intended to be experienced holistically.

In Dürer's image of the Woman (the tenth in his series of fifteen images), we note that, although very naturalistically portrayed, she is not immediately identifiable as Mary (Figure 10.5). While she has been depicted with the long flowing hair of the young Virgin, and with the iconographical features of the Woman (a crown of stars and standing on the crescent moon) and with the angelic wings given to the Woman at Rev 12:14, she more closely resembles a young woman from Nuremberg than the iconic figure of the Virgin. Perhaps she is intended to be neither Mary nor the church but rather a sort of everywoman figure. Dürer's Woman of 1498 is therefore very much in keeping with his revolutionarily naturalistic approach to the text. However, in his frontispiece to the Latin version of his Apocalypse book, published in 1511, in which John is depicted envisaging the Woman and Child (in a foreshadowing of the Velázquez image we shall shortly turn to), she is far more traditionally Marian (Figure 10.6). Here she is depicted as an older, more regal Mary/Woman of Revelation 12, holding the Christ child close to her and wearing a larger, more ostentatious crown. The Woman seems to represent John's visionary inspiration, rather than functioning as a character in the narrative, as is the case in the previous image. The latter perhaps represents the unattainable archetype of the 'Woman as perfect mother-figure' of some of the more pessimistic feminist critiques of the Woman while the former affords the figure an altogether more human resonance.

Diego Velázquez's pair of paintings *St John the Evangelist on the Island of Patmos* and *The Immaculate Conception* were executed in Seville in c. 1618 in the wake of celebrations there in 1617 to mark a papal decree defending the doctrine of the Immaculate Conception and prohibiting public criticism of it. Both paintings feature the Woman Clothed with the Sun. In the first image we see John (described

**Figure 10.5** Albrecht Dürer, *Apocalypse* Series, c. 1498. *The Woman Clothed with the Sun.* London: British Museum. © The Trustees of the British Museum.

as the Evangelist, but obviously the author of Revelation) in a dark wood ecstatically transfixed by his vision in true Baroque style, his pencil poised over the empty page on which he will write, as instructed (Figure 10.7). He is an earnest and beardless young man, seen by some commentators to be a self-portrait of the artist.[27] In the top left-hand corner of the painting we see what it is he is transfixed

**Figure 10.6** Albrecht Dürer, *Apocalypse* Series, 1511. Frontispiece, London: British Museum. © The Trustees of the British Museum.

by, an evocation of the Woman being pursued by the Dragon. This is tantamount to claiming that this scene from Revelation 12, with its sharp visual focus on the battle between the forces of good and evil, here symbolized by the Woman and the Dragon, embodies the essence of Revelation itself. The Woman herself in this image is an ethereal shadowy figure, her defining feature being that she is bathed in light (see Rev 12:1 which tells us that she is clothed with sun).

The Woman is also the main subject of the second painting, *The Immaculate Conception* (Figure 10.8). What stands out here are also the sources of light within the painting: the translucent moon on which the Woman stands, the white and

**Figure 10.7** Diego Velázquez, *St. John the Evangelist on the Island of Patmos*, c. 1618. London: National Gallery. © Bridgeman Art Library.

grey clouds from which she seems to appear and the corona of stars above her head. Light also falls on the mysterious and symbolic forms below her feet. These objects, include a fountain and an enclosed garden, visual references to the Song of Songs and also Revelation 21 and 22, the New Jerusalem, in which the water of life is situated (Rev 21:6; 22:1) The inclusion of these symbols suggest an implicit comment regarding the Woman's function as a precursor to or forerunner of the New Jerusalem. Most striking of all in the second Velázquez painting is the Woman herself. When hung next to the first painting, as they often are in the National Gallery in London, the Woman appears huge, a visual counterpart to John (they stand at 135.5 x 102.2 cm). Like Dürer's woman, this is a very young, local girl (some say she was Velázquez's fiancée), and, as already mentioned, there is no attempt to idealize her or her features, or to disguise her youth. But in her rapt devotion the ordinary girl is transfigured, a Madonna one can believe actually existed, and in this sense she acts as a mediator between the divine and the human,

**Figure 10.8** Diego Velázquez, *The Immaculate Conception*, c. 1618. London: National Gallery. © Bridgeman Art Library.

rather than a character in a narrative, as was the case with earlier evocations of the figure.

Nearly two hundred years after Velázquez, William Blake produced a series of four watercolours of the Dragon and the Beasts for his main patron Thomas Butts (they were part of a much larger series of watercolours of Revelation that he was producing for Butts around 1805–1809). This image is the second in the series and is titled *The Great Red Dragon and the Woman Clothed with the Sun: The Devil is Come Down* (Figure 10.9). It is hard to see the Dragon, menacing as he is, as wholly evil. He is, after all, flying with angel-like wings, and there is some suggestion that he may be a chrysalis on the road to a more perfect nature. Whether the human body is emerging from the beast or vice versa is unclear. And is the Woman's expression and gesture one of terror or of something else? She certainly seems more than a match for the Dragon with her impressive wingspan. Her gesture of resistance via her outstretched arms mirrors the intimidatory gesture of the 'Dragon', suggesting that good and evil are far closer than Revelation, with its

**Figure 10.9** William Blake, *The Great Red Dragon and the Woman Clothed with the Sun*, c. 1805. New York: The Brooklyn Museum of Art. © Bridgeman Art Library.

recurring binary oppositions, would have us believe. This could be seen as a welcome or unwelcome subversion of the literal meaning of the text depending on your viewpoint regarding where the essence or *Sache* of Revelation is to be found. If it is Revelation's absolute certainties and polemic that appeal, then the suggestion that good and evil are more fluid will not. If it is seen however as a call to seriously question the power structures of our own time and 'worldly things', despite their superficial attraction, then Blake's image of the Woman and the Dragon will have resonance.[28] In feminist terms, some of the strength that can be inferred via a 'recovered' reading of the Woman in Revelation 12 is finally brought to the fore in Blake's image.

It is interesting also to note the presence of human figures at the bottom of the image, appearing as the flood of Rev 12:16 (created by the Dragon to engulf the Woman) subsides after the intervention of (Mother) earth. What role do they play in this drama, and whose side are they on? As so often, Blake leaves us with more questions than answers. What is important to note from our perspective is the way in which Blake, like those who came after him, has in this series, which focuses just on the Woman and the Beasts of Revelation 12–13, offered us a snapshot of the apocalyptic drama, in an attempt to engage with the essence rather than the detail of the text of Revelation.

If Blake's image is hard to interpret, the same could not be said of Odilon Redon's *fin de siècle* lithograph of the Woman from his Revelation series of 1899, commissioned by the art dealer Ambroise Vollard (Figure 10.10). Redon (1840–1916) was a French painter and printmaker. His earlier work (up until 1900) consisted mostly of macabre black and white lithographs of mythical, fantastical and religious subject matters (he was interested in Hinduism and Buddhism as well as Christianity). Following a personal revelation around the end of the nineteenth century, Redon's style changed to become both more colourful and more abstract. His image of the Woman was made at the very end of his first artistic period. Here the Woman is a Loie Fuller-type dancer, rising suggestively out of a dark background into the sun, in a style that is redolent of Redon's visions of sensuously seductive, half-mythical

**Figure 10.10** Odilon Redon, A Woman Clothed with the Sun (Rev. 12.1), 1899, © The Museum of Modern Art/Licensed by SCALA/Art Resource, NY.

women of this era.[29] The Dragon is dealt with separately in a later image, chained in the pit envisaged in Revelation 20. Revelation was by this point on the cusp of becoming a secularized text, a compendium of images for uses quite different from the original intention, hinting at transgression and suggestions of *fin-de-siècle* evil. This image is a good example of this key trend and introduces a worldliness to the visual reception of the Woman which can be seen to jar with the underlying thesis of Revelation itself, which in many ways functions as a counter-cultural critique of the worldly materialism of its own time. Indeed, Wilson argues that the lithographs that Redon was producing at this time are redolent of the religious ambivalence that he was undergoing in the late 1890s. These works, dark, mysterious and menacing, certainly sit at the cusp of Redon's radical transition from an artist of macabre black and white images to that of a more joyful colourist.[30]

Perhaps closer to the spirit of Revelation are our final examples, which come from the end of the twentieth century via two anti-establishment Chicana artists, Yolanda and Alma Lopez. Yolanda Lopez is an American painter, printmaker and film-maker who now resides in San Francisco. Her *Virgen de Guadelupe* series dating from 1978, which we will focus on below, was internationally acclaimed and gave her a platform to continue to explore the Chicana (Mexican-American) experience and to challenge some of the stereotypes associated with that identity through her art.[31] Alma Lopez was born in Mexico but lives and works in Los Angeles. She is an artist-activist specializing in digital prints and murals and also holds a post at the UCLA. Like Yolanda Lopez, she has used her art to challenge Chicana stereotypes as well as gender-based, homophobic and racial discrimination. Both women have attracted criticism for their at times irreverent images of the Virgin Mary.[32]

Yolanda Lopez's *Virgen de Guadelupe* series, dating from 1978, is itself an updating of the famous Virgin of Guadelupe image, one of the most revered icons in Latin America. The vision that inspired the Virgin of Guadalupe iconography saw Mary appear to Mexican peasant Juan Diego in 1531 in the guise of the Woman Clothed with the Sun.[33] Her image was reportedly imprinted on his cloak, now housed in a nearby basilica. All her attributes are the same as in Revelation 12 with the additional detail that the moon on which she stands is supported by a cherub. Lopez was troubled by the iconography of the Virgin of Guadalupe, the most famous version of which hangs in the Basilica de Guadalupe in Mexico City. She found her demure downcast gaze and perfect 'white' appearance at odds with the Chicana experience of religion that she seeks to represent in her work.[34]

In Lopez's triptych, the conventional image of the Virgin as a young white woman has been replaced with contemporary working class Mexican women. The first (*Portrait of the Artist as the Virgin of Guadelupe*) is the artist herself as an exuberant, muscular running Virgin, who clutches a snake (a visual reminder of the Dragon of Revelation 12) around its neck. In a surprising detail, she tramples the cherub who traditionally supports her, although Davalos argues that the 'Virgin' is actually jumping over the angel, representing her freedom from societal anchors (Figure 10.11).[35] The second of the paintings is of Lopez's own mother, Margaret F. Stewart, depicted at her sewing machine, bespectacled, unadorned and far from glamorous (although Lopez reports that she *was* glamorous as a younger

**Figure 10.11** Yolanda Lopez, *Portrait of the Artist as the Virgin of Guadelupe*, 1978.  Used by permission of the artist. Image courtesy of The Chicano Studies Research Center, UCLA.

woman) (Figure 10.12).[36] But she is a strong working woman who is making her own destiny in the form of the Virgin/Woman's traditional gold-starred cloak that she is sewing. The snake is now coiled tightly around the body of the sewing machine, part of the subject's sewing accessories and subdued by her labour. *Margaret F. Stewart: Our Lady of Guadelupe* is a comprehensive re-envisioning of the Woman of Revelation 12/Our Lady of Guadelupe. This Woman is non-white, does not have an 'ideal' or airbrushed body and stares out past the viewer in a rejection of the demure downturned gaze of many of the other Women we have discussed. However, she possesses a certain strength and constancy that both evokes the Woman and makes her relatable. The third image is of the artist's grandmother, Victoria Franco, who is, according to Lopez, stoically and calmly waiting for death (Figure 10.13). The cessation of her earthly struggles (including with her sexuality) is here visually celebrated via the dead (skinned) snake that she holds.[37]

**Figure 10.12** Yolanda Lopez, *Margaret F. Stewart: Our Lady of Guadalupe*, 1978.  Used by permission of the artist. Image courtesy of The Chicano Studies Research Center, UCLA.

In this triptych, Lopez has self-consciously used a well-established Western European art form and re-worked it to express her Chicana interpretation of the Woman Clothed with the Sun/Virgin. The naming of the figures in the three images was, for example, a very deliberate action, done to counteract the cultural 'invisibility' that often plagues women of Chicana origin. The series can very much be seen in terms of the church working from below and of reclaiming the imagery of the orthodox church for an alternative audience. Davalos is surely correct when she talks of the series in terms of Lopez complicating and enriching the figure of the Woman/Virgin of Guadalupe rather than trying to eliminate previous versions.[38] These images both need the context of the previous images we have looked at in order to exert their full liberating power and at the same time offer those other images an alternative 'ending'.

Alma Lopez's photo-montage from 1993 re-imagines the Woman Clothed with the Sun/Virgin of Guadelupe as a young Mexican girl (http://www.elandar.com/online_stories/06_01_01/window7.html). A kitsch yet arresting image, the

**Figure 10.13** Yolanda Lopez, *Guadalupe: Victoria F. Franco*, 1978.  Used by permission of the artist. Image courtesy of The Chicano Studies Research Center, UCLA.

girl stands on a crescent moon and has fancy dress butterfly wings instead of the eagle's wings of Rev 12:14. In the background is a montage of images from the border between Mexico and the USA, including a patrol car and an old map, symbols of enforcement and of the erosion of boundaries. There is a prominent piece of graffiti of the Virgin Mary on a section of the border fence, providing an iconographic nod to the long-standing link between the girl/Woman Clothed with the Sun and the Virgin herself. This Woman of Revelation 12 stands at this famous border crossing, menaced not by the red Dragon but by the more pervasive forces of poverty, suspicion and violence that are all connected with the migrant experience. Alma Lopez has successfully 'updated' the image of the Woman of Revelation 12, making her relevant for our own age, from a more overtly political angle than Yolanda Lopez's images which carry their political message under a veneer of domesticity.

## *Conclusion*

The introduction to this contribution asserted both the significance of Revelation 12 in terms of playing a key role in understanding Revelation and in terms of its rich history of interpretation. Engagement with selected moments from the visual reception of this chapter and of the Woman Clothed with the Sun in particular was also put forward as a useful way of illuminating both the chapter and its historical interpretative emphases as well as possibly offering a more rounded picture of the Woman than some feminist critics might allow.

Taken as a set of images, the visualizations surveyed above have indeed pictorialized many of the key trends set out in the interpretative summary of Revelation 12 given above and in doing so illuminated elements of the chapter in significant ways. The first three examples discussed were visualizations of the Woman from the Bamberg, Trinity and Dürer Apocalypse series, who all employed an episodic, narrative approach to the visualization of Revelation. They tended to focus on the conflict narrative between the Woman and the Dragon. Apart from *Bamberg*, which depicts a physically imposing, non-Marian Woman, *Trinity* and Dürer both portrayed the Woman as demure and passive. The Marian interpretation was particularly strong in *Trinity* and in Dürer's frontispiece for his 1511 Latin edition of the series. In these images, the Woman and the Virgin are one and the same. These images were followed by examples from Velázquez from 1618, which can be said to typify the Counter-Reformation approach, if not to the Woman, then certainly to the figure of Mary. Once again therefore the interpretation offered is resolutely Marian. In what can be seen as a bolder exegetical step, following in the footsteps of Memling, Bosch and Dürer, Velázquez has condensed the whole of Revelation into two images that offer an incisive visual commentary on the essence of the text. The Woman and her struggle with the Dragon is presented as the exegetical key to Revelation as a whole. Mary herself is a pious young girl who, we suggested, is caught by Velázquez in the moment of transfiguration, a mediator between the divine and human realms. Blake, although idiosyncratic in his artistic style, produced an image of the Woman which is in keeping with his own theology in which good and evil are less binary opposites and more part of a continuum. Thus, here we see a Dragon who is more human than Beast, perhaps an allusion to his fallen state as one who was cast down from the heavenly realm and a Woman who is able to forcefully resist him. Here perhaps we also see shades, not of the Marian interpretation but of the 'inner struggle' perceived by Methodius to lie at the heart of Revelation 12. The Redon image, a lithograph which typifies the French *fin-de-siècle* aesthetic and a more decontextualized approach to the task of visualizing Revelation, perhaps also reveals shades of this motif of 'inner struggle', although in this case, this struggle is framed more in terms of the artist's own struggle with his faith. In terms of the Woman, we note that in this series, the Woman and the Dragon are depicted in completely separate images, thus taking the focus away from their conflict narrative. Although Redon's Woman is no longer the idealized virginal figure of the earlier images, she is still objectified and strangely passive. It is not until the final images in this survey that the figure of the Woman is offered an alternative visual representation in the form of images created by Mexican-American artists Yolanda and Alma Lopez. Both artists view the Woman through the Marian prism, to be sure, but they also infuse her with the energy and fortitude of the Liberation movement and Chicana feminism, thus helping to free her from the passivity that had characterized many depictions of the Woman since the Late Medieval era.

To what extent then is there mileage in using these images to construct a more hopeful vision of the Woman in feminist terms? To return to Yarbro Collins's assertion that the presence of the Woman in the narrative of Revelation is evidence of some acknowledgment of the 'feminine aspect of the divine', this is surely echoed in the images discussed in this contribution. In nearly all of the images, in keeping with the source text itself, the Woman is presented as the central figure, and the 'star' of the visual narrative as it were. Her presence is undeniable and in this sense the Woman is the opposite of the 'invisible women' that Yolanda Lopez seeks to champion. Neither is she the subject of overt misogyny in these images, as is the case with images of the Whore of Babylon of Revelation 17, for example. From early on in the visual history of this figure, artists either delighted in portraying this figure as a contemporary courtesan or prostitute (see for example Dürer's image of the Whore of Babylon from the same *Apocalypse Series* of 1498, in which she is depicted as a Venetian prostitute) or in showing her grisly destruction (see for example the twelfth-century *Hortus deliciarum* image of 'The Whore of Babylon Cast to her Death' in which the Whore is graphically speared to death by angels).[39]

Clearly the two women are presented in Revelation, on one level, as contrasting models of femininity, one an innocent mother, the other a destructive, egotistical enchanter of men and acquirer of riches (Rev 17:1–6). But they are at the same time symbols of wider cosmic forces. Babylon, like the Sea-Beast of Revelation 13, signifies Rome. While he represents the military power of the state, she represents the seductive power of Roman ideology and religion (Roma) and later came to be regarded as the evil face of the papacy, both in Dante and in the polemic and potent imagery of the Protestant Reformation (see for example Lucas Cranach the Elder's *Whore of Babylon* of 1522 in which she is depicted as wearing the papal triple tiara).[40] As already discussed, although the Woman of Revelation 12 was interpreted from an early stage as representing Mary, a plurality of interpretations and visualizations were still extant. Thus while the imagery of the Whore of Babylon has been restricted almost exclusively to misogynistic and polemical uses, the Woman has received a more diffuse and open treatment in visual terms.

However, it would of course be completely wrong to claim that there are not troubling aspects about the visual history of the Woman of Revelation 12 from a feminist perspective. Far from it. Apart from the *Bamberg* image which stands as a fascinating early counterexample to this trend, the visual reception of the Woman up until Blake presents an almost uniformly demure, often passive figure. She is presented as the ideal of feminine obedience, purity and (white-European) beauty, interchangeable with the Virgin in that regard. Some may argue that images such as Velázquez's *Immaculate Conception*, despite its exegetical brilliance (when taken in combination with *St John the Evangelist on the Island of Patmos*) have contributed to the punishing and damaging cultural ideal of womanhood that real women have been judged by for centuries. However, some of the later visualizations by Blake and Yolanda and Alma Lopez suggest that there are other and more positive ways of representing the Woman that crucially do not lose touch with the source text of Revelation 12. That politically engaged female artists want to create images of the Woman is highly significant. This has certainly not been the case with the figure of the Whore of Babylon for example. And in creating their personal and non-idealized images of the Woman, which must be viewed from within the visual history of Revelation 12 and the Virgin to retain their full effect, they suggest, I argue, that the figure *can* be redeemed from a feminist perspective.

## *Notes*

1 See R. Bauckham, *The Theology of the Book of Revelation* (Cambridge: Cambridge University Press, 1993), 80–84, on the significance of Rev 10 as a turning point within the narrative.

2 I. Boxall, *The Revelation of St. John* (Peabody, MA: Hendrickson Publishers, 2006), 173.

3 See J. Kovacs and C. Rowland, *Revelation: The Apocalypse of Jesus Christ* (Oxford: Blackwell Publishing, 2004), 134–46.

4 Kovacs and Rowland, *Revelation,* 134.

5 See E. Cady-Stanton, *The Woman's Bible: The Original Feminist Attack on the Bible* (Edinburgh: Polygon Books, 1985), 183; A. Yarbro Collins, 'Feminine Symbolism in the Book of Revelation', *Biblical Interpretation* 1:1 (1993): 24; E. Schüssler-Fiorenza, 'The Words of Prophecy: Reading the Apocalypse Theologically', in *Studies in the Book of Revelation*, ed. S. Moyise (Edinburgh and New York: T&T Clark, 2001), 9–13; T. Pippin, *Death and Desire: The Rhetoric of Gender in the Book of Revelation of John* (Louisville, KT: John Knox Press, 1992); A. Jack, 'Out of the Wilderness: Feminist Perspectives on the Book of Revelation', in Moyise, *Studies in the Book of Revelation,* 149–62.

6 Pippin, *Death and Desire,* 57–68, 100–105.

7 See especially N. O'Hear, *Contrasting Images of the Book of Revelation in Late Medieval and Early Modern Art* (Oxford: Oxford University Press, 2011); N. O'Hear and A. O'Hear, *Picturing the Apocalypse: The Book of Revelation in the Arts over Two Millennia* (Oxford: Oxford University Press, 2015). See also N. O'Hear, 'Images of Babylon: A Visual History of the Whore in Late Medieval and Early Modern Art', in *From the Margins 2: Women of the New Testament and their Afterlives,* ed. Joynes and Rowland (Sheffield: Sheffield Phoenix Press, 2009), 311–33; N. O'Hear, 'Seeing the Apocalypse: Pre-1700 Visualizations of Revelation', in *The Book of Revelation and its Interpreters: Short Studies and an Annotated Bibliography,* ed. I. Boxall and R. Tresley (Lanham and London: Rowman & Littlefield, 2016), 85–124. See also D. Apostolos-Cappadona, 'Imagining Salome, or How *la sauterelle* Became *la femme fatale*', in *From the Margins 2: Women of the New Testament and their Afterlives,* ed. Joynes and

Rowland (Sheffield: Sheffield Phoenix Press, 2009), 190–225, on visualizations of Salome through the ages.

8 See S. Lewis, *Reading Images: Narrative Discourse and Reception in the Thirteenth-Century Illuminated Book of Revelation* (Cambridge: Cambridge University Press, 1995), on 'reading' the mediaeval apocalypse manuscripts.

9 For more on the concept of visual exegesis, see N. O'Hear, *Contrasting Images*, especially 199–241 and N. O'Hear and A. O'Hear, *Picturing the Apocalypse*, especially 28–37 and 284–94.

10 Boxall, *The Revelation of St John*, 174–77.

11 See further, Kovacs and Rowland, *Revelation*, 134–46.

12 Kovacs and Rowland, *Revelation*, 135.

13 Quodvultdeus, *De symbolo* 3, *PL* 40, 661 (430 AD). Quoted in M. P. Shea, *Mary Mother of the Son* (San Diego, CA: Catholic Answers, 2009), 112. See B. J. Le Frois, *The Woman Clothed with the Sun* (Rome: Orbs Catholicus, 1954), 45, on Oecumenius.

14 N. O'Hear and A. O'Hear, *Picturing the Apocalypse*, 113–15.

15 Kovacs and Rowland, *Revelation*, 136.

16 Kovacs and Rowland, *Revelation*, 144.

17 N. O'Hear and A. O'Hear, *Picturing the Apocalypse*, 115. This particular identification is from a North German Apocalypse Commentary, the Alexander *Apocalypse* Commentary, c. 1242, extracts from which accompany the *Master Bertram Apocalypse Altarpiece* of c. 1400 now housed in the Victoria & Albert Museum, London.

18 The papal bull which proclaimed the dogma of the Immaculate Conception was not promulgated until 1854 by Pius IX.

19 Kovacs and Rowland, *Revelation*, 135.

20 Kovacs and Rowland, *Revelation*, 140–44.

21 Kovacs and Rowland, *Revelation*, 137–38, 145. See also G. A. Allan, 'Joanna Southcott: Enacting the Woman Clothed with the Sun', in *The Oxford Handbook of the Reception History of the Bible*, ed. M. Lieb, E. Mason and J. Roberts (Oxford: Oxford University Press, 2011), 635–48 on Joanna Southcott.

22 F. van der Meer, *Book of Revelation: Visions from the Book of Revelation in Western Art* (London: Thames & Hudson, 1978), 103.

23 F. van der Meer, *Book of Revelation*, 95.

24 For more on Trinity see *The Trinity Apocalypse*, ed. D. McKitterick (London: The British Library, 2005), and N. O'Hear, *Contrasting Images*, 11–42.

25 F. Van der Meer, *Book of Revelation*, 159.

26 See N. O'Hear, *Contrasting Images*, 142–75 on Dürer's *Apocalypse* series as a prime example of visual exegesis of Revelation. The Dürer *Apocalypse* books were around 38.8 x 29.1 cm in size and the images are all full-page images. While the Trinity manuscript is a similar size (43.5 x 32 cm), the images are much smaller (tending to take up around one-third to one-half of a page).

27 D. Carr, *Velazquez* (London: National Gallery, 2006), 134.

28 See N. O'Hear and A. O'Hear, *Picturing the Apocalypse*, 288–94 on contrasting interpretations of the meaning of Revelation.

29 See M. Wilson, *Nature and Imagination: The Work of Odilon Redon* (Oxford: Phaidon Press, 1978).

30 Wilson, *Nature and Imagination*, 48–54.

31 See K. Davalos, *Yolanda M. Lopez* (Los Angeles: UCLA Chicano Studies Research Center Press, 2008).

32 See further http://almalopez.net/ORindex.html.
33 See Kovacs and Rowland, *Revelation*, 137; Davalos, *Yolanda M. Lopez*, 87–88.
34 Davalos, *Yolanda M. Lopez,* 88.
35 Davalos, *Yolanda M. Lopez,* 91.
36 Davalos, *Yolanda M. Lopez,* 91.
37 See Davalos, *Yolanda M. Lopez,* 93, on Mesoamerican snake symbolism. Here the snake represents not so much evil as the cycle of life and death.
38 Davalos, *Yolanda M. Lopez,* 95.
39 See N. O'Hear, 'Images of Babylon'; N. O'Hear and A. O'Hear, *Picturing the Apocalypse*, 155–75, on visualizations of the Whore of Babylon.
40 See Bauckham, *The Theology of the Book of Revelation*, 35–39, on the Roman symbolism of the Sea-Beast and the Whore of Babylon; Kovacs and Rowland, *Revelation*, 177–89; N. O'Hear and A. O'Hear, *Picturing the Apocalypse*, 155–75, on the textual and visual history of the Whore of Babylon.

CPSIA information can be obtained
at www.ICGtesting.com
Printed in the USA
LVHW081052241219
641578LV00002B/6/P